Creating Masculinity in Los Angeles's Little Manila

Popular Cultures, Everyday Lives

Popular Cultures, Everyday Lives

Robin D. G. Kelley and Janice Radway, Editors

Creating Masculinity in Los Angeles's Little Manila

WORKING-CLASS FILIPINOS AND POPULAR CULTURE,
1920s–1950s

Linda España-Maram

Columbia University Press   New York

Columbia University Press
Publishers Since 1893
New York Chichester, West Sussex
Copyright © 2006 Columbia University Press
All rights reserved

Library of Congress Cataloging-in-Publication Data
España-Maram, Linda.
Creating masculinity in Los Angeles's Little Manila :
working-class Filipinos and popular culture, 1920s–1950s /
Linda Espana-Maram.
p. cm. — (Popular cultures, everyday lives)
Includes bibliographical references and index.

ISBN 978-0-231-11592-6 (cloth : alk. paper)
ISBN 978-0-231-11593-3 (pbk. : alk. paper)

1. Working class—California—Los Angeles—History—20th century.
2. Filipinos—California—Los Angeles—History—20th century.
3. Masculinity—California—Los Angeles—History—20th century.
4. Popular culture—California—Los Angeles—History—20th century.
I. Title. II. Series.
HD8085.L73E86   2006
305.38'89992079494—dc22   2005033842

Printed in the United States of America

For my parents,

Lydia and Criscencio Nueva España

CONTENTS

ACKNOWLEDGMENTS

The production of this book was very much a collective effort. The Filipino oldtimers who welcomed me into their homes and shared their life stories deserve special recognition for breathing life into this work. Their recollections and retrospections give urgency to the need preserve a usable past for the present and future generations.

This book began as a dissertation in the Department of History at UCLA, where George J. Sánchez, Norris Hundley, George Lipsitz, and Don Nakanishi nurtured my interest in urban popular culture and provided exceptional guidance in exploring the theories, practice, and possibilities of understanding, and writing about, discursive performances among immigrants and Angeleños of color. The high caliber of their mentorship and the appreciation of the structure of historical analyses that they instilled in me would take the length of another book to fully acknowledge. The contributions of Leila Zenderland, Michael Steiner, José Moya, Gerald Greenfield, Jane Rhodes, Sandya Shukla, Valerie Matsumoto, Michael Salman, Vicente Rafael, Tania Azores, Herminia Meñez, Nenita Pambid-Domingo, Elizabeth Pastores-Palfy, Howard De Witt, and colleagues who offered comments and suggestions when I presented my work in conferences further enriched this study.

This book bears witness to the dedication and expertise of research librarians. I thank Dorothy and Fred Cordova of the Filipino American National Historical Society in Seattle, Washington; Helen Brown of the Pilipino American Research Room and Library in Los Angeles; and Carolyn Cole of the Los

Angeles Public Library for their support and for making all materials from these libraries available. The assistance of Jeff Rankin of the Department of Special Collections, UCLA; Janet Ness of the University of Washington; Paul Wormser of the Pacific Southwest Regional Branch of the National Archives; Michael W. Salmon of the Amateur Athletic Foundation of Los Angeles; John Ahouse of USC; and George Rugg of the University of Notre Dame were vital in helping me locate and retrieve materials.

In addition to these librarians, I thank Criscencio Nueva España for his assistance in conducting some of the oral testimonies and for translating the more complex Tagalog and Ilocano phrases; Mario Escalona and Noemi Escalona for contacting additional oral history participants; "Uncle" Royal Morales for introducing me to many of the Angeleño oldtimers; and Manolo Evalle for providing original artwork for this book. The quest for sources has necessitated numerous research trips over the years. I am grateful to my friends and family for their hospitality: in Seattle, I thank Rene Batingan for contacting Lorna and Vic Salinas; Medy Ignacio; Greg Choy and Catherine Ceniza Choy; and, in northern California, Aurora and Mario Escalona, and Cynthia Maram.

Several organizations provided financial assistance throughout the research, writing, and revisions of this work. Grants from the Department of History, the Institute of American Cultures, and the Center for the Study of Women at UCLA supported the initial stages of research, and an American Fellowship from the American Association of University Women assisted me in completing the dissertation on which this book is based. A UC Chancellor's Postdoctoral Fellowship in the Department of Ethnic Studies at UCSD afforded me the privilege to again work with George Lipsitz, whose brilliant insights were indispensable in the further development and revisions of the manuscript. His unequivocal support and our conversations over the years inspired me to finally complete this book.

The editors at Columbia University Press—Anne Miller, Peter Dimock, and Anne Routon—have been extremely accommodating and patient throughout the years as challenges in my personal life repeatedly delayed the publication of this book. The questions, comments, and suggestions of the two initial anonymous reviewers proved invaluable in the process of refining the arguments in the manuscript. Robin D. G. Kelley graciously stepped in, despite his own demanding research agenda, as I struggled with the final stages of the manuscript. His enthusiasm, critiques, and vision provided the impetus for me to finish this book.

At California State University, Long Beach, I thank my colleagues, particularly my department chair, John Tsuchida; vice-chair, Cassandra Kao; and Lloyd Inui in the Department of Asian and Asian American Studies; and Luis Arroyo, Jayne Howell, Dorothy Abrahamse, and Frank Fata for their support and sage counsel. I am grateful to the many colleagues who served on the Scholarly and Creative Activities Award committees for granting me release time from teaching in order to polish the manuscript. Jeane Relleve Caveness, Ferdinand Arcinue, Liz Labrador, Paulino Lim, Zeus Leonardo, Ma. Luis Calingo, Maria de la Cruz Besnard, Vincente Noble, and Atilio Alicio are remarkable allies in creating spaces for Filipino American scholarship and networks in the university.

I am privileged to be in the company of cohorts whose creativity and scholarship inspire me and whose friendships sustain me. John Nieto-Philips, Catherine Ceniza Choy, Rick Bonus, Anna Sandoval, Theodore Gonzalves, Oscar Campomanes, Kimberly Alidio, Arleen de Vera, John Rosa, Nayan Shah, Miroslava Chávez-Garcia, Ernesto Chávez, Augusto Espiritu, M. Evelina Galang, Karin Aguilar-San Juan, Dean Toji, Maythee Rojas, Alison de la Cruz, Gregory Rodriguez, Vu Pham, Rowena Robles, Maria Ana Quaglino, Juan Benitez, and Rumi Yasutake have, consistently and without reserve over these years, given of their time, energy, and good humor. I am further indebted to Nancy Fitch, Martin Manalansan IV, Chris Friday, Omar Valerio-Jiménez, Eve Oishi, Barbara Kim, Damon Woods, Michael Willard, and Feng-ying Ming for reading parts of the manuscript and providing perspectives that strengthened its contents. Dialogues with members of the Asian Pacific American History Collective and with participants of the workshops sponsored by the collective compelled me to more deeply think about the "place" of my own scholarship and its connections to the research, writing, and teaching of Asian Pacific American history. Jeffrey J. Rangel deserves special recognition for always sharing his expertise on art, ethnicity, and social movements at significant moments of the writing process and for his generosity of spirit at the most critical junctions of life.

Shout outs to my students, Constancio Arnaldo Jr., Peter Aguila, Cecille Basila, Michael Blanco, Jerico Cabaysa, Brian Campos, Roland Dulla, Derrick Engoy, Kevin Enomoto, Lisa Gee, Miguel Gregorio Jr., Branden Lew, Rachel Matsuda-Hager, Angie Holdeman, April Mascardo, Christian Mendoza, Oliver Panopio, Jocelyn Poblete, Michelle Quijano, Anne Ramis, Winnie Raquedan, Ned Realiza, Lisa Refuerzo, James Riturban, Wesleigh Santamaria, Todd

Takahashi, Eileen Trimor, Princess Ventus, Anne Ugalde, Odessa Ugalde, Pason Wang, Andy Wu, and Jennilee Yoon for presenting me with compelling reasons for why this work on Filipino American history is significant, not only for its scholarly content but also, perhaps more importantly, as a way for them to think about negotiating their own identities and reflecting on the roots of Filipino/a and Asian American expressive cultures in America.

My friends Haim and Elaine Asa, Gayle Brunelle, Susan Greenfield, David Rosales, Marcos Quaresma, Bara Salmon, Bernie Visser, Luis Carlos de Acevedo, Vera Paschoal, and Merce Cuenca Raya have kept me sane throughout the seemingly endless revisions of this work. My yoga practice, while not consistent by any stretch of the imagination (least of all mine), has nevertheless offered an oasis of tranquility, and I thank my yogis David Jones, Craig Villani, and especially Jeffrey J. Rangel.

My family has been, and continues to be, an invaluable source of strength, pride, and many happy surprises. My sister, May Nueva España; brother, Rey Nueva España; and brother-in-law, Wesley B. Maram, bestowed, depending on the need, extraordinary support or threats to my well-being as I sought to complete this book and get on with my life. Members of my transnational family have provided, in their own ways, tremendous sustenance. In the United States, I thank Sesinando Evalle; M. Liza Agsalud; Ryan Charles Agsalud; Aurora and Mario Escalona; Cynthia Maram; Denise, Ian, and Luna McCullough; Eve Maram; Dennis Fernandez; Ligaya Evalle; Bernadette, Myron, Victoria, Abigayle, and Hunter Ashby; Eve Thomas; Ireneo, Perla, Rachel, and Marc Lastrella; Manolo, Ferol, Mikel, Miles, Suzanne, and Nicole Evalle; Jonathan, Darice, Noah, and Nathan Maram; Patricia George; Kennedy George; and Leah Alletto. I thank Florence, Victor, Heidi, and Erwin Flores in Australia; and Rosario, Eligio, Elinita, Elirose, Eligio Junior, and Emrane Macatangay; Antonio and Christine May Evalle; Eden, Edgar, Ella, Jerome, and Rafael Nueva España; Alice, Imelda, and Aida Nueva España; Rene and Felita Batingan; and my *ninong* and *ninang*, Romeo and Constancia Lacson in the Philippines.

Sheldon L. Maram did not live to see the publication of this book, but his guidance and intellectual contributions—his passion for history, for narratives that give voice to the struggles and triumphs of ethnic minorities and workers—are reflected in the pages of this work.

Finally, I thank the spirit of my *lolos* and *lolas*, Patrocinio and Benjamina Evalle and Castor and Rosario Nueva España, for raising Lydia Evalle and

Criscencio Nueva España to be intelligent, strong individuals and loving parents. I know there were times when they, who are chemical engineers, pondered how their daughter became a historian, but their enthusiasm and belief in my scholarship always matched my own, and it is with my deepest respect, admiration, and love that I dedicate this book to them.

Creating Masculinity in Los Angeles's Little Manila

SOUTH CHINA SEA

BABUYAN ISLANDS

ILOCOS NORTE

ABRA

ILOCOS SUR

LA UNION

LUZON

PACIFIC OCEAN

PHILIPPINE SEA

THE PHILIPPINES

100 MILES

100 KILOMETERS

MINDORO

SAMAR

PANAY THE VISAYAS

LEYTE

CEBU

PALAWAN

NEGROS

SULU SEA

MINDANAO

ZAMBOANGA

DAVAO

JOLO

CELEBES SEA

The Philippines. (Original artwork courtesy of Manolo Evalle)

INTRODUCTION

Filipino Immigration to California and the Contours of Filipino Immigrant Studies

Dahil sa iyo, nais kong mabuhay	Because of you, I want to live
Dahil sa iyo, hanggang mamatay.	Because of you, until I die.
Dapat mong tantuin wala nang	You must know that there is no
ibang giliw	other love
Puso ko'y tanungin, ikaw at ikaw rin.	Ask my heart, it's you and you alone.
Dahil sa iyo, ako'y lumigaya	Because of you, I am happy
Pagmamahal ay alayan ka	To you I offer my love
Kung tunay mang ako, ay alipinin mo	If you must make me your slave
Ang lahat ng ito'y, dahil sa iyo.	Then I am willing, because of you.
Kung tunay mang ako, ay alipinin mo	If you must make me your slave
Ang lahat sa buhay ko . . . dahil sa iyo.	All my life, I am willing . . . because of you.

"Dahil Sa Iyo" (Because of You) has become somewhat of a theme song among Filipinos in the United States.[1] It is one of the most recognizable melodies, a staple of many Filipino cultural events, communal gatherings, and documentaries about the experiences of Filipino Americans. During the 1920s and 1930s, the haunting ballad ranked among the most requested musical numbers in the taxi dance halls frequented by Filipino workers.[2]

By the time the love song reached this stage of popularity, however, certain features within its structure had already been transformed, while other elements remained intact. In the Philippines, the ballad was a *harana*, a serenade traditionally sung by a male suitor to his beloved. This courtship ritual was usually accompanied by the strumming of only one instrument, the *kudyapi*, a six-string guitar.[3] Further, "Dahil Sa Iyo" exemplified a serenade particular to Tagalog, the dialect of Filipinos in a specific area of Luzon.

Filipino immigrants transplanted "Dahil Sa Iyo" to agricultural camp socials and urban commercialized dance halls in California, but instead of the strains of a lone guitar, a full orchestra usually performed the ballad. Initially, Filipino musicians composed the whole band, but, later, mixed Filipino and Anglo orchestras also performed the song. Eventually translated into, although very rarely sung in, English, "Dahil Sa Iyo" was never translated into Ilocano, the dialect of Filipinos from the provinces of northern Luzon.[4] These Ilocanos, who constituted the vast majority of Filipino immigrants in the 1920s and 1930s, were only vaguely familiar with the rudiments of Tagalog. Indeed, some Ilocanos said that a number of them learned how to communicate in Tagalog from their compatriots in the United States. In learning Tagalog, they expanded their cultural repertoire to include the more popular songs like "Dahil Sa Iyo."

The cultural intermingling that characterized the growth in popularity of "Dahil Sa Iyo" among Filipinos in the United States demonstrates one way the diverse community called itself into being through everyday life experiences. The incorporation of the ballad as part of the Filipinos' coping strategies shows their need to formulate an ethnic identity and exhibit some solidarity. Through commercialization, the ballad facilitated a unity and self-definition among groups of people who came from different regional backgrounds. Subjected to American policies of "benevolent assimilation" in the Philippines but segregation in the United States, Filipinos used songs to nurture a native dialect. A "womanless" immigrant group due to profit-driven American capitalists who paid for the migration of only male laborers and because of antimiscegenation laws in California, Filipinos nevertheless upheld the sentiments of romantic love and courtship in their songs. But the commodification of the ballad did not transform multicultural Filipinos into a single society. While the Tagalog song expanded the boundaries of community, Filipinos also reinforced their differences by talking or singing in their own regional dialects.

This study traces the importance of popular culture in the lives of Filipino laborers from the 1920s to the 1950s as they negotiated viable ethnic identities and created a male, working-class culture in Los Angeles's Little Manila, one of the major centers of urban Filipino group life in California. Previous studies of these laborers' experiences beginning in the 1920s have often failed to explore the dynamic cultural transformations taking place in the creation of an immigrant identity based on youth, ethnicity, and notions of masculinity within the confines of a working class. These few studies, generally master's theses from the period, tend to focus on Filipino fraternal associations, labor unions, and social movements in explaining the creation of group identity. They look at Filipino laborers only as immigrants, only as workers, or only as members of organizations. They neglect to take into account that the creation of an identity is a multilayered process, by which negotiations take place within a variety of settings and activities. Filipinos, who simultaneously were gendered subjects, immigrants, workers, and consumers, also pieced together an understanding of their collective identity by what they chose to do in their everyday life routines, including leisure activities. This study traces how working-class Filipinos in Los Angeles developed strategies that defined, modified, and expressed their realities, a process that the historian George Lipsitz has described as "cultural indeterminacy, picking and choosing from many traditions to fashion performances and narratives suitable for arbitrating an extraordinarily complex identity."[5]

The formulation of this identity cannot wholly be discerned through traditional sources. It is an understatement that Filipino voices in the making of their own histories in the United States are generally not preserved in official documents and archives. Popular culture, however, opens up critical inquiry into social relations not only among Filipinos themselves, but also between the immigrants and the host society. Filipinos, legally locked out of the political arena through U.S. imperialist policies in their homeland and racist legislation on the mainland, engaged in oppositional strategies by publicly questioning presumptions of, for example, sexuality in taxi dance halls and white supremacy in sporting arenas. These commercialized leisure centers offered opportunities for Filipinos to create meaning and construct an identity through their own standards of cultural production.

Filipinos are the largest immigrant group from Asia in the United States today. They are the second biggest Asian American ethnic group, constituting 18 percent (1.8 million) of Asian America nationwide. In California, where one in every three Asian American lives, Filipino Americans make up almost 23 percent of the state's Asian American population.[6] Despite their numerical significance, they have attracted few researchers, and most of those have concentrated on immigration since 1965. Unlike the earlier wave of Filipino immigrants in the 1920s and 1930s, preferences given to professionals and family reunification under the 1965 Immigration Reform Act ushered in this "new" wave of Filipino immigration, which initially consisted of educated and highly trained specialists in certain fields, particularly health care, engineering, and accounting. Once established, these immigrants joined Filipinos from the earlier immigration period in using the provision for family reunification to petition family members in the Philippines to join them in the United States. While the Immigration Act of 1990 limited the quantity of family-sponsored visas, Filipinos have used the act's preference for employment-based petitions to continue to come to the United States. As a result of immigration legislation since 1965 and natural birth rates, the contemporary Filipino American population is more diverse than the previous wave of immigrants.[7]

This study seeks to redress the imbalance in Filipino American scholarship by focusing on Filipinos who came to California from the 1920s until the late 1930s, a period when single young men made up the vast majority (94 percent) of the group.[8] Agents of American agribusiness recruited these immigrants from the rural areas of the Philippines for agricultural work, first in Hawaii and then on the U.S. West Coast. This wave of Filipinos virtually stopped by the 1930s, largely because of the Tydings-McDuffie Act of 1934, which established, among other things, a quota of fifty Filipino immigrants per year.[9] This study also includes an examination of the disparate experiences of these men during World War II: as part of the zoot suit scene in Los Angeles and as soldiers in segregated units of the U.S. armed forces sent to the Philippines to help liberate their homeland from Japanese forces.

Unskilled agricultural workers constituted the vast majority of immigrants who came to California beginning in the early 1920s. Filipinos were in demand as another source of exploitable labor because U.S. exclusionary policies beginning in 1882 had effectively restricted the immigration of other Asians who had worked in California's fields and Alaska's canneries. Filipinos were also easier to recruit because the Spanish-American War of 1898, American imperialism, and the defeat of large-scale indigenous resistance to U.S. occupation had resulted in the Philippines becoming a colony. Filipinos, as U.S. "nationals," were not subject to immigration restrictions or quotas at that time. Like other Asians in America, however, Filipinos could not vote, own land, buy homes, or apply for U.S. citizenship.[10]

The first large wave of more than 2,000 Filipinos arrived in California in 1923. This figure represents a threefold increase over the number of Filipinos in California in the previous year. Young men formed the bulk of this group, with 84 percent being under thirty years old.[11] By 1930, men made up 94 percent of the Filipino immigrant population. In that year, more than 45,000

Filipinos resided in the continental United States, most of them (67 percent) living and working in California.[12] The vast majority (80 percent) became migratory laborers. They traveled in groups to agricultural centers like Delano, Stockton, and the San Fernando Valley on the outskirts of Los Angeles to harvest crops and to canneries in the Pacific Northwest and Alaska. During the off-season, they returned to their Little Manilas. In these ethnic quarters, the migrant laborers joined their urban-based compatriots, who usually found employment in the service-oriented industries, working as domestics, janitors, porters, or dishwashers.

Los Angeles's Filipino community from the 1920s until World War II flourished in the downtown area, roughly demarcated by San Pedro Street on the east, Sixth Street on the south, Figueroa Avenue on the west, and Sunset Boulevard on the north.[13] Twenty-one-year-old George Weiss and his father, who came to Los Angeles from the Philippines in 1916, were among the earliest settlers during this period of immigration. Weiss's grandfather was from a wealthy Jewish family from Philadelphia, Pennsylvania, and he went to the Philippines on a commercial venture. In Manila, he married a "Spanish girl" and they had one child, George's father. The elder Weiss built a successful mercantile business, which he left to his wife and son when he returned to the United States for health reasons. George's father became one of the wealthiest merchants in the Philippines and eventually married a Filipina, but she died giving birth to George in 1895. When World War I broke out, father and son immigrated to Los Angeles, where, as the younger Weiss recalls, they settled in "a small house on the South Side of town where my father and I started on what we thought was the greatest adventure in our lives. . . . The buildings of the town astounded me." They opened a general store on South Vermont Avenue, by Sixty-seventh Street, which George continued to operate after his father's death in 1923.[14]

The more significant stream of settlement started in 1924, when 721 Filipinos who landed in Los Angeles's port decided to remain in the city. Some members of this group established a restaurant, a barbershop, and an employment agency between Commercial and Second Streets, by Main and Los Angeles Streets. Two years later, another 1,277 Filipinos settled in Los Angeles, and a second barbershop and employment agency were launched. In 1929 an additional 1,176 Filipinos migrated to the city. A Filipino graduate student conducting research in 1933 estimated that by that year, there were about 6,000 Filipinos living in Los Angeles and the services in Little Manila had expanded to include twelve restaurants and seven barbershops.[15] By 1935, Filipino-owned businesses like the L.V.M. Café at 113 East First Street, Basa and Nocon's Café at 111 North Los Angeles Street, the Lunch Counter at 116½ Weller Street, the Manila Portrait Studio at 128 Weller Street, and the *Philippines Review*, a major Filipino immigrant newspaper published by the fraternal order Caballeros de Dimas-Alang from its offices at 126–128 Weller Street, served the largely Filipino clientele.[16]

While workers constituted by far the largest portion of the Filipino Angeleño community, there was a small group composed of "fountain-pen boys," self-supporting students who came to the United States primarily to complete their education. These students chronicled the experiences of their companions, the full-time and migrant Filipino laborers. Graduate students who studied with sociologist Emory Bogardus at the University of Southern California (USC) contributed some of the earliest works, mostly theses and dissertations, focusing on contemporary developments of the 1930s and 1940s.[17] The fountain-pen boys' assessments of the workers' lifestyles, however, generally reflected the students' acceptance of then-prevailing attitudes regarding the laboring class. Not surprisingly, they expressed an aversion to and opposition toward the workers' recreational activities. The studies emphasized what the students perceived to be the state of decline in the Filipino community because the workers patronized places like the gambling dens in Chinatown and the taxi dance halls, where they danced with Anglo women in timed, ritualized sequences.[18]

Despite the limited analyses and biases of these theses, they are important because they present the urban aspect of Filipino experiences. Scholarship on this wave of Filipino immigrants to California have tended to focus on the living and working conditions faced by the workers in rural areas.[19] Filipino immigrant history has also been examined through the larger prism of Asian American experiences. H. Brett Melendy's *Asians in America* represents one of the earliest works to chronicle the comparative histories of Filipinos, Koreans, and East Indians in the United States. Although this work is not driven by analysis, Melendy's accessible narrative provides a good starting point for uncovering Filipino American history. Ronald Takaki's *Strangers from a Different Shore* and Sucheng Chan's *Asian Americans: An Interpretive History* are syntheses that contain significant sections on Filipino Americans, while more recent syntheses like Helen Zia's *Asian American Dreams: The Emergence of an American People* and Robert G. Lee's *Orientals* tend to focus more on East

Asians and include only limited segments on Filipino Americans.[20] Edited volumes by Shirley Hune and Gail M. Nomura, *Asian/Pacific Islander American Women: A Historical Anthology*; Kandice Chuh and Karen Shimakawa, *Orientations: Mapping Studies in the Asian Diaspora*; and Martin F. Manalansan IV, *Cultural Compass: Ethnographic Explorations of Asian America* include recent scholarship on, and by, Filipino Americans. Vicente L. Rafael's edited work *Discrepant Histories: Translocal Essays on Filipino Cultures* comprises articles centered around the legacy of U.S. imperialism in the Philippines and transnational Filipino culture.[21]

The sparse literature on Filipino American history has nevertheless produced insights into the experiences of these immigrants. Studies of the pre–World War II period include exploitation in the workplace, militancy in organizing unions, and memberships in fraternal organizations and mutual-aid societies. But Filipinos were *simultaneously* immigrants, gendered subjects, laborers, members of an aggrieved population, and consumers. The working out of a viable collective memory among these young men took place within a variety of settings and through what they chose to do in their everyday lives. This book examines how these workers negotiated an identity based on youth, ethnicity, and heterosexual masculinity through the aesthetics and public performance of brown bodies in leisure centers that catered to Filipino patrons and how these areas subsequently came to be contested terrains with the dominant society. One of the key issues in this study is that the parameters of notions associated with "American" youth and masculinity sprang from the philosophies and language of specific classes whose construction of particular social realities at given historical moments served their interests. But the meanings associated with these categories are not static, nor do they go unchallenged. Further, qualities attributed to "youth" and "masculinity" change over time for a variety of reasons. As the historian Gail Bederman posits, "at any time in history, many contradictory ideas about manhood are available to explain what men are, how they ought to behave, and what sorts of powers and authorities they may claim, as men."[22]

For Filipinos, excluded from the established social, economic, and political structures that in any event privileged whiteness as a component of the dominant's society's construction of manhood and, by extension, power, wage work and cultural practices provided viable avenues through which they measured and asserted masculinity. With the vast majority finding employment only in the lowest-paying, most physically demanding and demeaning sectors of the labor market, Filipinos developed a hierarchy of masculinity based on the occupational dangers of the workplace. Alaskeros, Filipinos who worked in the canneries of Alaska and the Pacific Northwest, were at the highest echelon of this structure because these men faced the harshest living and working conditions. As the labor historian Chris Friday suggests, Alaskeros commanded deference among Filipino laborers because many Filipinos felt that "to be an Alaskero was to be a survivor, a toughened veteran of the canneries. Filipinos so desired to be part of that select group that a few stowed away aboard steamers headed for Alaska."[23] Popular culture practices offered another channel wherein to stake Filipino masculinity. Indeed, since young men constituted 94 percent of the Filipino immigrant population, expressive cultures among Filipinos *were* about masculinity. Removed from the supervision of parents and community elders in the Philippines, the young men flocked to the commercialized leisure centers to work out, wrestle with, and claim what it meant to be Filipino men within the context of a racist host society. The Filipinos' participation in the thrills of risking hard-earned wages to best opponents and the house in Chinatown's extralegal gambling dens and in the sensual pleasures of dressing up for a night on the town sent white workers, legislators, and policing agencies scurrying to contain these public displays of Filipino virility. By flaunting "improper" behavior, Filipino workers carved niches of autonomy where they fought against restrictions on space, expanded the opportunities for alternative expressions, and, in the process, established an identity of their own. By looking at *what* they chose to do with their free time and *where* they chose to do it, we can better understand the solidarity they displayed in mass social movements, despite some internal conflicts along class and regional lines.

To examine this process, this study draws from paradigms developed in contemporary cultural analysis from various fields of inquiry, especially ethnic, labor, and gender studies. This approach integrates factors—including gender, class, race, and unequal power relations—that add depth to studies of transformations wherein identity, values, and social relations are negotiated within, and among, groups of people. As the historian George Lipsitz argues, cultural studies "open up for sustained analysis the everyday life activities of popular culture consumers, youth subcultures, and ethnic minorities. Most important, they provide sophisticated and convincing arguments about the ways in which the commonplace and ordinary practices of everyday life often encode larger social and ideological meaning."[24] In negotiating identities and building viable communities through popular culture practices, Filipino workers engaged the host society in a debate over the nature of "American" culture.

This discourse over meaning is wrought with friction. Battles over resources and traditions transpire as the more powerful group seeks to legitimize its dominance by presenting the status quo as the normal, desirable, and irrevocable reality not only through physical coercion but also through ideological, political, and cultural processes. The Italian intellectual Antonio Gramsci describes this schema of power relations as "hegemony." He explains that defending this position requires vigil, because members of marginalized populations engage in "counter-hegemonic" strategies that seek to subvert the dominant ideology by presenting the viability of alternative ideas, expressions, and experiences. Gramsci understands that hegemony was a contested milieu and that "in order for the working class to challenge [the] existing order, and become hegemonic in its turn without becoming dependent on intellectuals from another class, it must create 'organic' intellectuals of its own."[25] To better their positions, these "organic intellectuals" strive to form a "historical bloc," provisional coalitions rallied around oppositional ideas. The struggle to create an identity thus involves the interplay of factors, including unequal power relations, that sometimes retard but occasionally advance the aggrieved population's stance in what Gramsci hails as "wars of position."[26]

Beginning in the late 1960s, scholars in cultural studies expanded on Gramsci's concepts of hegemony and struggle to look at the ways marginalized populations, including the working class and ethnic minorities, develop channels of alternative expressions in a world increasingly bombarded by products of a commercial culture and consumerism. They posit that popular culture functions neither as a structure of social control imposed from above nor as a concrete representation of class consciousness. Rather, popular culture exposes contested meanings and illustrates a multivocal struggle within society. The working out of these contradictions transpires not only in courtrooms or during outbreaks of mass movements but also through cultural processes, in the daily life experiences of people, wherein meanings are created, challenged, defended, or reformulated in an unending cycle of contestation. As Stuart Hall, one of the most influential cultural theorists, puts it, the struggle *for* hegemony takes place "in the complex lines of resistance and acceptance, refusal and capitulation, which make the field of culture a sort of constant battlefield. A battlefield where no once-for-all victories are obtained but where there are always strategic positions to be won and lost."[27]

An emphasis on how popular culture provides sites for negotiating identity in an ongoing struggle imparts persuasive arguments that marginalized populations are not so easily swayed or controlled through commercialized products. Some scholars in the fields of working-class, popular culture, gender, and ethnic studies have effectively incorporated this approach to examine how immigrant and ethnic laborers forged distinct working-class cultures and viable communities despite constant attempts by the dominant culture's agencies—including bosses, middle-class reformers, and the police—to regulate the behavior of the poor and working class in and out of the workplace.[28] These studies provide compelling evidence that the struggle to create identities and solidarity occurs not only through activities associated with institutions but also through the cultural processes that happen in daily life and through individual choices. As the historian Roy Rosenzweig argues, even "where conventional expressions of class conflict—unions, strikes, radical political parties—were muted, leisure time became an arena of class struggle in which workers and industrialists fought over who would control life outside the work place."[29]

This work uses theories, concepts, and methodologies developed in cultural studies to examine the development of an ethnic, working-class culture among Filipinos. Because the livelihood of the vast majority of Filipino workers dictated a migratory lifestyle, this study pays particular attention to the creation of a portable community as a way to call itself into being, wherever it was. Filipinos, relegated to working in closely supervised positions and living in ghettoes, created a vibrant street culture where recreational centers became important gathering places for sharing experiences and cementing bonds through informal networks. The solidarity, however tenuous, produced in this communal system helped numerous Filipino laborers weather the turbulent period of organizing labor unions and the lean years of the Great Depression.

As the economic slump deepened, unemployed Filipinos desperately explored alternative means of acquiring money, food, and shelter. Chinatown's gambling dens offered some of these amenities, providing temporary refuge and complimentary meals to players. These extralegal establishments, however, increasingly became the focus of the city officials' and reformers' campaigns for eradication. But because gambling and bordellos flourished in the original Chinatown until its final destruction, this study includes an examination of the support that ethnic vice industries received not only from

Asian patrons but also from Anglo working- and middle-class men and the Los Angeles Police Department.

In addition to gambling in Chinatown, Filipinos bet heavily in sporting events, especially boxing matches. Between the 1920s and World War II, a number of Filipino pugilists garnered fame and championship titles. Despite the marginalization of Filipinos, these athletes legitimized a space for self-definition by defying the dominant society's assumptions about race and ability. Pugilists became symbols of Filipino aspirations, and the ring emerged as an important cultural space wherein ethnic laborers created their own heroes, who in turn became a part of the stories that Filipinos told themselves about themselves.

The intensely masculine subculture of the gambling dens and the sporting life among Filipinos reflect the overwhelming majority of men in this wave of immigrants. But these young men sought female company, and one of the most convenient ways was to patronize the taxi dance halls scattered throughout Little Manila. These leisure centers often hired Anglo women from the Southwest and Midwest as dance partners, and interethnic relations in the halls became a focus of reform societies' crusades. This study examines how the mixing of working-class brown men and white women in ritualized dance sequences became a public, visible site for the struggle over issues of ethnicity, class, sexuality, and gender relations within the larger American culture.

By the early 1940s, taxi dance halls that employed Anglo women were closed to Filipino patrons. Some Filipinos, generally the more recent immigrants, became part of the zoot suit scene around Los Angeles, continuing to nurture a vibrant dance subculture in the segregated black-and-tan cabarets of the city. Given the controversies surrounding the so-called zoot suit riots in 1943, this study analyzes how clothing and adorning the body became significant emblems of ethnicity, masculinity, and identity. Dress also took on important meanings for Filipinos who joined the U.S. armed forces and donned the uniform of the country whose policies made the Philippines a colony and whose racist ideology relegated the immigrant Filipinos to the lowest rungs of the socioeconomic ladder. Soldiers of the First and Second Filipino Regiments, segregated units of the U.S. Army, went to the Philippines to help free their homeland from the Japanese.

While all aspects of Filipino immigrant and Filipino American history are in their early stages, there are adequate materials from which this study draws. The students' theses from the 1930s, for example, despite their biases and limited analyses, contain useful material and promote new challenges for inquiry. Some of the theses provide maps that plot the location of Filipino establishments and depict the changing boundaries of Little Manila during these years. Newspapers, theses, and government records, however, expose only part of the process of negotiating identities. The life stories and testimonies of Filipino laborers themselves flesh out this study. Where possible, information given by the workers themselves was correlated with data from other sources. While oral history presents its own limitations, including the interviewees' selective memory, spoken recollections set into print give agency to people whose lives did not revolve around the written word. As the historians Tamara K. Hareven and Randolph Langenbach persuasively argue, "what is important in oral history is not merely the facts that people remember but how they remember them and why they remember them the way they do."[30] Oral testimonies of the experiences of Filipinos during the 1920s, the Great Depression, and World War II—including those from interviews that I conducted, those gathered in the collections of the National Pinoy Archives of the Filipino American National Historical Society in Seattle and the Washington State Oral-Aural History Program, and the previously unused transcripts of the "Racial Minorities Survey: Filipinos" conducted by members of the Federal Writers Project during the 1930s—compose an important portion of the sources for this work.

This study on the impact of popular culture practices on the creation of an ethnic, predominantly male, working-class culture in Los Angeles's Little Manila from the 1920s to the 1940s allows us to see that for Filipino workers, mass-produced newspapers, gambling dens, commercialized boxing matches, and taxi dance halls were as important as fraternal associations, mutual-aid societies, and labor unions for the construction, affirmation, or rejection of identities. This focus on Los Angeles sheds further light on the often neglected urban experience of these Filipino immigrant laborers. In broader terms, this study contributes to the histories of immigrant, working-class populations of the city itself by uncovering the stories of a community whose geographic locations no longer exist. In the post–World War II years, as Los Angeles's gentrification programs for the downtown area intensified, the rooming houses, recreational centers, and other buildings once frequented by the Filipino oldtimers in Little Manila were razed to accommodate the expansion of Little Tokyo as a tourist attraction and the construction of the

Harbor Freeway (Interstate 110).[31] But in the recollections and memories of the *manongs*, Little Manila continues to be alive with the exuberance of their youth, the value of their hard work, the pleasure of one another's company, and the intricate complexities of being Filipinos in America.[32] And these sentiments, after all, are at the very core of what this book is about.

1. MAKING A LIVING

The Meanings of Work and the Struggles for Solidarity

"All roads go to California and all travelers wind up in Los Angeles," Julio said. "But not this traveler. I have lived there too long. I know that state too damn well. . . ." "What do you mean?" I asked. Suddenly he became sad and said, "It is hard to be a Filipino in California."

—Carlos Bulosan, *America Is in the Heart*

In 1927 Manuel Fiores boarded the *Santa Maria*, a large merchant freighter with mixed cargo making a routine Manila–Panama run. Although only twenty-two years old, Fiores was already a seasoned mariner, having worked on his uncle's boat, a combination trader and diving ship, since he was twelve years old. He had started out as an apprentice, working with the rest of the crew collecting and trading coral, pearls, and copra around the Philippines and the South Seas. He stayed for six years, learning about the sea and the business, until he became dissatisfied with his $6 monthly wage. He approached his uncle for a raise, and he agreed to increase his salary to $10 on the next trip. When they returned to Manila's port after five months, however, the uncle reneged on the arrangement. Fiores quietly accepted the money, packed his meager belongings, and went ashore to look for a new job. The captain of the *Santa Maria* offered him a beginning monthly wage of $12, with the agreement that if things worked out, he would increase the salary to $16. Fiores recalled that the evening before the ship set sail for Panama, "I was so excited I could hardly sleep. It seemed that I was off on a great adventure and it turned out to be that I was."[1]

Fifteen days outside Manila, the *Santa Maria* ran into a fierce storm that blew it and its crew hundreds of miles off course. For two weeks, the angry tropical winds ripped at the vessel's sails and rigging and the turbulent waves tore into the ship's hull, leaving the freighter waterlogged and in danger of sinking. With most of the twelve-member crew exhausted or sick and the rations and potable water almost gone, the captain ordered the navigator to head for a port, any port. Eight days later, in the middle of the night, the crippled *Santa Maria* ran aground on a beach in Mexico.[2]

The Mexican government helped the stranded Filipinos by arranging for their transportation north to the port of Los Angeles, where they could board a ship bound for Manila. Upon his arrival in the City of Angels, however, Fiores decided "to stay in America for awhile. . . . I just quietly faded out of the picture and went about securing myself a job. I met a number of Filipino boys, and after a few days went to working as [a] cleaning boy for a restaurant in Los Angeles. I worked at nights and mopped and swept until I could hardly straighten up. The sea was swell compared to that job."[3]

While Fiores's spectacular misadventure at sea and his dramatic arrival in Los Angeles are atypical for the vast majority of Filipino immigrants, his experiences once in the city itself, including the informal networking for employment and the physical aches and pains associated with the strenuous jobs that remained open to Fiores and other Filipinos, mirror the lives of many of his compatriots. This chapter examines the meaning of work and the formation of a working-class solidarity among these ethnic Angeleños who were, in the late 1920s, the second significant wave of Filipino immigrants and the latest group of Asians in the United States.[4]

Because of the dominant society's racism and discriminatory practices and because of the Filipinos' lack of training in skilled and semiskilled trades, these immigrants were concentrated in low-status, labor-intensive jobs at or near the bottom rungs of the socioeconomic ladder. The majority of Filipinos became migratory laborers in the agribusiness and extractive industries in the Pacific Coast states. The transitory nature of their work and their desire for shared experiences compelled Filipinos to forge portable communities to maintain connections among the members of this highly mobile population.

Filipinos used these informal networks to obtain information about jobs and housing as well as to keep in touch with their compatriots along the migration circuit.

The interlocking system of community became crucial as the Great Depression deepened and thousands of Filipinos lost their jobs. Many displaced workers used the network to locate kin, friends, and townmates from whom they could seek assistance. They relied on *utang na loob*, the Filipino traditional system of mutual aid, to help them weather the devastating consequences of the national economic slump. *Utang na loob* (literally, an internal debt) is an informal arrangement of communal assistance practiced extensively throughout the Philippines and is arguably the most powerful underpinning of Filipino social relations, dictating that assistance received must be repaid. As one Filipino scholar explains, it is a process by which "a Filipino can expect help and protection from his family and kin group, [but] he also has obligations to them. If he can render service and hospitality, return support and provide protection, he is obliged to do so. If he does not, he is likely to be regarded as *walang hiya* (shameless)," and being considered shameless "must be avoided at all cost."[5] For Filipino laborers, portable communities, informal networking, and *utang na loob* emerged as important elements for survival and for forging a nascent working-class solidarity during the turbulent years of the Depression.

Beginning in the 1920s, at least three identifiable groups of immigrants made up the bulk of the Filipino community in Los Angeles. A small number of Filipinos came to continue their education as self-supporting students usually employed in the service-oriented sectors, particularly as domestics. Another small group of Filipino Angeleños, those who had completed their tour of duty in the U.S. armed forces, especially the navy, shared this job market with the part-time students.[6] The largest category of Filipinos, however, consisted of unskilled, migratory laborers principally from the northern rural provinces of Luzon in the Philippines. In part because U.S. exclusionary policies starting in 1882 effectively restricted the immigration of the other Asian groups who had worked in the emerging U.S. agribusiness, representatives of American agricultural industries, starting with the Hawaiian Sugar Planters' Association, went to the islands to recruit Filipino laborers beginning in the early twentieth century. These agents actively sought Filipinos because their country, as a result of the Spanish-American War of 1898, American imperialism, and the defeat of large-scale Filipino resistance to U.S. occupation, was a colony of the United States. Unlike other Asian immigrants, Filipinos were thus considered U.S. "nationals," carrying U.S. passports, and as such were not subject to immigration restrictions or quotas, but, like other Asian immigrants, Filipinos could not vote, own land, buy real estate, or apply for U.S. citizenship.[7]

Despite active recruitment campaigns by U.S. agribusiness representatives who portrayed the United States as *the* proverbial pot of gold and the eventual mass migration of Filipino laborers to Hawaii and the U.S. West Coast, Filipino immigration cannot wholly be explained by the traditional and rather reductionist view of economic push-pull principles. As a number of scholars have convincingly argued, immigration is also part of a social process that can be traced to the patterns of migration and means of survival in the country of origin.[8] In urban areas like Manila, for example, American recruiters generally wound up unsuccessful in securing enough laborers. This failure resulted primarily from the relative availability of jobs in the city and because many urban workers had little desire to relocate to the rural sugar and pineapple plantations of Hawaii.

The recruiters proved more successful in the countryside, especially in the northern hill provinces of the big island of Luzon. The vast majority (70 percent) of the first recruits to Hawaii came from the heavily populated Ilocano provinces like Ilocos Norte, Ilocos Sur, and La Union.[9] In a country where the average density (excluding the capital city of Manila) was 90 people per square mile, Ilocos Sur and La Union ranked as the two most crowded provinces, encompassing, respectively, 492 and 459 people per square mile.[10] In addition, the agriculture of rice production, which the Ilocanos depended on for their livelihood, was underdeveloped. Further, the government persisted in ignoring pleas for reform in an existing land-tenancy system where the absentee landlord got most everything from the harvest and the farmers and their families were left with little to support themselves until the next season.[11] Given these exigencies, the Ilocanos' willingness to emigrate reflected the survival mechanism already developed in these populous regions: outmigration.[12] Philip Vera Cruz, who left the small town of Saoang in Ilocos Sur in 1926 to immigrate to the United States, recalled that "when I decided to stay in California, I guess I was unconsciously carrying on the Saoang tradition of migrant work, for when the grape season was over in Delano we would work on lettuce in nearby MacFarland and Wasco or pack grapes for growers in other areas."[13]

The first large group of more than 2,000 Filipino laborers, most of them Ilocanos, arrived in California in 1923.[14] This figure represented a threefold increase over the number of Filipinos in California in the previous year. The majority of these Filipinos (84 percent) were reemmigrants from Hawaii who had worked in the sugar and pineapple plantations. But between 1924 and 1930, as steamship lines established better direct routes from Manila to Pacific Coast ports like Los Angeles, San Francisco, and Seattle, more immigrants began arriving directly from the Philippines. By 1928, 57 percent embarked in Manila, while only about 35 percent came from Hawaii, with the remaining 7.6 percent coming from other ports.[15]

Young men formed the bulk of these immigrants; 84 percent were under thirty years old. By 1930 men made up 94 percent of the Filipino immigrant population on the U.S. mainland.[16] The predominance of males in the immigration patterns of Filipinos to the contiguous United States in many ways reflects the intertwining of social conventions from the homeland and the economics of agribusiness in the American West. While some Filipinas *did* migrate for reasons such as the pursuit of education, employment, and escape from arranged marriages and other familial pressures, the majority were not encouraged, or expected, to leave the country. As the historian Sucheng Chan points out, "In [Asian] societies where girls were reared to serve men and procreate, respectable women did not travel far from home."[17] Single women were further restricted since, as one Filipina writer posits, traditional custom dictated that "an unmarried Filipina stays at home *as long as she is unmarried.* In her later years she becomes the respected aunt whom the younger members of the family look up to [emphasis in original]."[18] In addition, recruiters for U.S. businesses did not particularly want women for California's fields, since the growers preferred men for the migratory labor force that best characterized the agriculture industry. The combination of these factors resulted in an immigrant community in which, between 1920 and 1929, Filipinas constituted only about 6 percent of the Filipino population in California.[19]

Maria Garcia Cardoz was one of the rare Filipinas in Los Angeles during the 1930s. The youngest daughter of seven children, she and her siblings were forced to work after they were suddenly orphaned. Cardoz found employment as a caregiver for the sickly wife of an American army officer stationed in Manila. When the couple decided to return to the United States for the wife's health, they asked the twenty-year-old Cardoz to accompany them. They eventually settled in Santa Barbara, California, because of its warm climate, but the wife's health did not significantly improve. Cardoz recalled that "while I was in Santa Barbara I met a young fellow countryman who was [a] cook and houseboy for a family there. We fell in love but I refused to think of marriage until my employer was well. I didn't have long to wait. After a year she died." Cardoz married, and she and her husband moved with her employer to Beverly Hills, where the widower intended to start a business. But the enterprise failed, and the entrepreneur moved to the East Coast, leaving the couple with two months' salary apiece. After five months, Cardoz's husband finally secured a steady job as a cook in San Pedro. Two years later, he began his own business, opening a small lunch counter in Wilmington, a city by the port of Los Angeles, which he then expanded into a bigger café on Fish Harbor. In California, Cardoz said, "I married the boy of my choice . . . [and] we have two children who are going to school and they are going to make a name for themselves, I'm sure. My education was limited and I want them to have enough to ensure their future."[20]

By 1930, more than 45,000 Filipinos resided in the continental United States, the majority of whom (67 percent) lived and worked in California.[21] By 1933, an estimated 65,000 Filipinos had arrived, with more than one-fifth of that population (about 12,000) living in Los Angeles County.[22] Of these immigrants, about 4,000 stayed in the city of Los Angeles on a year-round basis.[23] This figure reflects an approximate twofold rise in the numbers of Filipinos living in Los Angeles within five years: in 1928 there were only about 2,500 in the city.[24]

The vast majority (80 percent) of Filipino immigrants on the Pacific Coast became migratory laborers. During the growing season, they traveled in groups to agricultural centers in California, including Delano and Fresno to harvest grapes, the Salinas area to pick lettuce, and Stockton to harvest asparagus.[25] A number of these laborers and some self-supporting students, the Alaskeros, migrated to Alaska during the summers to work in the salmon-canning industry.[26] During the winters, several thousand flocked to urban areas to work in temporary jobs, usually in the service industries, until the next growing cycle. These migration patterns primarily account for the fluctuating, seasonal population of Filipinos in California. In Stockton, a principal agricultural center in northern California, for example, the Filipino populace dipped to about 3,000 in the winter months but swelled to more than 8,000 during the growing and harvesting seasons of spring and early summer.[27]

Filipinos constituted the largest Asian immigrant migratory workforce in

California's agribusiness almost upon their arrival, in part because U.S. immigration laws had already restricted Chinese and Japanese immigration, in part because a large number from these groups had left the fields for employment elsewhere, and in part because initially, Filipinos worked for the lowest wages. While they followed the growing and harvesting seasons of California's produce, they eventually came to dominate the asparagus and lettuce industries, providing the "stoop labor" necessary to tend and reap these crops. Growers claimed that the Filipinos' youth, agility, and relatively shorter physiques made them more adept at continually having to bend down to attend to the plants, but as one farm worker bitterly recalled, "Shit. I'm a short Filipino but it was just as hard for me to bend over as any big white guy. Some of those growers didn't even know how difficult it was out there, bending over with the sun beating down on you."[28] Filipinos who performed this stoop labor in the lettuce fields of Salinas for eight to ten hours a day earned 15 cents an hour until 1933, when the wages increased to 20 cents an hour.[29]

Employers often provided housing for the migrant workers, but these quarters were usually nothing more than flimsy bunkhouses with the minimal provisions. One grower, who favored hiring Filipinos because they were single men, explained that "these Mexicans and Spaniards bring their families with them and I have to fix up houses; but I can put a hundred Filipinos in that barn [pointing to a large firetrap]."[30] Some camps had communal buildings for bathrooms and showers, although the sanitary conditions there were almost nonexistent. Philip Vera Cruz, who lived in a labor camp while working in Delano, recounted how "the kitchen . . . was so full of holes, flies were just coming in and out at their leisure, along with mosquitoes, roaches, and everything else. . . . The toilet was an outhouse with the pit so filled-up it was impossible to use."[31]

In the fish-processing industries of the Pacific Northwest and Alaska, Filipinos had begun to replace the earlier groups of Chinese and Japanese workers by 1921. After the growing season, a number of Filipinos made their way to Seattle's Chinatown, where they signed on with contractors, usually Chinese and Japanese, and waited for the ships to take them to Alaska. A few Filipinos eventually became contractors and some served as foremen of Filipino crews, but the majority filled the unskilled, most laborious, tedious, and lowest-paying positions along the processing line.[32] Vera Cruz, who worked in the Alitak cannery as a filler for one season, described the canning process: "First, the butchers cut off the fish heads and sent the fish to the fishwater where they were cleaned. Then everything went through a machine that cut them up and canned them. My job was to pull out the underweight cans from one of the conveyor belt lines, fill them up to the required weight, then put them back on the main line that then took cans through a sealer machine. That was all I did, a repetitious performance that made me dizzy watching all those cans in motion like a flowing stream of water." But Vera Cruz, like the other Alaskeros, quickly learned that unlike jobs in the agricultural sector, employment in the canneries meant relatively improved living conditions and higher wages. In the Alitak cannery, he recalled, the workers' bunkhouses were better maintained, food was provided, and "there was a cook, baker, dishwasher, and a couple of waiters even. . . . I received $500 for those two months of work which was good money then."[33]

In Los Angeles and other cities, Filipinos most often found employment in the service-oriented sectors, working as houseboys, chauffeurs, bellboys, kitchen helpers, dishwashers, busboys, or a combination of these jobs in part-time positions. In 1930 an estimated 11,441 Filipinos in California worked in these occupations.[34] But because the vast majority of these young men came from farming provinces in the Philippines, they had very limited previous experiences in these posts. Like the earlier European and Asian immigrants who came from rural communities, these occupations often served as an introduction to the urban labor market.[35] As a Filipino student at the University of Southern California in 1929 quipped, "most of us were initiated into American life by washing dishes 11 to 13 hours every day."[36] Another youthful Filipino, who attended a community college in 1935 but worked as a "schoolboy" for a family, recalled that when he first started, "I didn't know anything about cooking or cleaning the house. Yet the lady was good enough to show me everything she did. I learned to clean, to prepare dinner. I washed dishes when they were through eating. I later got another job for $15 a month still cooking and cleaning. . . . This job lasted until I graduated from Santa Monica Junior College and went on to UCLA for one year."[37]

For fountain-pen boys, Filipinos who came to the United States with hopes of attaining an American education, employment as domestics in private homes was a practical alternative to the migrant lifestyle that the majority of Filipino immigrants were forced to adopt in order to survive. Other Asian immigrant students to California, particularly the Japanese, had used this route to continue their studies from the end of the nineteenth to the early twentieth century. These "Japanese schoolboys" earned their room and board by performing household chores. At the peak of Japanese male migration, between 1904 and 1907, an estimated 4,000 Japanese schoolboys worked in San Francisco. One historian notes that although they received only token weekly earnings, about $1.50 in 1900 and $2 by 1909, "the job itself was the education: it provided the new immigrant with an opportunity to learn English and become familiar with American customs."[38] Many Japanese immigrants viewed working as domestics as temporary first jobs, and the majority shifted to agriculture and other urban employment, particularly gardening, as soon as they could. By 1930, the Japanese schoolboy had vanished.[39]

The demand for domestic labor, especially among urban, middle-, and lower-middle-class families where the homemaker had at least a high school education, increased considerably from the turn of the century until about World War II. The historian Phyllis Palmer shows that even during the Great Depression, homemakers who could possibly hire some help, even those in the lower-middle- and middle-class brackets with annual earnings between $500 and $3,000, managed to do so. Palmer argues that this reliance on hiring domestics, even among the lower middle class who could usually afford only part-time help, "reveals how central domestic labor was to a household's self-definition as middle-class."[40] Hiring and supervising domestics to provide the hallmarks of the middle-class home, including a comfortable and orderly residence, well-groomed children, and wholesome meals, became an important part of the dominant ideology and practices associated with the "proper" middle-class homemaker, or those who aspired to be so.

The demand for young Filipino domestics increased during the late 1920s, in part because of the exodus of Japanese male servants and in part because Filipinos proved to be good workers.[41] Filipinos who worked as domestics seemed to be eager to please their employers. A young Filipino who worked as a houseboy told a researcher in 1928, for example, that he spent every afternoon poring over American cookbooks so he could prepare the evening meals.[42] In the Pacific Coast states, Filipinos joined other Asian men, particularly the Chinese, and the larger group of female immigrants—including Japanese "picture brides," women of color, as well as single, working-class Anglo women—in forming a pool of part- and full-time domestic servants. Financial need, discriminatory practices, a lack of skills that locked them out of better-paying factory and "clean" jobs, language barriers, and limited alternative occupations compelled these workers, mostly women, to seek a source of livelihood characterized by disadvantageous hours, low status, and miserly wages.

Unlike industrial laborers, domestic workers faced irregular work hours, unregulated pay scales, and long stretches of drudgery in solitude. The length of labor demanded from the domestic worker, which ranged from seventy-two to eighty-four hours a week as opposed to the average workweek of fifty to fifty-nine hours put in by industrial workers, was a major source of tension between employees and employers, especially in the case of female domestics who had responsibilities for their own homes and families. One female maid in Los Angeles appealed to then First Lady Eleanor Roosevelt to standardize work hours, writing that "it has reached the point where [domestic service] employment is nothing less than slavery and is bondage for those engaged in it—for the hours are from 6 A.M. till 9, 10 and later into the night."[43] The relative lack of labor-saving appliances, even in middle-class homes, contributed to the long hours that made domestic service time-consuming and physically exhausting. Accounts by Japanese American women who worked as domestics in San Francisco during the 1930s illustrate how "employers stressed hand labor. Workers were expected to scrub floors on their hands and knees, wash clothes by hand, and apply elbow grease to waxing and polishing."[44] Mrs. Murakami, who started working as a domestic in 1921, recounted the rigors associated with domestic work, describing how "people wanted you to boil the white clothes. They had a gas burner in the laundry room. . . . When you did day work, you did the washing first. And if you were there eight hours you dried and then brought them in and ironed them. In between you cleaned the house from top to bottom."[45]

Despite facing the same meager wages, long hours, and poor working conditions that beset female domestics, some Filipino fountain-pen boys worked as live-in house servants because the job extended advantages that migratory labor, the alternative major field of employment open to them, did not offer. Foremost was that working as domestics facilitated their goals of going to school. They could stay in one place, and they could generally count on having some semblance of room and board within a reasonable distance from the university. In addition, the relative flexibility of hours and the task orientation of personal service allowed them to attend classes during the day. In the 1933/1934 academic year, about eighty-one fountain-pen boys lived, worked, and attended post–high school institutions in Los Angeles. The majority of these students attended community colleges, particularly the Los Angeles Junior College (40) and Woodbury College (2). The remainder went to four-year universities, principally the University of California at Los Angeles

(14) and California Christian College (12). In 1937/1938 the number of self-supporting students dropped to fifty-six, but with most of them attending four-year colleges, notably the University of Southern California (15) and the former California Christian College, renamed Chapman College (13). USC had nine graduate students in addition to the fifteen undergraduates.[46]

Miguel Lawagan's description of his life as a fountain-pen boy is illustrative of the experiences of many Filipinos in the Pacific Coast states. Lawagan worked as a live-in houseboy for a family to support himself while he went to school. During the week, his days began at 6:00 A.M., preparing and serving breakfast to the family and then washing and putting away the dishes. By late morning, after some light housekeeping chores, and while the husband and wife were at work and the children were in school, he walked a mile to the university for early afternoon classes. In late afternoon, he walked back to pick up the children from school and then to the house to start preparing the evening meal. His duties often lasted until past 8:00 P.M., after he put the children to bed. Barring any emergencies and additional chores, like dinner parties, Lawagan would then begin studying for his classes. On the weekends, Lawagan's duties included cleaning the entire house plus preparing an additional meal, lunch. His weekly wage averaged about $10, plus room and board. He recalled that "sometimes I had money, but most of the time I didn't. I couldn't even go to the movies. . . . You hate to spend your nickels, if you had any. So you stayed home, to study. Or look around for [another] job, but there wasn't any."[47]

Fountain-pen boys in Los Angeles encountered these same patterns of work, school, and wages. Severino Corpus, for example, emigrated from a farming village in the Ilocano-speaking region of the Philippines in 1929 specifically to pursue an education in an American university. He arrived in Los Angeles with a high school diploma but penniless, although he eventually found a full-time job as a cook in a private residence. As a self-supporting student, Corpus worked his way through an undergraduate degree from Chapman University and took graduate courses at USC.[48]

Other Filipinos, like those who had finished their tour of duty with the U.S. armed forces, viewed working in domestic service, especially as cooks, as a feasible source of livelihood. Because the Philippines was a U.S. colony, there were American bases in the islands where Filipinos could join the U.S. armed forces. A number of young Filipinos joined the U.S. Navy as a way to make a living and escape the grinding poverty they knew in the Philippines. The majority of these sailors worked in the naval kitchens and mess halls, where they learned how to cook. Johnny Garcia was seventeen years old and from a poor family when he joined the U.S. Navy in Manila in 1917. In the service, Garcia earned about $20 a month working in the mess hall of the USS *New York*. By 1934, he had worked his way up to a cook on the USS *Pennsylvania* when a swinging boom on the ship struck him in the chest. He spent most of the next eighteen months in recovery and was honorably discharged from the navy with a disability pension. Garcia went to Los Angeles and worked as a houseboy "in order to be doing something. The work is light and I earn my living that enables me to save the pension I receive from the government. . . . As soon as I feel better I am going to try and get a better job as a cook either in Beverly Hills or Pasadena."[49]

Filipino houseboys no doubt faced some of the same difficulties voiced by numerous female domestics: exploitative practices of the employers/homemakers, inadequate time off and rest periods, paltry wages, and the employers' refusal to acknowledge workers' independent lives. An immigrant Jamaican woman who worked as a housekeeper/cook for $10 a week in Los Angeles during the 1930s complained that "the employers here seem to think that you should be glad to work all day and night for a small salary."[50] There are indications, however, that some of the young, single Filipino houseboys received perquisites that helped cushion the more adverse conditions of the job, perks not usually accorded to their young, single, female counterparts. One of the perks allowed to a Filipino domestic in Los Angeles was the use of the employer's car during one of the housekeeper's two days off. "When I get the car," he said, "I usually take my girl friend for a ride and a dance at some classy place."[51] Additional privileges were often extended to the fountain-pen boys. One researcher noted that "if the family takes an interest in him (and many do!), he may get his laundry done free, be taken on trips, encouraged in his studies, and allowed a certain freedom of the house. [One Filipino student] employed by a family . . . was allowed the use of the dining and living rooms to entertain a small cosmopolitan group of friends."[52]

Whatever fringe benefits Filipinos received, however, came with a price. As the sociologist Judith Rollins articulates in her work on the inherently unequal power relations between female domestics and their female employers, "exploitation may be just as powerful when it is disguised in maternalism, in gift-giving, and in tolerance for irresponsibility. It is the motivation for and the belief system behind such apparently benevolent gestures that make them, in fact, highly beneficial to the employer at the psychological expense of the domestic."[53] While Rollins's work on the complex patterns of benevolence/exploitation in domestic labor focuses exclusively on the relations between women, her analysis is applicable to the business of hired help in the home in general. For Filipinos, because of gender considerations, paternalism played an equally significant role in making the young men more dependable servants for the family. Seaman Johnny Garcia, for example, was assigned as the personal cook for a rear admiral in the U.S. Navy. But his duties were not confined to the ship. The officer took him to his home during shore leaves as a domestic and on family trips abroad as a personal servant. Garcia recalled that he "soon became a permanent fixture in [the admiral's] household where I made it my business to be especially helpful to his wife. . . . Many were the presents that I received from him through his wife. He didn't want to appear kindhearted."[54]

In part through the psychological controls described by Rollins, some employers were able to effectively curb their employees' working-class activities beyond the workplace so that they did not interfere with the family's requirements for a dependable servant. Eddie Manzoa had been working as a domestic for a family in Los Angeles for nine years. One evening, he was arrested by the Los Angeles Police Department after a fistfight erupted in one of the many dance halls frequented by Filipinos along downtown's Main Street. Manzoa's employer, the husband, bailed him out. After the arrest, Manzoa avoided the dance halls, recalling that "it hurt his [the employer's] feelings that one of his family should get in trouble. He did not tell me that I shouldn't dance but I did not want to hurt his feelings so I have never gone back. He knows this and appreciates it."[55]

In addition to domestic work, an avenue of potential employment open to a few Filipinos in the Los Angeles area was the motion picture industry. Because of L.A.'s proximity to Hollywood, Los Angeles's ethnic communities have frequently provided bit players, extras, and, in a few cases, actors in starring roles, in movies that required an ethnic flavor. The most popular Asian American movie stars of the 1930s, Anna May Wong, Philip Ahn, and Luke Keye, hailed from Los Angeles's Chinatown. The community, located east of the film capital, had become a particularly important source of Chinese and Chinese American players in the 1930s, when the Japanese invasion of China attracted the attention and imagination of the Hollywood community. In 1934, when Metro-Goldwyn-Mayer began filming the movie version of Pearl S. Buck's novel *The Good Earth*, Chinatown supplied the thousands of Chinese and Chinese American extras.[56]

The stereotype of the "yellow peril" arguably played a significant role in the demand for East Asian actors as extras in Hollywood movies. In her work examining Hollywood narratives of race, inter-Asian sexual relations, and American identity, Gina Marchetti posits that "for the most part, Hollywood's depiction of Asia has been inextricably linked to the threat of the so-called 'yellow peril.' Rooted in medieval fears of Genghis Khan and Mongolian invasions of Europe, the yellow peril combines racist terror of alien cultures, sexual anxieties, and the belief that the West will be overpowered and enveloped by the irresistible, dark, occult forces of the East."[57] However, Euro-American actors, made up as "Asians," were almost always cast in the leading roles in the majority of these releases, with Asian and Asian Americans assigned bit parts to add "authenticity" to the films.

Throughout the 1930s, Chinese and Chinese American players received higher wages and remained in demand more than any other Asian group, but other Asian immigrants, including Koreans, Indians, and Filipinos, also found employment in the movie industry, most often as extras. Mohammed, for example, who immigrated from Calcutta and worked as a vaudeville performer around the United States until he finally settled down in Los Angeles, made his screen debut as a snake charmer and fire eater.[58] For Filipinos, screen time often meant work in movies with tropical island and jungle themes. Leo Aliwanag, who worked as an extra in several films, portrayed Filipino, Samoan, and Hawaiian "natives." Quite apart from the yellow peril stereotype of other Asians, the casting of Filipinos in these films more closely reflects what the anthropologist Fatimah Tobing Rony refers to as "'ethnographic cinema . . . the broad and variegated field of cinema which situates indigenous peoples in a displaced temporal realm." Rony posits that "ethnographic film reveals an obsession with race and racial categorization in the construction of peoples always already Primitive."[59] The casting of Filipinos in roles of island "natives," as "primitive" others, sustains the ways in which Filipinos were presented, most notably through World's Fairs, to the American public beginning at the turn of the twentieth century. Eager to display inhabitants of America's newest "possession" as a result of the Spanish-American War of 1898, social scientists and fair representatives brought indigenous Filipinos to the United States as exhibitions. On the fairgrounds, they were instructed to wear their "traditional" garb, reconstruct "authentic" villages, and perform "native" rituals, divorced from the reasons why those ceremonies would be executed in the first place, for the amusement of Euro-American and other fairgoers.[60]

But for Filipinos during the Great Depression, given the limited employment opportunities available to them, the lure of actually being on the silver screen, working with movie stars, and getting paid for it may be considered a step up the socioeconomic ladder. Robert Paz went from being a cook at the Brown Derby restaurant, then a posh meeting place for Hollywood's elite, to a steady job as an extra at Metro-Goldwyn-Mayer Studios after producer Sam Goldwyn spotted him and asked him to do a screen test for a South Pacific island movie starring Dorothy Lamour. Paz took a day off to take the screen test, recalling that "Dorothy Lamour saw me there and . . . she encouraged me that I should work in the movies. I have a chance to make pictures three times a year. . . . [The] pay is good. . . . I worked with Dorothy Lamour . . . with Gary Cooper . . . with Frances Farmer. . . . Who knows? If the war did not come, I could've been a leading actor."[61]

In the midst of the Great Depression, when the average daily wage of Filipinos was about $1, working as an extra represented an important source of additional income.[62] Leo Aliwanag drew an average daily wage of $25 to play parts like South Sea island natives. Aliwanag recalled that "$25.00 [a day], in those days, that's good money, you know." Furthermore, there was a potential for salary increases, up to $400, depending on the amount of acting they were required to perform and on whether they had a speaking part in the movie. Aliwanag received a substantial bonus when he delivered one line in *Alipang*, a film set in the southern city of Zamboanga in the Philippines. "So, they put me on the telephone and say something about, 'This is Zamboanga, calling,'" he remembered. "Just a few words, you know. They are giving me $25 a day, [plus] they give me $100 because I say a few words. That's big money."[63]

Besides being a source of supplemental wages, acting in films provided a welcome respite from the drudgery of the typical work patterns. One of the biggest film productions that hired Filipinos in the 1930s was director Frank Capra's *Lost Horizon* for Columbia Studios. The company recruited thirty-five Filipinos, at $15 a day each, to portray bandits. Veteran Filipino extras like Val Duran, Sammy Labrador, Jack Santos, Leo Abbey, Tommy Estrella, and Cachinaro Martin were cast in relatively bigger roles as the gang's leaders. One Filipino extra captured the festive atmosphere among his compatriots on location in Victorville, a desert outside Los Angeles. After they arrived by bus, "lunch was called, and there was a merry race for it. After-lunch found the gang either playing ball, going to a much-needed rest or indulging [in] penny-ante poker games." Following a day of rehearsal, the assistant director told the Filipinos to be ready for the next day's shooting at 5:30 A.M. The extra recalled that they were sound asleep "when suddenly . . . Moning Gonzales . . . hollered that it was already 5:30 A.M. Slowly, the boys started getting up to dress. Somewhere, one or two grumbled about it being still . . . so dark and early, and [Val] Duran volunteered that it was only 2 o'clock."[64]

Other Filipino entertainers, including musicians, scored their big break in the entertainment field by playing around the Los Angeles area. San Francisco–based Agcaoili Sabino and his orchestra began receiving better offers after a series of performances in and around L.A. Sabino, who graduated from San Francisco's Conservatory of Music and played the violin, recalled that "we played at theaters, nightclubs, and banquets, and for radio station KHJ in Los Angeles. One night we even played for Rita Hayworth in Pasadena. After that we got a lot of good jobs."[65]

In addition to potential work as extras and bit players, Filipinos enjoyed the aura of glamour that enveloped Hollywood and the chance for a firsthand glimpse into the movie star lifestyle. When Immanuel Tardez left the U.S. Coast Guard as a chief cook after six years, he set out for Hollywood, where, he recalled, "I hope[d] to see some of my screen favorites." Tardez eventually settled in Hollywood, working as a cook first for actor John Gilbert and then for producer Clifton Reed. For Tardez, one benefit of his job was being around celebrities and sometimes watching movies in various stages of production, noting that "I have a good time in Hollywood. I see many of the stars and sometimes when the boss [Reed] is nice he gets me a pass to the studios where I can see pictures being made. I get a great kick out of this."[66] Another Filipino houseboy who worked for a cameraman echoed these sentiments, remarking that one of the perks of his job was occasionally being able to "visit the studios and see all the stars."[67]

Even for Filipinos not necessarily desiring to work in Hollywood, Los Angeles and its environs proved to be desirable locations because they offered a variety of jobs and more diversions than the agricultural areas. A Filipino employment agent in Los Angeles constantly faced difficulties recruiting enough farm workers because "life is better here, they [Filipino Angeleños] say. They like the good times and conveniences of the city; they won't go into the [agricultural] camps."[68] Leo Escalona, for example, worked as a migrant laborer on various farms in the Pacific Coast states for two years until he came to Los Angeles, where he lived from 1932 until he was drafted into the U.S. Army in 1942. Escalona lived in Little Manila, in a hotel on First and Spring

Streets, and initially worked as a porter at the Club Century in Hollywood, earning $2 a day plus tips, until he found a better-paying position as a janitor in a convalescent hospital. In 1939 he landed a more lucrative job working as a handyman in an apartment complex on Los Feliz Boulevard, where he remained until he joined the army. Escalona claimed that work in the city was easier and steadier and paid higher wages than farm labor. "Plus," he winked, "[in Los Angeles] I could walk over to the movie houses on Broadway any time I wanted to, which was almost every day, for five or ten cents. I watched a lot of those sentimental movies. And I could also dress up once in a while. . . . I got me some fine suits and a pair of good shoes for going out."[69]

For Filipinos who liked urban life but preferred to work as agricultural laborers, the Los Angeles area was attractive because there were farms in the outlaying regions where Filipinos could work and still be within a reasonable distance from the city and its amenities. In the late 1920s, about ten Filipino crews were working in Los Angeles's citrus and vegetable industries, earning approximately $3.50 a day.[70] Bruno Tapang, for example, landed in San Pedro in 1928 and lived in Little Manila. He found a job picking lemons on the outskirts of Los Angeles, where he worked nine-hour days for about 25 cents an hour, plus a bonus of 7 cents a box. Tapang commuted between the city and the citrus grove by bus for three years, until he decided to try his luck in Alaska.[71]

Even for workers from other urban areas, Los Angeles was a preferred destination because of the relative availability of jobs. Vincent Mendoza, who was eighteen years old when he landed in Seattle in 1927, worked around Washington State until the Depression hit and he was unable to find employment. He and some friends worked in the Alaskan fish canneries for a season and then decided to head south to L.A., where another townmate lived. Mendoza and his friends were promptly hired as handymen and janitors in apartment complexes. Mendoza recalled that there was "lots of work in Los Angeles, if you're not lazy."[72] Indeed, a number of apartment managers remarked that they preferred to hire Filipinos because of their work ethic and well-groomed appearance. The manager of the Altonido Apartments in Hollywood said, "I like Filipinos, because they are honest, hard working and conscientious."[73]

Hotel and apartment managers throughout California hired Filipinos, sometimes preferring them over Anglo workers whom they regarded as sloppy, discourteous, and nearly constant complainers. Some no doubt employed Filipinos because they were desperate enough to work for lower

wages than Anglos, but most managers in the service and restaurant industries claimed to pay comparable wages and cited the Filipinos' overall good
manners, youth, and "exotic" appearance as important factors, especially if
they were hired in highly visible positions, like bellboys and elevator operators. Phil Riley of the St. Claire Hotel in San José, for example, said that the
Filipino busboys, janitors, elevator operators, and dishwashers employed in
the establishment since its opening in 1926 "have been most satisfactory. They
are neat, clean, careful of the equipment, and there is hardly any turnover. I
would hate to have to replace them with whites."[74]

The preference for Filipino workers in publicly visible positions because
they were youthful, polite, and well-groomed did not translate to better treatment outside the work environment. Like most people of color, Filipinos were
restricted by de jure and de facto segregation. Sam Figueras worked in the
lobby of the Los Angeles Theater for three months in 1931 until the theater
was forced to close because of poor attendance. As an employee of the theater,
Figueras was placed in a position that was in full view of the patrons, but when
he came to the theater as a customer, he was relegated to the seats toward the
rear. Figueras recalled that "in the theater they won't let you sit down by the
white people[;] they have to put you in the back where the Mexicans are."[75]

Whether working in the urban or rural sector, Filipinos occupied jobs
that were particularly sensitive to the increased work hours but declining
wages brought on by the Great Depression. During an era when other workers were succeeding in pushing for federal legislation to limit work hours,
protect union organizing, and provide minimum wages, retirement benefits,
and unemployment insurance through the New Deal, Filipinos were stuck in
occupations that followed preindustrial patterns of work that were generally
task oriented and labor intensive. Johnny Rallonza, who was a dishwasher in
a Los Angeles restaurant in the 1930s, remembers that when he first started
working, he received $45 a week for a nine-hour shift. But as the Depression
worsened, his wages plunged to $10 a week while his work schedule increased
to fourteen- and fifteen-hour days. Despite the hardships, Rallonza remained
with the restaurant because "I *had* to work! Too many people were out of jobs
and had nothing to eat and no place to sleep."[76]

One Depression-era study suggested that even before the full onslaught
of the Great Depression, the wages of Filipinos in Los Angeles had already
dropped between 15 and 33 percent over the late 1920s. For some Filipinos
working in the service-oriented industries between 1925 and 1930, work

hours remained the same, about eight to ten hours a day, but monthly salaries decreased, depending on the position. In 1925, for example, monthly salaries for a combination chauffeur and houseboy (including room and board) was about $125; a combination cook and houseboy (including room and board) was about $150; and a busboy (with board only) was about $80. Five years later, wages for these same jobs declined, respectively, from $125 to $95 (24 percent); from $150 to $100 (33 percent); and from $80 to $60 (25 percent). Furthermore, this downward swing was systematic. Average monthly salaries for Filipino elevator operators fell about 5 percent annually from 1926 to 1930, starting with $110 in 1926, and then dropping to $105 in 1927, $95 in 1928, $90 in 1929, and $85 in 1930, representing an overall 23 percent decrease within four years.[77]

Because of high rates of unemployment, Filipinos whose jobs included room and board, usually the domestics, fared relatively better during the Depression. At the very minimum, they at least had a place to sleep when numbers of their jobless countrymen were spending nights in the streets or, if they had a nickel, sleeping in all-night movie theaters. Chris Mensalvas, for example, was eighteen years old when he landed in Los Angeles in the midst of the Depression. He had no employment contract, no skills, and no friends in the city. During those lean years, he depended on charities for food and recalled spending his nights in "the theaters, the shows. There used to be a lot of all night shows. If you were smart you would go down there and sleep all night. Then in the morning you get out and go to the Soup Kitchens. May be [sic] you get a 7 cents cup of coffee. . . . A lot of us who got no rooms[,] especially the single guys . . . have to go to all night movies."[78] Some Filipinos also garnered additional compensation or other benefits for the long hours and paltry wages. Vincent Mendoza earned about $60 a month as a handyman in an apartment complex in Los Angeles, but he also periodically received bonuses from the owners and the tenants, especially during the holidays. Mendoza recalled that "they are very courteous. Christmas time when I am working sometimes they give me $150 for Christmas. . . . Some of them [tenants] buy me a shirt, bathrobe, . . . a half dozen of underwear."[79]

Wages among migratory laborers reflected the same fluctuations brought about by the nationwide economic slump. In Alaska's canneries, salaries for Filipinos in unskilled posts fell 40 percent between 1929 and 1933.[80] In California, a study by the state's Department of Industrial Relations estimated that Filipino migrant workers earned between 30 and 50 cents an hour or between

$2.50 and $5 a day during the 1930s. Sometimes their wages depended on the amount of crop harvested—for example, $1.10 per hundred pounds of asparagus, or 14 cents per crate of melons.[81] More recent accounts, however, indicate that these wage estimates for Filipino laborers were high.[82] As one historian points out, migrant farmers from the Dust Bowl expected to earn only about $2.50 to $3.00 for a day's work in California's fields during this same period. He argues that in comparison with the woes farmers faced in the midwestern states, these wages seemed promising, but "only in comparison with Hispanics, Asians, and blacks—groups plagued by severe racial discrimination—did the migrants' economic performance look good."[83]

Toribio Castillo, who worked in the Stockton area during the 1930s, recalled that workers felt "lucky" if they earned $2 for backbreaking twelve-hour days cutting celery or picking peaches.[84] Other migrant workers provided similar testimony. Celendo La Questa, Jacinto Sequig, and Florentino Mendoza remember making only $1 a day for fifteen-hour days performing backbreaking stoop labor like hoeing cabbage in the Salinas Valley.[85]

Despite exploitation and, especially for agricultural and cannery laborers, unsafe working conditions, Filipinos worked in the fields, fish-processing plants, and service-oriented jobs because these employment sectors remained open to them. Frank Coloma, who passed the civil service examination in Washington State, was nevertheless refused employment in Seattle and Tacoma. He then moved to Los Angeles, where he again passed the civil service exam to work in the post office, but again his application was rejected. He eventually found a job as a handyman/janitor in an apartment complex.[86]

The networks of jobs in agribusiness, fish canneries, and the service-oriented industry likewise gave some Filipinos optional ways of making a living should they choose to make changes in their lives. Toribio Castillo immigrated to the United States in 1928 to continue his education. However, he came from a poor family and arrived in California with no funds. To raise money, he immediately went to work as a migrant laborer around Stockton and Delano. After the season ended, he came to Los Angeles, where he found a job working at night and on weekends as a busboy/dishwasher in a diner. Castillo received a paltry wage, but he skimped and saved to support himself until he earned his B.A. in sociology from the California Christian College. After graduation, however, the only employment he could find was in migratory labor, so he again worked in California's fields. Eventually, he decided to enroll in graduate school, so he returned to Los Angeles and worked as a houseboy until he earned his master's in sociology from the University of Southern California. Because of pervasive racism, however, no employer hired him in a capacity commensurate with his advanced degree, and Castillo remained a domestic until World War II when he was able to lease land in Gardena, a suburb of Los Angeles.[87]

The relative availability of jobs in these sectors and the preference of some employers for Filipinos in those positions provided Filipino laborers with some room to negotiate the conditions of their employment. At the very least, Filipinos could withdraw their labor from a particular market. Vincent Mendoza, for example, quit his job at an apartment complex because he felt that the manager was too strict. He recalled that the shortest period he spent on a job was "when I was in Los Angeles, I worked for three months and I don't like the manager and I said, 'Go to hell. I am leaving.'"[88]

Other Filipinos, especially those in the service-oriented industries, developed different oppositional strategies that mitigated the indignities and verbal abuse from employers and from customers who associated them with servitude. The most common tactic was posturing as an overly sensitive person, easily hurt by any and all criticism or admonishments. The manager of an Oakland restaurant, for example, became more cautious about reprimanding the Filipino kitchen helpers and busboys after an incident where she "called [a Filipino employee] down only slightly for doing some of his work sloppily. He became gloomy and remained that way all day. In the evening I attempted to cheer him up and tell him that I hadn't meant to be abusive. At this he cried. That relieved him and soon he was cheerful again."[89] Indeed, the manager of the St. James Hotel in San José made it a point to compliment often the Filipino bellboys and elevator operators because they were excellent employees and he wanted to keep them. He realized that they are "very susceptible to flattery, [and] a pleasant word to the Filipino is as good as a coin."[90]

Despite the pervasive racism and discrimination that restricted marked socioeconomic mobility for the vast majority of Filipino laborers, several of them nonetheless sought to improve their lives within the realm of their working environment and the jobs open to them. Manuel Fiores, then a car mechanic in Los Angeles, earned about $30 a week, a significant income in 1937. Fiores, however, had spent the previous ten years working his way up to the position, starting out as a busboy in a restaurant in 1927 and then moving on to work in a gas station in Boyle Heights, where he earned $15 a week. In the eighteen months that he worked in the station, Fiores made it his business to learn how to be a car mechanic, and when he did, he "decided that I was worth more money and went about looking for a new place."[91]

Pride in doing their best contributed to this sense of self-worth among several Filipinos. Immanuel Tardez, who worked his way up from mess boy to chief cook in the U.S. Coast Guard and then landed a job as cook for the actor John Gilbert, sought to further improve his skills. He remembered that "I bought three cook books and memorized the recipes. I had heard about the fancy dishes that movie stars like and was determined that I should not be caught napping when the time came for me to do my stuff. I also experimented in the kitchen but had to stop when the butler started complaining about the bills."[92]

Filipinos also developed meanings of work and measures of respect by creating a hierarchical order based on the physical challenges of the jobs. The labor historian Chris Friday suggests that Alaskeros commanded the most deference among Filipino laborers, arguing that many Filipinos felt that "to be an Alaskero was to be a survivor, a toughened veteran of the canneries. Filipinos so desired to be part of that select group that a few stowed away aboard steamers headed for Alaska."[93] Indeed, several Filipinos who had worked in the canneries as part of the migration chain of labor continued to trek to Alaska every summer even though they had no compelling financial need to go. Peter Quintero returned to work on a freezer boat on the Yukon River for two months every year to process caviar during the annual salmon run. For the sixty-two-year-old Quintero, working in Alaska was more of an adventure, a reliving of his youth and a break from his daily routine, than an economic necessity. For the remaining ten months of the year, he lived with his cousin and his cousin's family in Seattle, mainly babysitting his cousin's four grandchildren.[94]

For most Filipinos, the growing cycle of crops and the annual run of fish dictated the rhythm of work, and the laborers' migratory lifestyle made the creation of viable ethnic enclaves exceedingly difficult. During the off-season, however, they generally returned to their Little Manilas. These communities provided some semblance of stability in their lives and opened up avenues for a few entrepreneurs. Little Manila contained Filipino restaurants and entertainment centers, some of them owned by Filipinos. Los Angeles's Little Manila in the 1930s flourished in the downtown area, roughly demarcated by San Pedro Street on the east, Sixth Street on the south, Figueroa Avenue on the west, and Sunset Boulevard on the north.[95]

Some historians have argued that Filipino laborers, even within the confines of their Little Manila, failed to construct a viable community because of the transitory nature of their work patterns. Ronald Takaki posits that Filipino enclaves functioned "mainly [as] gathering places for migratory workers. They were not places to live and build long-term communities."[96] But scholars like Takaki and political activists like Carey McWilliams, who makes a similar argument, miss the point. Filipino workers, precisely because their livelihoods depended on mobility, created networks of portable communities. News items and advertisements for hotels, restaurants, and services along the migration circuit that routinely filled the pages of Filipino ethnic presses attest to these systems of maintaining communal connections as Filipinos traversed between urban and rural spaces. Much like the newspapers of other immigrant and ethnic communities, the Filipino press "offered a reflection of a group experience.... It expressed a group's values, heritage, and changing sense of identity."[97]

A qualitative analysis of the extant copies of one of the major Filipino immigrant newspapers offers a glimpse of the realities faced by many Filipinos during the Depression. The *Philippines Review* was a major Filipino immigrant newspaper in Los Angeles during the 1930s.[98] It averaged eight pages and sold for a nickel a copy. The Caballeros de Dimas-Alang, a fraternal order, published the newspaper on the first and last Saturday of every month from its offices at 126–128 Weller Street. G. S. Moreno and Luis M. Tupas worked as managers. Florencio C. Aquino served as editor, and Manuel M. Insigne, Julian Bulaon, and W. L. Tambolero made frequent editorial contributions. As with most Filipino newspapers, the *Philippines Review* was published in English, in part reflecting the achievements of American educational institutions in the Philippines and in part recognizing that publishing in the numerous Filipino dialects was not economically feasible. Most of the immigrants came from Ilocano-speaking provinces and were not familiar with the several dialects, including Tagalog and Visayan, spoken by other Filipinos.[99] Newspapers also indicated a desire among those who arrived with little or no command of English for a medium of communication common with other Filipinos as well as a desire to know the language of the employer in order to get and hold jobs.

Datelines and stories in the *Philippines Review* exhibit many of the characteristics one would expect from an immigrant publication. For example, a number of news items and articles contained information about events in the

Philippines. This trend escalated after the passage of the Tydings-McDuffie Act in 1934, which promised Philippine liberation from the United States by 1945. The front page routinely featured news about the emerging Philippine government and the drafting of the new constitution. The debates between Manuel Quezon and Emilio Aguinaldo in their bid for the presidency of the commonwealth received full coverage. But news of events in the Philippines also delineated a contested terrain between the Filipino community and the larger society, the premise of American colonial policies toward the islands. The newspaper invariably expressed sentiments like "inspite [sic] of the pessimism expressed by selfish interests concerning our ability for self-rule, the Philippine Islands can point to thirty-seven years of progress in all branches of government unequalled by any other country in the Far East."[100]

The interlocking system of community implicit in the ethnic newspaper becomes most visible immediately before and after the seasonal migrations. In anticipation of the March trek to the canneries of the Pacific Northwest, for example, a slew of advertisements for establishments in Seattle, Washington, the way station for the Alaskeros, filled the February issues of the Los Angeles–based *Philippines Review*. Advertisements for services that could be found in Seattle included the New Manila Café on Sixth Avenue, the Rex Hotel on King Street, and the De Cano and Company Cannery Labor Agents on King Street.[101] In Stockton, the exodus farther north was likewise met in the *Philippine Examiner* with a string of advertisements from Sacramento, including the Kona Rooms on J Street, the Union Café on L Street, and the Grey Pharmacy on K Street.[102] Through the information from the ethnic press, Filipino migrant workers in Los Angeles and elsewhere knew that in Seattle they could stay at the Hotel Alps at 621 King Street for 35 cents a day or $2.25 a week.[103] By the same token, the return of the Alaskeros to the lower Pacific Coast states was met with anticipation by their friends and area merchants. A headline for the August issue of the Los Angeles–based *Associated Filipino Press*, for example, estimated that "Alaska Workers Due September 20. . . . to Spend $35,000." The paper announced that "more than seven thousand Filipinos who spent the entire summer working in Alaska salmon factories . . . are on their way to Southern California, having Los Angeles as their destination."[104]

Through commercials in the ethnic press, Filipinos also knew where compatriots could be found. This information proved salient for forging a geographically mobile community, given the lean years of the Depression, the pervasive nativist sentiments in the larger society, and a government that ignored their needs for survival. A spot ad for the Manila Garden in the *Philippines Review* advertised that, when in Salinas, workers can "while away idle hours wholesomely and pleasantly" in the establishment.[105] The *Philippine Examiner* in Stockton reflected a similar pattern. Routine advertisers included the L Street Restaurant in Sacramento and the Ninth Street Garage in Oakland.[106]

The assumption that Little Manila was unstable because it lacked permanent residents and buildings rests on an overly narrow definition of community as requiring a stationary population or a built environment. Because most Filipino laborers *had* to tailor a life in harmony with their migratory work patterns, they created a community that was versatile and, for them, functional. They took their communities with them. Information they found, and acted on, in their newspapers functioned as one mechanism of how the community called itself into being, wherever it was. Thus Filipino workers opened up arenas of struggle for space in an urban environment where powerful symbols of the dominant society, particularly "home" and "community," took on contradictory meanings. Leo Aliwanag always went "home" to Los Angeles between jobs that took him to Washington, Alaska, Chicago, and New York. "I roam around from one place to another," he recalled, "[but] my hometown was Los Angeles, you know. After I came from Chicago, get tired over there, go home to Los Angeles and go back roaming around again."[107]

Through its advertisements, ethnic newspapers like the *Philippines Review* also offered glimpses into a very public consumer culture of the Filipino community. Restaurants, dance halls, barbershops, and billiard rooms routinely took up a considerable portion of ad space. In a community limited spatially and whose patrons were mostly migratory laborers, services and entertainment centers thrived. In 1933, for example, there were seven barbershops, three pool halls, and twelve restaurants and cafés.[108] Five years later, despite an insignificant rise in the Filipino population because of the Tydings-McDuffie Act of 1934, which limited the annual quota of Filipino immigrants to fifty, in Los Angeles's Little Manila there were twelve barbershops, seven pool halls, and sixteen eating establishments.[109] The only nonentertainment enterprise that multiplied during these years was markets, growing from a solitary grocery store in 1933 to three shops in 1938, an increase that pales in comparison with the rapid development of recreation centers.[110]

The expansion and immense popularity of these leisure places dedicated to masculine pleasures testifies to the importance of public spaces for communal experiences in an immigrant bachelor subculture.[111] But the sites were also significant because they formed one branch of an informal employment network. In the pool halls and barbershops, not only did Filipinos learn about available jobs and prevailing wages, information they could also obtain from newspapers, but, more important, they gleaned particulars, including the disposition of possible employers and practical terms of negotiations for their labor, which were not readily available through other sources. Further, compensation for the information passed along this grapevine was based on reciprocity, rather than cash, which was a rare commodity among the workers. The exchange of "free" information was also critical because, typically, employment offices in Los Angeles charged anywhere from 25 cents to 10 percent of the first month's wages or as much as $10 as finder's fees for jobs.[112] Indeed, an economics graduate student researching the effects of Filipino immigration to the Pacific Coast in 1928 lamented that "employment agencies [in Los Angeles] are not able to furnish definite figures for the numbers in any occupation because so many Filipinos find positions through other avenues, such as the want advertisements in the daily papers, and through friends."[113]

Even when Filipinos turned to employment offices, being part of an existing network continued to be advantageous. Leo Aliwanag and a dozen of his friends were part of the fortunate few who weathered at least part of the Depression relatively well, working as stewards for faculty and about 800 students in a "floating university." Aliwanag was walking along Broadway in Los Angeles when he spotted a notice for "12 Filipinos wanted to go around the world" in the window of an employment agency. Curious, he went in to inquire, and the secretary asked him to bring back other Filipinos willing to work with him on the ship. Aliwanag went to his apartment complex and rounded up Pancho, Johnny, George, and nine more of his unemployed friends who, not quite believing such a job existed, nevertheless accompanied him to the employment office. Within an hour, the secretary had arranged for medical checkups for them with a doctor in San Pedro. When they mentioned that they had no money for her commission, she said they could pay her later, when they received their wages.[114]

As supervisor of the Filipino workers on the SS *Ryndam*, Aliwanag received the highest salary, $125 a month. But he and his friends supplemented their income handsomely by doing additional chores, like ironing shirts and running errands, for the faculty. They also received generous tips from the students, sometimes just for giving them extra ice cream for dessert or providing them with additional snacks. After only nine months at sea, however, the floating university docked in New York amid controversy. Aliwanag recalled that "when we reached Paris there were five girls pregnant... [and when] we went to the Mediterranean Sea, there were two more girls pregnant.... [In New York] we were [met] by... big crowds [and] others... [who] were very angry. Scandal ship."[115] Despite the abrupt ending of work in the floating university, Aliwanag had more than $1,000, even after sending a considerable amount to his family in the Philippines. He stayed in New York, working as a waiter at the Roosevelt Hotel, and then migrated to Chicago before eventually returning to Los Angeles.

In addition to the pool halls and barbershops in Little Manila, there were eating establishments, including the L.V.M. Café at 113 East First Street and Basa and Nocon's Café at 111 North Los Angeles Street, owned by Filipinos. These restaurants invoked images of family and home life to entice the bachelor Filipinos who formed the greater part of the workforce. Basa and Nocon's Café, for example, advertised that it was "the most ideal place in town. Prices very reasonable. Home cooking." The Lunch Counter, at 116½ Weller Street, ran a similar plug, proclaiming "Home cooking! Genuine Filipino Dishes."[116]

While advertisements for leisure centers and restaurants delineate a predominant bachelor society, commercials for cheap hotels in the ethnic press illustrate additional aspects of the Filipino experiences, a working-class lifestyle and de facto segregated housing in Los Angeles. Because of the alien land laws, Filipinos, like all Asian immigrants, were prohibited from buying land or property in the United States.[117] In any case, poverty and a migratory existence prevented the majority of laborers from becoming homeowners. Housing discrimination forced most Filipino workers in Los Angeles to live in the seedy hotels in and around Little Manila. A number of establishments in other parts of the city displayed signs that announced "No Filipinos Allowed," with numerous variations, including "No Filipinos or Dogs Allowed" and "Positively No Filipinos Allowed."[118] The Filipino author Carlos Bulosan remembers how, in Los Angeles, he and his brother were forced to live on "Hope Street, in the red light district, where pimps and prostitutes were as numerous as the stars in the sky. It was a noisy and tragic street, where suicides and murders were a daily occurrence, but it was the only place in the city where we could find a room. There was no other district where we were allowed to reside, and even when we tried to escape from it, we were always driven back to this narrow island of despair."[119]

Filipino workers' options for living accommodations in Little Manila also included the Union Hotel on 705 East Ninth Street, the Pacific Hotel on 121 San Pedro Street, and the Majestic Hotel-Apartments on Fourth Street. These facilities recognized the economic status and migratory nature of their customers' lives, advertising "moderate rates by day or by week," although some places that charged higher rates tried to entice them by emphasizing "hot and cold water in *every* room."[120] These cheap hotels, however, provided more than temporary shelter. Like the Mexican workers in the Los Angeles barrios examined by the historian George J. Sánchez during this same time period, Filipinos actively participated in the creation of a vibrant community in Little Manila through the personal choices they made.[121] This sense of community and fellowship was crucial during the Depression. These years hit the Filipinos especially hard. One study estimated that about 75 percent of the more than 12,000 Filipino laborers living in Los Angeles County lost their jobs.[122] In addition, New Deal legislation and the promises of a welfare state were meaningless to these immigrants because the Filipino exclusion law included in the Tydings-McDuffie Act of 1934 reclassified their status in the United States from U.S. "nationals" to "aliens ineligible for citizenship," effectively preventing them from receiving government relief through food and housing programs or the Works Progress Administration (WPA).[123]

One of the options open to Filipino workers was to turn to one another for support, banking on the traditional give-and-take inherent in the practice of *utang na loob*. Fabian Bergano, a migratory laborer who weathered three years of the Depression in Los Angeles, believed that Filipinos in urban areas were relatively more willing to assist one another than those in rural areas. While he found employment only in various menial jobs that paid little, Bergano stayed put in Los Angeles from 1929 to 1932 because "I feel that if I stayed in the city with lots of friends, you know how the Filipinos are[,] they have got to help each other even if they are not related."[124] Alfonso Yasonia echoed similar beliefs, relying on *utang na loob* when he lost his $17-a-week job as a busboy in a Los Angeles restaurant. Yasonia recalled that "I have a room with four other boys—when I am working I pay, and we all stay there. . . . When I am fired I go home and say to each of them, 'The room costs three dollars a week so each of you is going to pay a dollar a week.'"[125]

For some Filipinos, being able to provide solace to their countrymen and not have them rely on charity from outside the community became a source of pride. Johnny Rallonza, a migrant worker who eventually settled in Los

Angeles, proudly recalled that even in the midst of the Depression, he and his Angeleño townmates "never had to rely on the charity of soup kitchens to get something to eat." Rallonza worked as a busboy at the Tic Toc Tea Room in Hollywood, where he saved scraps of meat and vegetables from the dining room to take home to his apartment. At night, he would sneak as many as a dozen of his unemployed friends who had nothing to eat and no place to sleep into his small room in the Majestic Apartment-Hotels. They would cook a little bit of rice and stir-fry the pieces of beef and vegetables that he brought home from the restaurant into chop suey for dinner.[126]

Through the unending cycle of *utang na loob*, mutual aid and a sense of responsibility for one another's welfare frequently transcended institutions in the Los Angeles Filipino community and lessened their dependence on the larger society for assistance. Filipino applications for relief from the Catholic Welfare Bureau of Los Angeles and San Diego, the biggest private charity organization, numbered only 26 out of the annual total of 2,844 cases for the 1929/1930 fiscal year. Moreover, as the assistant executive director, Reverend James E. Dolan, reported, 14 out of these 26 petitions were requests for "minor services, such as information, direction, etc." The remaining 12 requests, said Dolan, were "actual major care cases," although he gave only 11 examples: "nine burials, one confinement case, and one budget case."[127]

However, because the vast majority of Filipino workers remained poor and the job situation erratic as the Depression worsened, personal commitments through *utang na loob* could not support all those in need. Filipino mutual-aid societies and fraternities sought to fill this deficiency, and the rapid growth of Filipino organizations gives some indication of a nascent ethnic solidarity. In Los Angeles, the headquarters of most Filipino associations, including mutual-aid societies and fraternal alliances, were in Little Manila, often on the same street or even within the same building. At one point, the main offices of the Filipino Patriotic Association of California, the Philippine American Club, the Philippine Catholic Club, the Philippine American Corporation Employment Agency, and the Caballeros de Dimas-Alang were all at 126 Weller Street.[128] At one time or another during the 1930s, at least twenty-four Filipino organizations served the community.

In general, there is a dearth of scholarly material on Filipino associations in the United States, with only bits and pieces available about some of the most prominent organizations, like the Caballeros de Dimas-Alang. In many ways, its history illustrates how some associations imported from the Philippines satisfied needs of Filipinos in the United States. Founded in Manila in 1906, the Caballeros promoted Philippine liberation from the United States. Dimas Alang was the pseudonym of José Rizal, the Philippine national hero who championed Philippine independence from Spain and who was subsequently executed by the Spaniards. In 1921 the Caballeros inaugurated its first U.S. branch in San Francisco, and by the mid-1930s twenty-six lodges existed in California, including one in Los Angeles. The fraternal organization provided its needy members with food, clothing, and funds for medical and burial expenses. Meetings were initially conducted in Tagalog, but because not all the members understood the dialect, English eventually became the official language. They retained Tagalog for ceremonies.[129] Along with the Caballeros, myriad other mutual-aid societies, including the Filipino Mercantile Association and the Filipino Brotherhood Association, attempted to fulfill the social and economic needs of Filipino immigrants. Other organizations, including the Filipino-American Christian Fellowship and the Filipino Federation of America, sought to address spiritual matters.[130]

The tremendous growth of fraternal associations and mutual-aid societies certainly attests to the process whereby Filipinos came to grips with the disparities in their lives and the difficulties in creating a sense of immigrant identity at a time when the host country was in the depths of an economic slump. But several obstacles also blocked that course. Privileged Filipinos, including those with post–high school or some university education and beneficial connections with the dominant society that most of the workers did not possess, led the majority of the ethnic social organizations and societies. For the laborers, the struggles for labor unionization as a means to mitigate the harsh circumstances and nurture some sense of Filipino identity better point to their heightening sense of ethnic and class solidarity.

Efforts toward unionization, however, proved to be problematic, in part because of the migratory nature of the vast majority of Filipino workers' lifestyles and in part because the National Labor Relations Act (Wagner Act), which protected workers' rights to unionize, did not extend to domestic and agricultural labor, sectors where Filipinos were concentrated. Despite the tremendous hardships, Filipinos pressed for unionization in order to fight for equitable wages, reasonable hours, and better, safer working conditions. Perhaps not surprisingly, the Filipino impetus to unionize was strongest in the two occupations where employment depended on a contractor and the most dangerous workplaces were found: California's agribusiness and Alaska's canneries.

In California, Filipino agricultural workers composed 42 percent of all nonwhite, unskilled labor in the fields by the mid-1920s. In part because of their visibility, these laborers suffered the brunt of anti-Filipino sentiments as charges of displacing white workers and lowering wage scales were heaped against them.[131] As the labor historian Howard De Witt points out, Filipino militancy emerged because "from 1926 to 1930 casual Filipino labor in agricultural communities was subjected to [every] imaginable racial taunt, verbal slur and social slight. Although seldom complaining publicly about their life in California, many young Filipinos developed attitudes of labor solidarity and ethnic identification for the first time in their lives."[132]

Campaigns for Filipino agricultural unionization were sporadic, and most strikes resulted in violent repressions and defeat. While small-scale outbreaks began as early as the 1920s, the first successful labor organization, the Filipino Labor Union (FLU), was not formed until 1933, when 700 Filipino lettuce pickers walked off the fields in the Salinas Valley. The strike failed, but in many ways, the solidarity garnered by the FLU signaled the emergence of Filipino activism and strength in California's fields.[133]

By 1934, the FLU had grown to more than 2,000 members, and it joined the Vegetable Packers Association, a predominantly Anglo union chartered by the American Federation of Labor, in a work stoppage in Monterey County. Anglo lettuce packers had initially joined the Filipinos in the strike, but then broke away and consented to arbitration with the growers. In the meantime, the growers summoned the California Highway Patrol, sheriffs' deputies, and armed vigilantes to terrorize and attack striking Filipino workers. Left alone, FLU members faced the brutal repression of the growers and their henchmen: striking Filipinos were beaten, stabbed, and shot. Vigilantes beat FLU president Rufo Canete and burned down his camp, forcing the hundreds of Filipino workers staying there to flee. Nevertheless, the FLU kept up the strike and eventually won its demands, including a 100 percent raise, from 20 to 40 cents an hour, improved working conditions, and the recognition of the union by the growers.[134]

Filipino workers organized to ameliorate working conditions, earn decent wages, and gain the growers' and cannery owners' recognition of their organizations as legitimate unions. This last issue was important to workers in order to remove Filipino contractors, thereby requiring the owners to bargain collectively with democratically elected union representatives and to pay the workers directly. Filipino laborers had long complained of Filipino contrac-

tors, who in many cases were just as exploitative and abusive as the growers and canners. The director of labor in the Philippines, Hermenegildo Cruz,
identified "absconding labor contractors . . . [who,] after receiving money from
the employer, get away with the money, leaving the laborers without their
wages" as a major problem faced by Filipino workers in the continental United
States.[135] Juan Castillo recalled that when he first arrived in the United States,
he found that Filipinos "could only depend on one job, and that is the Alaska
jobs, which is run by Filipino contractors. And, sorry to say, these contractors
have no regards for the [Filipinos]. They are only out for their own skins. The
condition became so bad that the boys were forced to do something about it.
The first thing that came to mind was to form a union to combat this vicious
system that is existing at this time."[136] Jesus R. Yambao recalled that the unionization campaign in the Alaskan canneries to protect workers' rights to fair
wages and safe working conditions went hand-in-hand with ousting contractors. "After 1944 when we get wise for ourselves," he said, "we joined the unions
[and] when we joined the unions we got more wages. When we went to Alaska
they were getting 35 dollars a month there but when we formed a union we got
more. . . . We eliminate the contractor."[137] Knowing that unionization threatened their economic position, contractors routinely undermined the workers' strikes. During the FLU work stoppage in California in 1934, for example,
Filipino contractors formed the Filipino Labor Supply Association, which furnished the growers with Mexican, Punjabi, and Japanese strikebreakers.[138]

Conflicts between Filipino workers and contractors highlight the limits of
ethnic solidarity. In general, contractors recruited laborers for jobs and in turn
received a portion of the workers' wages. In theory, contractors were supposed
to bargain with the owners for the fairest wages and for decent working conditions for their crews, collect the workers' salaries, and pay the men. While
some contractors lived up to their part of the bargain, others were unscrupu-
lous, taking advantage of their compatriots. As the sociologist and historian
Charles Tilly cogently points out, "Networks brought into being by immigration serve to create and perpetuate inequality. Lest anyone think that solidarity and mutual aid have nothing but gratifying results, we should recognize . . .
[that] members of immigrant groups often exploited one another as they
would not have dared exploit the native-born."[139] Eighteen-year-old immigrant Chris Mensalvas, for example, was approached by a labor contractor on
the dock as soon as he had landed in Los Angeles's port. Having no friends or
kin in the city, he went with the contractor. Mensalvas recalled that "the worse

part [was when] the contractors came and pick you on the docks. 'Okay, boys, let's go.' You don't even know where they were going to take you. They take you to these camps in California—Salinas, all those places, Stockton. . . . Those camps were terrible. But where else can you go when you just come from the Philippines? You have to stay there under their conditions." Because he did not know what else to do or where else to go, Mensalvas worked in the camps for the season, earning 25 cents an hour for backbreaking stoop labor. To boot, the contractor also charged Mensalvas for room and board after deducting his commission from Mensalvas's already meager wages. In order to escape working another season in the fields, Mensalvas fled to Los Angeles, where he worked as a houseboy while attending UCLA.[140]

For numerous Filipino workers in California's agribusiness and Alaska's canneries, the Depression years were a time of interethnic conflicts associated with unionization, brutal repression by employers, and plenty of defeats, but they also brought valuable ground toward their recognition as legitimate unions that negotiated directly with employers for equitable wages, safer working conditions, and humane hours of labor. The migratory lifestyle that Filipinos were forced to adopt in order to survive in their adopted country played a key role in connecting these movements, despite the geographic divide that loomed before them. Because Filipinos had to follow seasonal work, scores were involved in union activities in both California's fields and Alaska's canneries. Chris Mensalvas, who was snared by a Filipino contractor in Los Angeles and forced to work for a season in the agricultural camps, became one of the leading figures in the Alaskan cannery union movement, fighting for workers' rights and calling for the elimination of corrupt labor contractors. Mensalvas and his fellow union organizers routinely traveled between Alaska and California, and while they regarded Alaska as their primary residence, Mensalvas said that "there's not any town in California that you can mention that I have not been there [to help with union activities]. I've been in jail 5 to 6 times."[141] This pattern of transporting ideas and strategies through the migratory circuit was crucial in spreading the message of unionization in places where significant numbers of Filipinos worked. Mariano Angeles claimed that after he participated in the labor movements in California in 1935, he "was one of the first Filipinos who tried to put in the minds of Filipinos the advantage or the importance of unionism here in Seattle."[142]

By and large, however, the struggles for unionization were generally restricted to the fields and the Alaskan canneries. No comparable strikes were organized among Filipino workers in Los Angeles, and there were few union locals in the city.[143] Some Filipino labor organizers tried to unionize the small group of about 300 Filipino cannery workers on Terminal Island near Los Angeles's port, but the campaign failed, in part because of the unstable work schedules of the Filipinos. Although fishing and canning sardine, tuna, and mackerel were year-round occupations on Terminal Island, the Japanese managers hired Filipino laborers only sporadically, sometimes for merely two or three hours a day during slow periods and occasionally for twelve to fifteen hours a day during the heavy season. As a result, most Filipinos went to Los Angeles or to the agricultural centers in central and northern California for employment during the down cycles.[144]

Employment patterns of Filipinos in Los Angeles in part explain the relative absence of labor organizing in the city. The majority worked as domestics in private homes and in service-oriented industries, positions that have been historically difficult to unionize. Domestics, for example, spent the greater part of their job doing solitary work, isolated from their cohorts. In addition, the paternalism and maternalism associated with domestic service restrained many Filipino houseboys from confronting their employers and their exploitative practices. Eddie Manzoa, who worked for a family in Los Angeles for nine years, maintained that "I feel that I am as much a part of their household as their two young sons that I have practically raised. They leave the running of the house to me and when one of the children need spanking it is up to me to do it. We get along famously."[145]

Even if Filipino houseboys and their fellow house servants, the majority of whom were women of color, *had* been able to unionize, New Deal legislation that protected laborers' rights to unions and collective bargaining (section 7a of the National Industrial Relations Act and the Wagner Act, which supplanted it in 1935) excluded domestic workers. Without federal protection for organizing, some domestics attempted to better working conditions by campaigning for measures, including a maximum ten-hour workday, that would standardize the job's requirements nationwide. But bills introduced in Washington State and California in 1920, 1934, and 1939 calling for the regulation of domestics' work hours failed.[146]

Filipinos in the hotel and restaurant industries also faced tremendous setbacks in trying to unionize. Some turned to their Anglo cohorts for assistance, but since most mainstream culinary and service unions were chartered by the American Federation of Labor, they were prohibited by the AFL's constitution from both organizing and granting membership to noncitizens, especially "aliens ineligible for citizenship" like the Filipinos.[147]

The relative absence of a strong collective movement among Filipino Angeleños in the service-oriented sectors does not necessarily mean they did not develop strategies of resistance. Living in a major crossroad in the migratory circuit, Filipinos in Los Angeles were very aware of labor unionization efforts elsewhere, either through the grapevine or through their participation in the movement en route to the city. Before Vincent Mendoza settled in Los Angeles in 1937, he experienced the interethnic conflicts and violence associated with unionization in California's fields, working, unbeknownst to him, as a scab. Driving south from Seattle, Mendoza and his friends stopped in Stockton to try to raise some money to complete their trip to Los Angeles. A Filipino contractor approached them and offered them jobs, which they accepted. "And then, my gosh," Mendoza recalled, "we are working over there and they [Filipino workers on strike] come down and strike somebody and kicked the gate. . . . And then came the convoy, it was a mile-long convoy. Automobiles . . . and everything they barricaded the gate. The policeman got the rifles and . . . those strikers were forced to get in [the police cars] . . . and [the police had to] guard us when we are working."[148]

Given the nature of employment of Filipino Angeleños, the militant, confrontational style adopted by Filipino laborers in the agricultural fields and Alaskan canneries would not have been practical. As some scholars have explained, the location and social environs where the work takes place play a substantial part in the formulation of oppositional practices.[149] For Filipinos in Los Angeles, evasive tactics to improve their working conditions and strive for some semblance of autonomy proved to be more pragmatic. For domestics, one approach was to find their own lodgings, thereby reducing the time spent with and the demands of employers. Severino Corpus, a fountain-pen boy who worked as a family cook, lived at the Filipino Club on Winston Street.[150] Another option was to quit when the situation became intolerable. A Filipino houseboy who worked on Westlake Avenue for a doctor and his wife was ready to leave for his only day off when the woman called him back to clean up the mess the dog made in the house. At first he politely pointed out that he was not working that day, and he was already dressed to go downtown. He recalled that she then got very upset and sneered, "'Are there brown monkeys in the Philippines?' And yes, forgive me for this[,] I had to swear. This woman must be prejudiced, I thought. I said to her, 'Mrs. Miller, yes, there are brown monkeys in the Philippines. There are white monkeys, too. You'd better fix my time and I'm going to quit this day.' So without a word I went downstairs to the basement where I lived and really got my things. I went out and never went back."[151]

Filipinos who worked in the entertainment industry also faced obstacles in joining unions. The majority of mainstream organizations in the field maintained a requirement for U.S. citizenship, effectively locking out Filipino performers who may have wanted to join. As early as 1924, the American Federation of Musicians directed all its locals to ensure that members who were not American or Canadian citizens but who were eligible for citizenship in the country of their residence complete the process of naturalization within a "reasonable time . . . and, if he fails to do so, . . . erase his name from its membership list."[152] By 1938, officials of the Musicians' Mutual Protective Association in Los Angeles, Local 47 of the American Federation of Musicians, went one step further in passing a resolution that "all members of Local 47 twenty-one or more years of age shall hereafter be required, if foreign born, to become citizens of the United States in the shortest possible time provided by law, and that all such members be required to be registered voters."[153]

As laborers in service-oriented jobs, agriculture and extractive industries, and the entertainment field, Filipino immigrants developed meanings of work and pragmatic oppositional strategies to mitigate the harsh circumstances of their lives and to foster some semblance of working-class solidarity. Because the vast majority of Filipinos depended on patterns of migratory labor between urban and rural areas to eke out a living, they created portable communities that connected these experiences and that kept them in touch with their more stationary compatriots. News about acquaintances, living accommodations, possible employment, and unionization struggles traveled along the migratory circuit through coverage in their ethnic press or through word of mouth and helped Filipinos cultivate a nascent ethnic, working-class identity.

But as the Italian scholar Antonio Gramsci cogently argues, the negotiation of identities also occurs through the cultural processes, when marginalized populations engage in counterhegemonic strategies to impart traditions and experiences that differ from the larger society. Recreational activities among Filipinos elucidate Gramsci's observation. Because Filipino workers were relegated to the lowest-paying and most labor-intensive jobs, they explored alternative means of attaining some semblance of economic success in America. Games of chance in Chinatown's many gambling dens and lottery stands extended this possibility.

2. OF DICE AND MEN

Inter-Asian Relations and the Ethnic Vice Industry in Chinatown

> In California Professor [Paul S.] Taylor finds the Filipino
> considered a special problem by law enforcement officials.
> The statistics indicate that Filipinos "were arrested somewhat
> out of proportion to their numbers"; but Professor Taylor
> finds that "the explanation of this high percentage lies chiefly
> in the large proportion who were charged with offenses con-
> nected with gambling."
>
> —U.S. National Commission on Law Observance
> and Enforcement, *Report on Crime and the Foreign Born*

In 1937 Vincent Mendoza, his cousin, and two townmates packed their meager belongings, squeezed into their tiny, collectively owned Ford, and looked
around their Seattle neighborhood for what they thought would be the last
time. Mendoza's cousin and friends had just finished working the short Alaskan canning season and could not find jobs after their return to the Pacific
Northwest city. They decided to drive south to try their luck in Los Angeles,
and, at his cousin's urging, Mendoza agreed to join them. Mendoza recalled
that "the four of us in the small car, we carry our pots and pans, we carry our
groceries, [every] time we stop on the way to California, we cooked our food.
Make it cheaper, you know, don't eat in the restaurant. And then our car is
very slow and there is trouble in the carburetor, 'poop, poop, poop' . . . [and
it took us] five days to reach California."[1]

They arrived in Stockton, an agricultural center in northern California, at daybreak on the fifth day of their journey. They were broke, their food supply was almost depleted, and the car desperately needed repairs. To make some money to continue on their journey, they signed on with a labor contractor to harvest grapes, celery, and tomatoes. But even with the four of them employed, they estimated that at their wage of 25 cents an hour, they would have to work for more than two weeks to earn their goal of $15 a piece in order to stock up on rations, pay for the garage services for the Ford, and have enough money for gas to reach Los Angeles. Impatient to get on with their plans, Mendoza slipped into one of Stockton's many Chinese gambling dens with big hopes and 35 cents. He bet the entire amount on a lottery game, "and I make 'eight spot' so I got $365.00 . . . and then we fill up the car and we went to Los Angles with all our pack and pans and everything."[2]

This chapter focuses on the participation of young Filipino immigrants like Vincent Mendoza and his friends in extralegal activities, particularly gambling, not only as recreation to pass the time but also as a means of developing a version of socioeconomic mobility that was viable for an ethnic, working-class population. Because a majority of the games transpired in Chinese-owned gambling dens, the analysis examines how different Asian communities struggled for space in an urban environment that was generally hostile to Asians, immigrants, the poor, and other minorities. For Filipinos and other people of color pushed out of the workforce as the Great Depression deepened, the games of chance in Chinatown represented an alternative source of refuge and income.

The earliest record of Chinese presence in Los Angeles was in 1781, when some workers came to the pueblo as shipbuilders, but the first identifiable Chinatown in Los Angeles did not emerge until the early 1860s. The enclave originated east of the downtown business area near the Garnier Building, on Main and Aliso Streets, by Ferguson Alley on Calle de Los Negros, or, as racists called it, "nigger alley." Some Chinese businesses began to flourish in this neighborhood; in 1861 an herb shop, a restaurant, a curio shop, and four laundry services were already in operation. By 1890, Chinatown had defined geographic boundaries that would exist until the 1930s. The community was located around Los Angeles, Alameda, and Macy Streets, south of the central plaza. About 70 percent of the total Chinese population in Los Angeles lived in, or within walking distance of, Chinatown.[3]

The completion of the transcontinental railroad and escalating violence and racial antagonism from white laborers pushed Chinese workers out of the transportation, extractive, and agriculture industries. Chinese ethnic enterprises in Chinatown sought to provide jobs for these displaced workers.[4] Outside Chinatown, Chinese worked as unskilled laborers, cooks, domestic servants, fishers, and farmhands. Chinese Angeleños, for example, spearheaded the truck-farming enterprise. As early as 1880, some 208 (88.9 percent) of the county's 234 truck farmers were Chinese.[5] As the Chinese agricultural pursuits flourished, Chinese entrepreneur Louie Quan opened the City Market on Ninth and San Pedro Streets, where Chinese produce farmers could sell their harvest in one of the 200 stalls available. The surrounding area, extending to East Adams Boulevard, quickly became a satellite Chinese community in the first decades of the twentieth century.[6]

In addition to the legitimate, self-employed businesses, L.A.'s main Chinatown also housed a number of extralegal activities, including prostitution, gambling halls, and drug trafficking, in part because as in most cities, immigrants and the poor could afford to settle only in neighborhoods already deemed undesirable. Most of these areas invariably incorporated red-light districts. The immigrants' poverty and racial violence from the neighboring members of the dominant society maintained this segregation.[7]

The establishment and growth of Los Angeles's Chinatown exemplified these patterns of settlement, development, and violence. The small Chinese community began in and around an area that was already known for prostitute cribs on Alameda Street. The prostitutes around this area of "nigger alley" were mostly poor European immigrants and Anglo-Americans, but as more Chinese settled in the area, they began to displace the local residents. When the section became part of the Chinese community, Chinese women were imported for brothels to serve the largely male population of Chinese laborers.[8]

By the early decades of the twentieth century, there were two entrenched hubs of vice activities in Los Angeles that, not coincidentally, overlapped ethnic neighborhoods that also housed thriving, legitimate businesses: Chinatown, by the plaza, and on and around Central Avenue, by the African American district.[9] These sections emerged as an uneasy compromise among middle-class reformers, local politicians, the Los Angeles Police Department (LAPD), and the vice industries themselves.[10] As the sociologist Ivan Light argues, by the latter half of the nineteenth century, middle-class whites toured Chinatowns, including Los Angeles's, "to get a first-hand glimpse of the filth and depravity they expected to find."[11] In San Francisco, as the historian Nayan Shah chronicles, public health officials conducted both formal and informal inspections of the ghetto, accentuating how Chinese men and women—by living in "overcrowded" housing, "unventilated underground habitations," and the general "nauseating" atmosphere—presented dangers of epidemic proportions to the city's white residents.[12] Writing about segregation and ethnic vice in general and prostitution in particular, the historian Neil Larry Shumsky posits that "respectable" Americans tolerated tenderloin sections on the assumption that they provided spaces wherein the assumed uncontrolled sexual desires of immigrant and working-class men were met, leaving "decent" women safe in other sections of the city. "Such a district," he continues, "helped establish the boundaries of proper behavior; those who accepted the sexual norms of proper society avoided the district while those who rejected propriety frequented it."[13]

In Los Angeles, the exciting attractions to be found in the Chinese quarter did not escape the notice of its Filipino neighbors farther south on Main Street. The populace of Little Manila closely resembled that of Chinatown: single, working-class men constituted the largest portion of both communities. In 1930, 80 percent of the Chinese population was male, compared with 94 percent of the Filipino.[14] In addition, the Filipinos were young, with the vast majority of them being under twenty-four years old. In the gambling dens, these Asian immigrant communities of bachelors participated in titillating games of chance, with the ever-present possibility of winning the jackpot.

For the Filipinos, youth and being away from their parents for the first time in their lives contributed part of the stimulation. The immigrant experience of these Filipinos was distinct from that of other immigrants who may have come to the United States as adults or as children with their families. Familial tensions associated with consumption of commercialized entertainment and extralegal activities was relatively absent among these immigrants, because their parents and older kin remained in the Philippines.[15] John Mendoza, who immigrated to the United States in 1927, remembered that there were many difficulties in the community "because you know, [I was] seventeen years old, first time to get away from home[,] nobody tell you, 'Don't do this, don't do that.' Where as at home . . . you better look out, don't do anything wrong because you will be punish[ed] by your parents, but over here[,] nobody."[16] Subsequently, the peer group emerged as the primary network that set the social boundaries in the community. Ray Corpus, who immigrated when he was fourteen years old, recalled that in the Filipino community of the 1930s, "we were all males at that time, from L.A. to Seattle. . . . So what do we have to do? We were young so we go to Chinatown because there are a lot of, ah, things going on there. Taxi dances, prostitution, whatever, they were there. And of course young people like me at the time, I like to try everything to see what it looks like as opposed to, you know, [reading about] it in the books."[17]

Young, unbridled by parental supervision, but forced by poverty and de facto segregation to live in small, shoddy hotel rooms on and around Main Street, Filipinos took to the streets as an extension of their entertaining quarters. The walkways leading to the various recreation centers and the hotels became strategic meeting points in the Filipinos' social lives. Filipino foot traffic was so brisk that at least one researcher observed that "Filipino arrests in Los Angeles for blocking the sidewalk alone run proportionately high. In 1928–29, 46 of the total 80 arrested under this ordinance were Filipinos."[18]

The gambling dens in Chinatown became a fixture, along with the billiard rooms and the dance halls, of the lively street culture nurtured by the youthful Filipino immigrants. Twenty-three-year-old Alfonso Yasonia recalled that in 1929 L.A., "there were about fifteen gambling houses [in Chinatown], and you could go in and out without being searched. The Filipinos [who are between jobs or on their days off] go to the gambling houses in the daytime and about six o'clock they go home, dress up, and go to the barbershop. They put cologne on, and sticky, greasy pomade on their hair. . . . Later [they] go to the dance halls, like the Hippodrome in Los Angeles."[19] In 1929 there were more than twenty gambling houses fully operating in Los Angeles, despite the claims of District Attorney Buron Fitts that the city's dens had been closed down.[20] As an Asian immigrant group, Filipinos were among the most frequent patrons, second only to the Chinese, of this extralegal enterprise.

Chinatown offered two ways of wagering: in the gambling halls and through the lottery. The dens were usually open to Chinese and other patrons, including Filipinos and Japanese, and typically operated close to twenty-four hours a day, seven days a week. Employees included doormen, money-changers, dealers, pit bosses, and a runner, who collected the house's profits every day. Generally, a customer had to identify a secret password or be known to the guard in order to enter the halls. Sometimes there was a second scrutiny before admission to the gaming tables.[21] Filipino patrons, however, were ordinarily not subject to these body searches.[22]

Once in the den, there were a variety of games of chance from which, on average, the house got 5 to 10 percent of the bets. The most popular game was fan-tan. A number of small, colored disks (usually buttons) are put on ten-foot-long board, which is typically covered with a black-and-white tablecloth. Some of the disks are then covered with a cup, and the rest are set aside. The patron bets on numbers between one and four. The dealer then takes off the cup and starts eliminating the disks in groups of four until the amount of the residual buttons is between one and four, and the patrons who guessed the correct number win. *Pai kow*, another favorite game, is played with dominoes. Each player receives four blocks and bets against the house's four. The winners must have a better combination than the dealer.[23]

The other form of wager, the lottery, was available outside the gambling halls and transcended Asian immigrant patrons, although the tickets were usually available only in Chinatown. Because California's constitution banned lotteries and lottery stands, the Chinese sold tickets from behind the counters of legitimate businesses. An undercover Filipino journalist for *Ang Bantay* (*The Guardian*), a Los Angeles–based Filipino newspaper, reported that in Vallejo, as in all other cities throughout California, Chinese lotteries "are conducted under the guise of grocery stores, cigar stands, pool halls, dry goods stores, chop suey houses, and other places of the most unsuspecting nature," including the Hongkong Grocery Store and the Lucky Spot Cigar Stand.[24] In Los Angeles, establishments selling lottery tickets often posted employees outside their doors to screen potential informants as well as to solicit customers from the streets.[25] As another added precaution, lottery tickets were printed with Chinese characters that corresponded with numbers. *Baakgapbiu*, the Chinese lottery, was comparable to keno. The ticket contained numbers from one to eighty, and the patron could bet on up to ten "spots" (numbers) on the card. The winning ticket had to match the numbers drawn by the issuing house in its scheduled daily drawings.[26]

While Filipinos were as eager as the Chinese to participate in the Asian gambling dens and lotteries, relations between the Chinese hall owners and the Filipino patrons were tenuous. The tensions existed in part because the positions of the Chinese and Filipinos in the larger Asian immigrant community duplicated the pattern that Filipinos were already familiar with, and resentful of, from their experiences in their homeland. In the Philippines, Chinese and Chinese mestizos (usually, Filipinos with Chinese fathers and Filipina mothers) constitute a separate, elite merchant class, a position they acquired during the Spanish colonial rule. The Spanish outlawed Filipinos from small business enterprises and encouraged Chinese merchants to fill the role. During the Spanish period, Chinese settlers and mestizos came to form a distinct class, sometimes becoming local elite, by serving as economic mediators between the *peninsulares* and the *indios*. Although the Spanish lifted the ban on Filipinos in the early nineteenth century, the Chinese and Chinese mestizos had already established their status within the islands' socioeconomic hierarchy.[27]

Perhaps not coincidentally, one of the wealthiest Filipinos in the Los Angeles area in the 1930s, Arturo Gonzales, was a Chinese mestizo, the son of a well-to-do Spanish merchant born in the Philippines and a Chinese mother from an affluent family in Shanghai. Gonzales was only a boy when pirates murdered his father during a business trip. Mother and son continued to live in Manila, but with the outbreak of the Spanish-American War, they left for Shanghai to live with the mother's family. The grandfather renamed the boy Sen Lum and, despite his grandson's young age, began training him as a merchant, eventually sending the young man to Columbia University to earn his bachelor's and master's degrees. The grandfather and grandson became partners in a lucrative import-export business between the United States and Shanghai. When the old man died, Sen (Gonzales) inherited the business. He continued to run the company from his comfortable home in West Hollywood while a cousin in Shanghai managed the offices in Asia.[28]

Gonzales, however, was an exception. In part because of historical circumstances, most of the handful of Filipino entrepreneurs in California in the 1930s tended to concentrate in small, service-oriented businesses like barbershops and street vending.[29] A few opened Filipino restaurants, like the Brother's Café at 121½ West Second Street, the Filipino Café at 243 East Second Street, and the Ermita Restaurant at 121 South Los Angeles Street, which catered primarily to the large bachelor community in Little Manila.[30] "I wouldn't criticize Filipino people when it comes to business, but I don't think they are as successful as the Japanese or the Chinese," Fabian Bergano explained, "so with those times [the 1930s] I think the line of business to the Filipinos is not really profitable, because they don't have the know-how. . . . The businesses in the Philippines are controlled by foreigners."[31]

For other goods and services, Filipinos had to depend on the relatively numerous and more entrenched Chinese and Japanese businesses. But because of their experience with the Chinese in the Philippines, Filipinos viewed American Chinese merchants and small business owners within and outside their ethnic community with resentment. There were very few hostile outbreaks between the two Asian communities in Los Angeles, however, and Filipinos continued to patronize Chinese legal and extralegal enterprises. Nevertheless, as a contemporary sociologist pointed out, the Filipinos retained their suspicions, prejudices, and "hostile attitude" toward the Chinese. For their part, Chinese and Japanese immigrants, because they were "more economically settled and socially established . . . [were] apt to look down upon Filipinos where these [occupied] the least desirable occupations and living quarters in the community."[32]

Despite the tensions, inter-Asian relations were also symbiotic because both the Chinese and Filipino immigrant communities, to a certain extent, relied on gambling as part of an alternative ethnic economic support system. Restricted to slums, effectively locked out of well-paid legal jobs, and relegated to labor-intensive industries, both peoples searched for ways to alleviate problems of poverty and chronic underemployment. Like their African American counterparts who faced the same housing segregation and discriminatory policies in the legitimate workforce, Chinese and Filipinos turned to the ethnic vice industry to define a space for themselves in a hostile urban environment and to provide solutions to their individual and communal difficulties.

The social historian Mark H. Haller understands this relationship between marginalized communities and the ethnic vice industry. Writing about policy gambling, a form of lottery popular among African Americans in Chicago's South Side from the turn of the century until 1940, Haller convincingly shows that the activity supported an ethnic economy, becoming a basis for hope in a community devastated by the Great Depression as numerous legitimate black businesses failed and workers lost their jobs. Policy gamblers increased their prestige in the community and emerged as viable alternative institutions by supporting legal establishments, funding black teams and sporting events, and generously contributing to charity organizations.[33] Ivan Light emphasizes the significance of the ethnic vice industry as an alternative financial institution in supporting legal businesses in African American communities: racketeers have traditionally invested heavily in black-owned business while "numbers bankers have been virtually the only sources of business capitalization available to local blacks, lacking collateral or credit rating."[34]

Like African Americans, most of the Chinese were effectively disenfranchised from the dominant society's political and economic sectors through racist legislation and class domination. In Chinatowns, the ethnic vice industry emerged as an integral part of the community's alternative economic system. The game houses, for example, employed numerous Chinatown residents and paid better wages than the occupations open to the Chinese outside the enclave. These jobs became especially crucial during the lean years of the Great Depression, when work in general was hard to find. In addition, Chinese dealers could anticipate tips from generous winners and significant bonuses from the owners during holidays like the Chinese New Year. Because non-Chinese also patronized Chinatown's dens and lottery stands, the enterprise produced millions of dollars of income for the ethnic community. Revenues from the gambling halls were often used to bolster the neighborhood's local economy, including supporting legal Chinese businesses like restaurants and curio shops and providing assistance to the needy.[35]

For the Filipino patrons, playing games of chance in Chinatown, because gambling held possibilities of winning supplemental funds, became one way of redefining the American dream. Filipino immigrants had learned about this concept from a combination of sources, including their American teachers, labor recruiters and representatives of American agribusinesses, and letters sent home from Filipinos who had already immigrated. Because the Philippines was a U.S. colony, the American administrators in the islands established an educational system patterned after that in the United States and staffed by American missionaries and instructors. Colonial officials mandated that Filipino children attend these public schools, where the coursework included English and U.S. history. Mariano Angeles, who emigrated when he was about twenty-one years old, did so because "it [was] always my ambition to go abroad," having learned about the United States from the missionaries who lived as boarders in his family's home, his American teachers in high school, and a townmate living in Iowa.[36]

Once in the United States, however, the majority of Filipinos faced harsh living and working conditions and low wages. Several immigrants reasoned that if the proverbial pot of gold could not be had through long hours of strenuous labor, then perhaps Chinatown's various gambling dens might provide the solution. "All the money we make," recalled Toribio Martin Sr., who immigrated in 1926, "is not enough to maintain ourselves, you know, throughout the whole year. . . . [But there were] lots of gambling houses in Chinatown, we go down there and take a chance with our last money hoping that we [might] strike it rich."[37]

Because the winnings were substantially higher than the salaries that Filipino laborers earned within the same amount of time, profits from gambling were usually the only way Filipinos could get enough money in a lump sum to make tangible differences in their lives. When Alfonso Yasonia lost his job as a busboy in Los Angeles, he decided to work as an agricultural laborer for a while. To pass time in the evenings, he gambled in the various Chinese dens along the migratory circuit. In northern California, Yasonia won $400, an amount that represented more than six months' wages had he continued to work as a busboy in Los Angeles, where he earned $17 a week, and approximately sixteen months' salary for working as a farmhand at a time when the majority of Filipino laborers earned $1 a day for ten- to twelve-hour days. With his winnings, Yasonia decided to treat his friends to steak dinners in a restaurant, where they had to wait a long time to be seated and where the waitress was obviously reluctant to serve them. Yasonia recalled that after they finished eating, "I have plenty of change in my pocket—maybe five dollars worth—so I fill the saucer the waitress gives me with the change. And I tell my friends, 'We will come back here and you will see the difference in how they treat us!'" After the picking season, Yasonia and his friends returned to the restaurant on their way back to Los Angeles. "My friends say, 'We can't eat any more,'" he recalled, "but I told them, 'Eat, or don't eat if you don't want to, just order something.' So we go in and they wait on us right off—no problems at all. Then I see that money is power!"[38]

In addition to the potential tangible rewards that winnings in Chinatown held, Filipinos participated because the Chinese dens provided free food, beverages, and lodging for as long as the gambler played.[39] Leo Aliwanag recalled that he and his friends visited the halls "because it is free to eat.... You have soda water there free. And maybe in the afternoon one after another, they offer something [to] eat, you know. So naturally, the Filipino go there."[40] Complimentary fare was usually available on long banquet-style tables during the houses' hours of operation, typically starting very early in the morning until late into the night or even dawn of the next day. Some halls stayed open twenty-four hours a day.

The prospect of winning, plus free provisions and shelter, became especially attractive when thousands of Filipino workers became unemployed as the Great Depression deepened. Yasonia recalled that before he lost his busboy job in Los Angeles, "I wonder why the Filipinos go to the gambling house—why they don't want to work? But then I discover there is free donuts and coffee at the gambling house available twenty-four hours a day. So in the morning I don't have to worry about breakfast. In the afternoon there is a table full of all kinds of food—you just help yourself."[41] For some Filipinos, the steady availability of food balanced the loses they might incur in the dens. Felipe G. Dumlao remembered that "you go to the gamble house. . . . You never got hungry because coffee and doughnut in there, all day. . . . You go there and sit there, drinking coffee and doughnut anyway, you even win four time[s], three time[s] or a hundred time[s], you could eat that hundred doughnuts. . . . They [Chinese] won't stop you."[42]

While gambling and lotteries provided certain amenities to the Chinese and Filipino communities that were not available to them in the dominant society, the more affluent Anglo classes and their policing agents viewed the extralegal activities with wary eyes. Of course, legal gambling establishments for the rich, including the race track at Santa Anita and the luxurious game ships anchored the requisite three miles from the ports of Los Angeles and Long Beach, existed.[43] But as scholars like Sidney L. Harring point out, in American cities, "working-class vice areas received more attention than those of higher classes in the crackdowns that the police repeatedly undertook at the behest of reformers."[44] One of the reasons for the demand was that the upper classes and reformers viewed gambling, especially among the immigrant, ethnic, and laboring classes, as an infraction of the Protestant work ethic. Wealth and respect are achieved through diligent, honest work, *not* through winning a game.[45] That positions in these legitimate, well-paying jobs that allowed Asians in particular and women, immigrants, and people of color in general opportunities to ascend the socioeconomic ladder were basically nonexistent did not sway mainstream conviction in the ideology. The historian Ann Fabian posits that reformers during the American industrializing period of the nineteenth century denounced games of chance because "when gamblers, especially working-class gamblers, won, they ceased to labor and quickly adopted the airs of decayed aristocrats. Winning undermined the character of true and steady workers; winners grew distracted, lazy, and useless."[46]

Closely related to gamblers transgressing the work ethic was the perception that workers were squandering their time in useless pursuits and, furthermore, getting involved in the criminal ventures that the dominant society imagined were affiliated with most, if not all, working-class leisure activities. That the campaigns led largely by the privileged classes criminalized these enterprises in the first place, forcing them to operate surreptitiously, neither troubled the reformers nor quelled the inclination of the workers to gamble. Indeed, the single highest category for Filipino arrests in Los Angeles during the 1920s and 1930s was gambling, including patronizing the dens and possessing gambling paraphernalia and lottery tickets. Between 1928 and 1931, of the 1,360 Filipino Angeleños arrested, 348 (26 percent) were for gambling infractions.[47] This pattern also held true in San Francisco, where in 1929, 320 (37 percent) of the total 859 Filipino arrests were for gambling-related charges.[48] As for the Filipinos' gambling cohorts, Chinese and Chinese Americans, the arrest rates were higher in part because they were more numerous than Filipinos and in part because they also generally managed the gambling dens and lottery stands, activities that constituted separate, additional charges. In San Francisco in 1929, some 5,162 (92 percent) of the 5,604 Chinese arrests were for gambling, possession of gambling materials, and "keeping" gambling establishments.[49]

The data do not indicate how many Filipinos and Chinese were repeatedly apprehended for the same offenses, but even with the high arrest rates, these working-class immigrants were hardly "criminals." Gambling and gambling-related charges were, after all, misdemeanors. In addition, given the youthfulness of the Filipinos and the drudgery and harsh circumstances they typically faced in their daily lives, the immigrants viewed gambling as a source of excitement, not as a full-time career. Most immigrants probably echoed young Felix Tapiz's remark that "I never gambled before I came to this country. But I wanted adventure, and so I said, what is money anyway? It's only good to help you have a good time."[50] Furthermore, Filipinos did not willingly give up their jobs en masse or become lazy when they won the pot, as the dominant society believed of working-class gamblers.

From the 1920s until World War II, Filipino laborers, including those who gambled like Tapiz, composed significant proportions of the agribusiness and service-oriented sectors in the Pacific Coast states as well as the Alaskan canning industries. In addition, Filipinos who won money in gambling did *not* leave the workforce, in part because the pot was never that sizable a sum. Since Filipinos had limited capital from which to wager, they usually could not participate in the high-stakes games that generated the more lucrative returns. Moreover, Filipinos as a group tended not to be reckless bettors. While Filipinos, like all gamblers, invested tremendous amounts of hope in winning the big jackpot, the majority of Filipinos regarded gambling as a combination of one of the options among their recreational activities, as a means of getting complimentary food and beverages, and as a potential source of *supplemental* income. Many Filipino gamblers followed Alfonso Yasonia's cautious approach: when playing against the Chinese house, "you've got to be smart—when you make twenty-five dollars you quit because if you want more, maybe you go home with nothing. So when I make twenty-five dollars I don't play anymore. And when I get home, I got twenty-five dollars to put under the carpet. When I go the next day I put only a few dollars in my pocket."[51]

In addition to class conflicts with the dominant society and its police agents and despite the advantages that gambling provided to the Asian immigrant patrons, the extralegal industry also caused rifts within the Chinese, Filipino, and Japanese communities. The intraethnic conflicts illustrate the different perceptions of Asian identity politics, strategies of survival, and class stratifications among these ethnic Angeleños.

Japanese community leaders, with support from the imperial government, were the earliest and most aggressive in discouraging their working-class countrymen from patronizing the Chinese gambling halls for economic as well as moral reasons. This campaign began with the large-scale emigration of the Japanese around the end of the nineteenth century and continued through the early decades of the twentieth century. In Los Angeles, members of Japanese reformist societies routinely positioned themselves outside the doors of Chinese-owned lottery stands to dissuade Japanese workers from patronizing the establishments.[52] Yet, as the historian Lon Kurashige points out, the Japanese Angeleño laborers were hardly as problematic as the ethnic community's elites perceived them to be. While the workers were certainly not from the privileged classes, neither were they from the lowest rungs of Japanese society. And since gambling has been part of Japanese tradition since the Meiji period (1868–1912), "it should not have been surprising that the immigrants transplanted it to America."[53]

Among the Chinese, merchants and restaurant owners battled with tongs over the existence of vice industries in Chinatown.[54] Tongs, the largest of which were the Hip Sing, the On Leong, the Bing Kong, and the Suey Sing, had branches in every major Chinatown to control and protect the extensive extralegal operations in the community. These gangs engaged in various forms of racketeering, including smuggling Chinese prostitutes into the United States and paying off police and politicians. Their teams of mercenaries, the *boo how doy*, collected overdue gambling debts and kept rival factions and potentially unfriendly witnesses in check. Vice operators made monthly payments to the syndicates in exchange for these services, although some tongs also operated their own gambling resorts, bordellos, and opium dens. The ethnic vice industry represented the major source of income to the tongs.[55]

A number of Chinese store owners and restaurateurs, however, wanted the syndicates out of Chinatown for social and economic reasons. While some of these vendors indeed benefited from revenues of the industry, the merchants as a class were also the ones most likely to have families in Chinatown, and they wanted a good environment for their children. In addition, the tongs extorted money from these business owners for protection from police raids, assurance that the merchants felt they did not need because they operated legitimate businesses. Furthermore, because their livelihood depended in part on middle-class, non-Asian tourists, the merchants had a stake in eliminating vice and the multiethnic hoodlums whom the enterprises attracted in the Chinese enclave.[56]

Arguably, the most pressing reason to eradicate the vice industry was because of the recurring tong wars, which not only kept Chinese shoppers at home and Anglo tourists away from Chinatown but also endangered the lives of the merchants themselves. Because store owners and restaurateurs were forced to pay tribute to the tongs that controlled the area where their businesses were located, the merchants were considered members of those particular sects and, therefore, prospective targets of rival tongs during the wars. As a sociologist explains, "In wartime, tongs put a price ('a pie') on the head of all members of the hostile tong or tongs. The more affluent and conspicuous a tong member, the more 'delicious' his 'pie.' Tong officials and interpreters attracted the highest bounties, but merchants, because of their prominence, merited higher bounties than other rank and file tong members, and many merchants died in tong wars."[57]

Among Filipinos, the controversies surrounding gambling likewise exposed social and economic issues associated with the workers' participation in the extralegal activities. Although the types of gambling differed between the urban and rural areas, most were illegal and could take place only in clandestine locations, elements that no doubt added fuel to the danger and thrills already inherent in playing games of chance. In the urban areas, Filipino laborers flocked to the gambling halls in Chinatown because they represented one of the few recreational centers open to Filipinos. In addition, these Asian immigrant communities were usually clustered closely together, so the gambling houses and lottery stands were readily accessible by foot. In Los Angeles, for example, Chinatown was only a few blocks from Little Manila. For Filipino Angeleños, it was only a short walk to place a wager on *baakgapbiu* or pass some time playing fan-tan and *pai kow*.

In predominantly agricultural areas like Stockton, Watsonville, and the San

Fernando Valley on the outskirts of Los Angeles, the major form of wagering was *sabong-sabong*, or cockfighting. In the Philippines this blood sport was legal and extremely popular, and Filipino immigrants brought the *sabong* with them to the United States. Cockfighting was widespread among the Filipino, the Mexican, and even some Anglo farm workers. Sammy Escalona recalled that "those Anglos had more fighting cocks than [even] the Filipinos and Mexicans, and they were better cared for, too. . . . The whites would bet thousands of dollars on their cocks." Because cockfights were illegal, the participants had to be familiar with code words in order to know when the fight was and whose roosters were scheduled. This information gave bettors a chance to look over the cocks and decide on which to wager in advance of the match. "Yeah, in the old days I [used to] go to a lot of cockfights," Escalona chuckled, "when a *sabong* was arranged, we'd pass around [word] that 'there's a picnic on so-and-so day . . . [and] so-and-so and so-and-so will bring chicken' and everybody know[s] what 'picnic' and 'chicken' mean. So on that day we go off to the far end of the fields, you know, where there's lots of cover."[58]

Self-appointed community leaders objected to gambling in part because of the economic deficits created in the Filipino community. Indeed, even Hermenegildo Cruz, the director of labor in the Philippines, lamented that gambling, particularly in the urban areas, was one of the major activities that Filipino immigrants engaged in across the continental United States. Cruz estimated that approximately half the annual combined wages of all Filipinos in California in the early 1930s, nearly $40 million, "are lost across the gambling tables of the Chinese."[59] Given that most Filipino workers earned about $1 a day during the Great Depression, this amount represented a substantial loss of income not only in the ethnic community but also in the Philippines because of the loss in potential remissions that the immigrants might have sent home to their relatives.

But the halt in remittances to the Philippines during the Great Depression was more a reflection of the hardships faced by Filipino laborers due to the economic slump in the United States than what the ethnic community leaders and officials in the Philippines assumed to be the workers' massive losses in gambling. Before the onslaught of the Depression, Filipino immigrants regularly sent bank drafts to their families in the islands. Herman de los Santos was typical of those doing so. He had emigrated from the Ilocos provinces to California in 1924 and eventually found a job as an elevator operator in the Ritz Hotel in Los Angeles. Thereafter, he steadily sent money orders, "a little money" to help the family, through his sister in the Philippines.[60] Money orders from Filipinos in the United States, including Hawaii, to the Philippines, particularly to the Ilocos region, represented considerable sums in both countries throughout the 1920s. In 1927, for example, an estimated 81,615 money orders, totaling more than $4 million, were sent to the Philippines.[61] Foreign money orders sent by Filipinos from Stockton alone were calculated to be about $1 million.[62] The following year, 110,670 money orders exceeding $5 million were dispatched to the islands, and in 1929, more than $6 million was transferred through 128,757 bank drafts.[63] Indeed, the sheer quantity of postal orders and other financial instruments sent to the archipelago propelled the governor general of the Philippines to recommend that more money service stations be made available to Filipinos because "of the immigrants who continuously send their savings to their families in the Philippines through the money order system."[64]

By the 1930s, intraethnic controversies related to gambling, including the attempts of the ethnic press and its personnel to discourage the practice, came to a head when the editorial staff of the *Philippines Herald-Tribune*, a Los Angeles–based newspaper, published an open letter to B. G. Aquino, the publisher of the Stockton-based *Philippines Star Press*. Concluding with "yours for better ethics in journalism," the *Herald-Tribune* publicly challenged Aquino to explain:

1. Why is it that in the year 1933 you ran the advertisements of the Vernon Athletic Club [in Los Angeles], a notorious gambling establishment, which had preyed on hundreds of Filipinos before it was finally closed by the Police?
2. Why is it that for months, nay years, you have, on and off, [run] in the Philippines Star Press the advertisement of Charley Yusida, under the guise of a "Japanese Club" in El Centro, California, but which is in fact a gambling joint patronized by hundreds of Filipinos during the harvest season?
3. Why is it that you have, for months now, [run] in the Philippines Star Press the advertisement of a certain establishment in Pismo Beach where gambling goes on uninterrupted?
4. Why is it that for months, even years, you have [run] advertisements in the Philippines Star Press of place[s] of gambling and prostitution under the guises of pool halls, restaurants and rooming houses?

5. Why is it that for months you have advertised in the Philippines Star Press a spot called "Joe's Place" in Imperial Valley, where gambling is going on all the time and which is situated right in the center of the red light district?

6. Why is it that for many months now you have solicited the advertisements of several establishments in Los Angeles, appearing in the Philippines Star Press under the guises of laundries and cigar stores but are in reality gambling joints and vice resorts?

7. And why do you always suppress articles against the existence of gambling resorts and houses of prostitution in Imperial Valley, Pismo Beach, Guadalupe, and other towns where these resorts prey on the Filipinos, whose money should otherwise be [spent] with your other advertisers conducting legitimate and honest business establishments?[65]

But despite the active participation of the Chinese, Filipinos, and other minorities, Chinatown's gambling halls, bordellos, and opium dens could not have survived without the regular support of Anglo patrons. As the sociologist Ivan Light argues, "White demand permitted many more . . . Chinese to find employment in the vice industry than would have been possible on the basis of co-ethnic patronage alone."[66] While the bulk of Anglo customers in Chinatown were working-class youths, ruffians, or thieves and other "undesirables," the tongs provided some semblance of anonymity and guaranteed discrete levels of security from police raids for its "better class" of Anglo customers. Precautions, such as lookouts and secret passages from the cribs and dens that led directly to the streets, allowed these customers to escape arrest in the event of trouble.[67]

Chinatown's vice lords could offer assurances of safety and privacy to its select Anglo patrons and protection to its subscribing Chinese business owners because tongs regularly paid off the LAPD. [68] In part because of this practice, Chinatown had become synonymous with graft and corruption in the mind of the public and especially in the campaigns of the city's reformers, although the Chinese were not the most successful vice operators in Los Angeles even during the 1920s and 1930s. At the top of the criminal hierarchy were native-born Euro-Americans and first- or second-generation Italians and Jews.[69] Mickey Cohen, who was born in Brooklyn but grew up in the Los Angeles suburb of Boyle Heights, was arguably the most prominent Angeleño mobster until Benjamin "Bugsy" Siegel came to town in 1936.[70] And despite the notoriety associated with Chinatown's bordellos and the tongs who smuggled women from China to the United States, Italians, like Marco Albori (Albert Marco) and Augusto "Chito" Sasso, were the leading and most effective brokers of Los Angeles's prostitution rings. Thus while the Chinese and some African Americans were prominent in their respective ethnic enclaves, they filled only the middle ranks of the vice industry. Mexicans, Filipinos, and most African American operators made up the bottom ranks of the underworld.[71]

The development of a lucrative vice industry was possible to a degree because, as one writer notes, "in Los Angeles, the police didn't fight crime; they protected it, controlling and directing vice and gambling. . . . Police protection of gambling and vice was standard practice."[72] The LAPD was established in 1869, with the first central station located on First Street, between Broadway and Hill Street in 1897. At its inception, there were no physical or mental requirements to join the force, but the job held low status and salaries were meager, with skilled workers earning more than the officers. In addition, before the turn of the century, jobs in the LAPD were part of a patronage system, and the police paid more attention to forging political alliances than to enforcing the laws.[73]

Initially, the LAPD was reluctant to do anything about the ethnic vice industry in Chinatown, since most officers believed that the Chinese were only "engaging in their natural passions." Besides, they were doing it behind closed doors in Chinatown. When middle-class reformers and several city officials began demanding the suppression of brothels and gambling within city limits, some police officers began to see the advantages of the vice industry. Graft and corruption increased in the process of criminalizing these ethnic, working-class enterprises. Vice lords began actively seeking police "protection" from raids and arrests for themselves as well for their clients and select customers. Many officers used these bribes to supplement their low income from the force.[74]

The police department made several attempts, including a reorganization of its vice squad into a more active unit staffed with supposedly more trustworthy officers, to satisfy the reformers. Chief of Police James Davis, for example, threatened to dismiss any captain who did not keep his division clean. But hardly anyone in the force was disciplined because the rates of raids and arrests in the city showed vast improvements. This increase in law enforcement, however, was largely because leaders of the extralegal enterprises and the police had arrived at some kind of understanding, including an agreed-on number of raids per month on the marginal operations in Chinatown, Sonoratown by the central plaza, and the African American district along Central Avenue. On occasion, police officers even arrested some of the more disorderly Anglos, Filipinos, and African Americans hanging around Chinatown in order to keep the peace. In exchange for the tong leaders' "cooperation," the metropolitan squad ordered its officers not to cross north of Aliso Street, the southern boundary of Chinatown.[75]

The police had no serious intention of closing down the Chinese or any other vice industry. Indeed, even Filipino community leaders who applauded the officers' intensified efforts to stem gambling clearly understood that the activities were only intermittent. During one of the cyclical periods, for example, a Filipino newspaper gave kudos to the LAPD and city officials "for the present campaign against the underworld," but was nevertheless resigned that "to all appearances it is simply one more campaign reaching a climax. Soon there will be an interval of quiet or indifference or physical inability to match strength with the underworld, and commercialized vice will be, in effect, conducted under the very noses of the peace offices. That has been the general experience here [in Los Angeles] and everywhere."[76] The existence and smooth operation of extralegal activities in the city had become as important to the LAPD as it was to the tongs and other owners of vice enterprises.

Chinatown and the Chinese vice industry particularly emerged as a key target of Los Angeles's campaigns for a "clean" and "pure" city because of the stereotype of the mysterious and secretive "heathen Chinee." This pervasive image had fueled numerous ruthless attacks on Chinese Angeleños. One of the most vicious anti-Chinese riots occurred in Los Angeles's Chinatown in October 1871. The events surrounding the massacre remain unclear, but most accounts agree that mobs looted the district and lynched eighteen to twenty-one Chinese residents after an Anglo man was accidentally killed in the neighborhood.[77]

Crowded into Chinatown because of poverty, enforced residential restrictions, and fear of violent attacks from the dominant community, Chinese appeared to validate these views of them as unassimilable and unacceptable immigrants. This image, coupled with the recurring tong wars, prevented many Angeleños from visiting Chinatown. Reports of the filthy conditions in Chinese restaurants only added to the reluctance of potential tourists to eat there. In 1916, for example, a health inspector described the kitchens in Los Angeles's Chinese district as "filled with rubbish and decaying matter, swarming with flies, overrun with cockroaches and rats. Vermin swarmed in the slime found in the rotting boards under the unsanitary, leaking sinks. In the rear of one restaurant there was a large, deep hole near the cellar door, filled with several feet of water and . . . a dead chicken and rotting garbage floating in the water polluted the air throughout the neighborhood."[78] For the most part, people went to Chinatown to gamble, patronize bordellos, or smoke opium, not to eat. The corrupt police and tongs, therefore, had a stake in continuing the lucrative vice industry. At the same time, Chinese entrepreneurs faced a continuing struggle to improve their community's unfavorable image and to oust the extralegal activities from Chinatown.

By the early 1930s, Harry Chandler, the publisher of the *Los Angeles Times*, felt that Chinatown and its vice industries were "too colorful" to be near the city's central plaza. He supported, and pushed for, a train station to be built over the Chinese district. By 1933, demolition of the area began, and its Chinese residents were left to their own devices to find other accommodations. By 1936, Union Station, a project of the Works Progress Administration (WPA) under the New Deal, stood over what was once Los Angeles's Chinatown.

With the demise of Chinatown, Chinese Angeleños moved to three areas: the New Chinatown, China City, and the City Market district. These neighborhoods clustered around the Civic Center, off Spring Street. The New Chinatown developed with tourism as an economic base. It contained a number of Chinese businesses, including restaurants, curio shops, and Asian markets, as well as housing tracts extending from Figueroa Street to Elysian Park. China City, unlike the New Chinatown, which was operated largely by Chinese, was initiated by non-Chinese, mainly Anglo, businesses, with no provisions for Chinese residential areas.[79]

The vice industries did not flourish as they once had in these new Chinese areas, and the extralegal activities that survived quickly went underground or formed their own means of internal regulation. To a certain extent, these arrangements developed because the Chinese syndicates were weakened when a number of their most powerful leaders and members were killed in the tong wars of the previous decades. The newer tongs recognized that there was more profit in attracting middle-class Anglos and tourists, so their leaders supported the shift of the community's economic base from vice to tourism, although they continued to operate some extralegal enterprises in the back rooms of restaurants and shops. Because tongs, repackaged as "merchants' associations" and "chambers of labor and commerce," had a stake in eliminating violence in Chinatown, they used their power to protect the public's safety in the enclave.[80]

In light of the demolition of the old Chinese quarter and the limited number of gambling dens and lottery stands in the New Chinatown, some Filipinos turned to legitimate gambling operations, including the racetracks. Carlos Miguel, who worked as a ranch hand on the outskirts of Los Angeles, recalled that "I bet a little at Santa Anita sometimes when I am able to go[,] which is not so often as I have to sneak away. I haven't won or lost much as I hold myself down to four dollars betting money when I go. I like it though and it is swell fun even if you don't win."[81]

Charges for gambling and gambling-related infractions among Filipino Angeleños, however, continued to be the highest single category for arrests throughout the Depression. In 1936/1937, for example, 152 (29 percent) of 523 Filipino arrests were for gambling (107), visiting lottery stands (22), possession of lottery tickets (7), possession of a gambling device (9), and "gambling conducting" (7).[82] The consistently high arrest rates for gambling among Filipinos, despite the reduction of extralegal Chinese houses that they could patronize and the limited number of legal establishments available to them, suggests that Filipino gamblers found other places for putting down their wagers. One of these sites was sporting events, particularly boxing matches. The betting was especially heated when a Filipino pugilist faced a non-Filipino opponent. In the 1937 bout between the Filipino community's favorite son Ceferino Garcia, the Bolo Puncher, and Glen Lee, the Nebraskan Wildcat, there was a wagering frenzy in Little Manila. A Filipino sportswriter observed that "gamboleers in First Street [are] tabbing the bolo puncher to beat Lee in short order." Not surprisingly, bookies in the ethnic enclave were giving 2 to 1 odds in favor of Garcia, and the sports editor of one of the Filipino newspapers anticipated that "thousands of Garcia's countrymen working in the [agricultural] camps in the neighboring cities who have been waiting for this match are expected to flock to the Grand avenue fight emporium [the Olympic Auditorium] to fill up all available space in the gallery."[83]

In light of the demolition of the original Chinatown and the marked absence of gambling dens and other more intriguing attractions in the new Chinese district, prizefights emerged as an alternative source of wagering. The possibility of getting extra money by gambling on the prowess of Filipino athletes was one of the attractions associated with the tremendous popularity of boxing matches among Filipino workers. Unlike fan-tan and lotteries, boxing highlighted the brown male body by giving it the pivotal role. Instead of watching colorful fan-tan disks or counting black dots on white domino blocks, Filipino eyes focused on the glimmer of powerful brown muscles. This passion for boxing, however, did not necessarily mean that the Filipinos stopped going to the Chinese quarter. Like other Angeleños and tourists, Filipinos took advantage of the "wholesome" atmosphere of the new ethnic enclave to shop in Asian markets and to eat Chinese food in supposedly more sanitary restaurants without anxieties associated with getting caught in LAPD raids or tong wars. For Los Angeles's Chinese residents, the relocation and the transformation of their community's socioeconomic base from extralegal enterprises to a tourist center evinced patterns of resiliency and tenacity in how marginalized peoples develop strategies for survival in an openly hostile environment.

3. FROM THE "LIVING DOLL" TO THE "BOLO PUNCHER"

Prizefighting, Masculinity, and the Sporting Life

> Professional boxing's an odd sport, an anachronism, a throwback to the days of dogs, pits, and bears. Yet it persists because, at its core, it's brutal and honest, a contest of courage and skill. . . . Is it any wonder, then, that one of the quickest ways to a Manong's heart is to talk fight and fighters?
>
> —Peter Bacho, "A Manong's Heart"

Weighing in at 153¾ pounds, the contender stepped into the ring for his first attempt at the American Middleweight Championship crown. A deafening hodgepodge of cheers, whistles, applause, and disapproval rose from the near-capacity crowd of 12,000 boxing fans gathered in New York's Madison Square Garden that brisk October evening in 1939. Ceferino Garcia, the Filipino Angeleño community's favorite son, demonstrated his famous right uppercut for fans and foes alike as his way of greeting. Reigning champ Fred Apostoli, favored at 5 to 8 and weighing in at the maximum limit of 160 pounds, met Garcia in the center of the ring, impatient to defend his title in a scheduled fifteen-round bout.[1]

Garcia kept up a volley of powerful blows, including his renowned "bolo punch," a powerful right uppercut, which rocked Apostoli in the first round. A bolo punch to the chin, quickly followed by a left–right combination, sent an already-dazed Apostoli to his knees for a count of two. Apostoli got up, but Garcia's swift straight right and left hook knocked him down again, this time for a count of nine. By the fourth round, Garcia had inflicted a bleeding gash under the defending champ's chin, while Apostoli cut Garcia near the right eye with a left hook in the fifth round. By the sixth round, Garcia was leading Apostoli on competition points, winning four of the rounds.

Two minutes and seven seconds into the seventh round, it was all over. After a series of fierce, well-placed bolo punches to Apostoli's jaw and head, the bleeding, badly beaten champion went down for the third time, slowly sinking his forehead onto the canvas. Standing over Apostoli's collapsed body, referee Billy Cavanaugh began the count and then spread both arms to signal the end of Apostoli's reign. Lifting Garcia's arm, Cavanaugh proclaimed the new middleweight champion.[2] The exuberant crowd hailed its new hero.

With victories garnered by Filipino boxers like the Bolo Puncher, the sporting life, especially prizefighting, played an important role in the formulation of heroes and notions of heterosexual masculinity among Filipino immigrants of the 1920s and 1930s. Boxing matches were arguably the most popular organized recreational activity attended by Filipinos, and, unlike other leisure activities such as gambling in Chinatown and dancing with Euro-American women in taxi dance halls, this passion for prizefighting did not generate rabid disapproval from the small self-appointed elite of the community. In countless ways, the sporting life represented a common ground for both middle- and working-class Filipino boxing aficionados to carve out a cultural space wherein they celebrated the champions who in turn became a part of the stories they told themselves about themselves. They energized the hollows of coliseums, investing meanings to words like "manliness," "fair play," and "courage" that reflected their particular circumstances at the intersection of race and class in their adopted country.

Because Filipino boxers fought against pugilists of other ethnicities, this chapter also examines relations that usually transcended the arena. Looking at the interaction between marginalized populations during recreational periods provides insights on how they established alliances, although temporary, during often intense social movements like unionization drives. The cumulative effect of the success and recognition that many athletes of color achieved in marginalized sports like boxing and segregated leagues arguably influenced the eventual integration of professional teams beginning in the late 1940s.

The ring also represented a contested space between Filipino boxers and recruiters, trainers, managers, promoters, and athletic association officials from other communities. While the particular meanings associated with the sporting life provided Filipinos with agency in defining their individual and collective selves, a number of elements outside the community determined the course of organized sports. Athletic organizations like the National Boxing Association and the California Boxing Commission regulated the rules and weight categories of the games. Furthermore, the recruiters, trainers, managers, and promoters who made the critical decisions, including the amount and disbursement of the purse, the pairing of pugilists, and the location of fights, were usually white entrepreneurs. The arena also represented a tug-of-war among reformers, particularly assimilationists who argued that sports were mechanisms toward the "Americanization" of working-class immigrants, members of the medical profession who stressed the physical dangers of boxing, and the clergy who questioned the morality of prizefighting.

The migration of Filipino sports figures to the United States stemmed directly from the colonial relationship that defined U.S. efforts to support its military and political domination of the islands through policies of "benevolent assimilation." These policies included the regulation and suppression of indigenous cultural production and the promotion of American-style education of Filipinos first by American soldiers and then by American missionaries and teachers. Instruction in American sports, including boxing and baseball, became part of the indoctrination of Filipinos into "good" colonials. The subordination of Filipinos in their homeland, however, was not the only objective of the United States. As an imperial power, it also sought out which of its colony's citizens could best serve its purposes. This process began with the *pensionado* program, with the U.S. government sponsoring the best Filipino students to study in American universities. Upon the completion of their degrees, these students returned to the Philippines, where colonial administrators placed them in influential positions with expectations that they would support U.S. policies and institutions.[3] Later, as the emerging agribusiness in Hawaii and then California needed laborers, recruiters enticed poor, landless Filipinos to work in U.S. fields. When Filipinos demonstrated exceptional abilities in sports, especially boxing, American trainers and managers went to the islands, taking the most promising young athletes to the United States.

Filipinos and Filipino immigrants in the United States found their idols in these pugilists. Boxing enthusiasts celebrated victories, challenged unpopular decisions, and lamented loses in both countries. Commuting between the

United States and the Philippines, fighters became a force that bridged the Filipino and Filipino American experiences. As athletes, they challenged the stereotypes of the "little brown brother" uttered by the colonizers in their homeland and the image of the dirty, lazy "brown monkey" deployed in the racist language of their adopted country.

The earliest Filipino boxer to gain distinction was Francisco "Pancho Villa" Guilledo, the Living Doll, who, at twenty-one years old, knocked out Johnny Buff and captured the 1922 American Flyweight Championship at Ebbets Field, Brooklyn. At 110 pounds, Villa was outweighed by the defending champ, who tipped the scale at 114¼ pounds. The bout was intense, with Villa landing powerful left hooks and right crosses at close quarters that sent Buff staggering for most of the ten rounds of fighting. Twenty-seven seconds into the eleventh round, with Buff suffering from a badly bruised nose and blood flowing from a split lip, gums, and left eye, Buff's second threw in the towel as a sign of defeat. After the grueling title bout, the New York Times proclaimed that "the new champion impressed the large crowd with his victory. Popular in the extreme prior to the battle, Villa added many new admirers to his legion of friends through the workmanlike manner in which he attained the title. The Oriental champion was the master throughout."[4]

Villa gained popularity with both Filipino and non-Filipino boxing enthusiasts. Even when Frankie Genaro won the U.S. title from Villa in May 1923, the new champ muttered, "What's the use? You can beat him all you want but he's the guy the fans go for, he's a living doll."[5] Indeed, three months later, at the World Flyweight Championship bout, Villa, not Genaro, was chosen to defend the U.S. title.[6] The Living Doll went on to defeat England's Jimmy Wilde for the 1923 World Flyweight Championship before a crowd of 40,000 fans at the Polo Grounds in New York. By the second round, Villa exploded a right to the defending champ's jaw, the likes of which Wilde later confessed he "didn't get over."[7] One minute and forty-six seconds into the seventh round, with the defending champ's eyes almost closed and blood dripping freely from a broken nose, Villa's short right hook landed squarely on Wilde's jaw, sending him down on the canvas for the count.[8] Villa successfully defended his world championship title over the English contender Frankie Ash in Brooklyn in 1924.[9] Villa's extraordinary feats led George L. "Tex" Rickard, the most prominent boxing promoter of the 1920s, to rank Villa as the number-one fighter of 1924, characterizing the year in boxing as one that witnessed "the continued supremacy of Pancho Villa in the flyweight class."[10]

The Living Doll's explosive rise in the U.S. boxing circuit was part of a process started in the Philippines. Born in 1901 to a landless family in the sugar-cane-producing province of Iloilo, the young Guilledo traveled to the capital city of Manila to find a better job. In the city, he made contact with Frank Churchill, who managed the stadium and ran the Olympic Club, a training gym for Filipino amateur boxers. Watching the young man train during those early days, Bill Miller, who eventually became Villa's publicity manager in the United States, recalled that "even then [Villa] was the star of the *novatos* (the beginners)."[11] By 1919, in his first professional fight in Manila, Villa knocked out his opponent, Australian flyweight champion George Mendres, in three rounds. Villa's fighting record in the Philippines was already outstanding when Churchill brought him to the United States in 1922.[12]

When Villa died unexpectedly in July 1925, American sportswriters vied to name the next Filipino champion. Within months of Villa's death, Norris C. Mills anticipated the advent of a "Filipino boxing invasion," naming Filipino fighters such as Angel de la Cruz, "Battling" Candelosa, Varias Milling, and Kid Moro as future champions in the lighter weight divisions. Mills urged American promoters to quickly recruit these boxers, forecasting that they "will find their gate receipts mounting with these men fighting in American rings, for most of them possess knock-out punches and have their share of cleverness and, what is more important, are game to the core."[13]

In the meantime, Bill Van, writing for the *Knockout*, a weekly newspaper dedicated to boxing, dubbed Diosdado "Speedy Dado" Posadas as Villa's most likely successor when Dado wrested the Pacific Coast Bantamweight and Flyweight Championships from the Jewish fighter David "Newsboy Brown" Montrose at Los Angeles's Olympic Auditorium in 1931. Van declared that "Dado's win over Brown was decisive. He fairly outclassed Brown and when little Dado, the Brown Doll, goes back to Madison Square Garden he will be hailed as the new Pancho Villa. Dado has class—he has color—he will do more to create interest in the boxing game than any man we know of."[14] Still other sportswriters made projections. *Ring* magazine's Harry B. Smith announced that no one rates with Little Dado, California's bantamweight champion, who is "the best Filipino fighter seen in this country since the days of Villa.... [Little] Dado is a shrewd boxer and can stand a punch."[15] The 1930s and 1940s represented an era of substantial successes by Filipino boxers and champions, notably Pablo Dano, "the wild and rugged Filipino bull of the Pampas," and Benjamin "Small Montana" Gan, the Filipino Flash, who became the 1935 American flyweight champion when he beat Italian American Joseph "Midget Wolgast" Loscatzo in ten rounds.[16]

In spite of the victories garnered by these Filipino pugilists and the prophesies of the *Knockout* and the *Ring* as to whom Villa's crown belonged, countless Filipino immigrants of the 1930s believed that Ceferino Garcia, the Bolo Puncher, was the Living Doll's long-awaited successor as champion. Garcia's manager in the Philippines, Jess Cortes, had brought the nineteen-year-old amateur fighter to the United States around 1930. Two years later, Cortes ended the relationship, leaving the still-unknown Garcia in the hands of a new manager, George Parnassus.[17] Under Parnassus's charge, the welterweight Garcia steadily improved his craft and, by 1934, showed promise, knocking out opponents like Andy DiVodi in the first round, Peter Jackson in three rounds, and Joe Glick in two.[18] By 1938, Garcia had fought and, more often than not, knocked out most fighters in his class division, forcing his manager and several fight promoters on a desperate countrywide search for suitable opponents. One Filipino sportswriter delightedly proclaimed that "very few fighters dare risk their chins against Garcia's bolo punch, which is usually deadly."[19]

Despite, or more likely because of, Garcia's slow start and spotty boxing record until 1934, he captured the imagination and admiration of his countrymen. Through his consistent show of strength and skill in the ring and his sheer determination in his difficult ascent to a world championship title, Garcia also earned the respect of others in the boxing world. In his first venture for the World Welterweight Championship, Garcia lost by decision to the defending champion Barney Ross in a gruesome fifteen-round bout. Bill Henry, the *Los Angeles Times*'s sports editor, covered this 1937 "Carnival of Champions" boxing tournament in New York's Polo Grounds, where Ross was the 4 to 1 favorite. Regardless of Garcia's loss, Henry proclaimed that "the hero of the four and a half hours of slugging was Ceferino Garcia of California . . . [who] wore the carmine badge of courage and stole the show." Henry continued: "The bolo punching Filipino, hitting one punch to the champion's two but carrying more real murder in one of his lethal wallop than Ross had in a dozen, came from behind in the last four rounds with an exhibition of gameness that forced a highly partisan audience to forget their prejudice in appreciation of the Filipino's courageous comeback."[20]

In subsequent bouts, Garcia gained fame for this bolo punch, a deadly combination of right uppercuts and half hooks. The development of this boxing technique exemplified Garcia's drawing on his experiences from the

Philippines and applying them to his life in the United States. The delivery, a series of sharp, fast punches, grew out of a skill he first learned as a boy, working in the sugarcane fields with his family in the Philippines. To harvest the sugarcane, the laborer holds up a handful of stalks, bends down, and, with quick strokes of the sharp bolo knife, cuts the canes swiftly and as close to the ground as possible. Transferring and perfecting this technique in the boxing ring, Garcia, at 5 feet, 6 inches, and weighing 154 pounds, eventually became the twenty-fourth middleweight champion in 1939 when he knocked out the Italian American defender Fred Apostoli in seven rounds.[21] Nat Fleischer, publisher of the *Ring* and the foremost boxing commentator of the day, rated this championship bout as the "most thrilling fight" of 1939, ranking it among the ten outstanding fights of the year.[22]

That boxing matches were widely attended by Filipino laborers is an understatement. Full-capacity crowds typically showed up in Los Angeles's Olympic Auditorium, San Francisco's Dreamland Arena, and Stockton's Civic Auditorium when Filipino fighters were scheduled. In Los Angeles, Toribio Castillo remembered how the Filipino community looked forward to Tuesday evenings when boxing matches usually took place downtown. "On those nights," he recalled, "even washing dishes for ten hours didn't matter. We went. Some of the workers, they tried to make sure their work was done quickly, especially if they had no tickets. When the big boys [champions] are in town, you can't even see the end of the [ticket] line. Sometimes the fights start right there [between ticket buyers], everybody scrambling for tickets and all. You could call it a pre-game show."[23]

Filipinos filled local boxing venues and traveled for hundreds of miles to attend a bout that featured not only titleholders like the Bolo Puncher, Small Montana, and Speedy Dado, but also up-and-coming pugilists like Ralph Mano and Varias Milling. The automobile, central to the migratory employment pattern of the vast majority of Filipino laborers, took on an alternative significance in their lives during these trips. It became the vehicle that transported them from exploitative, mundane jobs for which they earned marginal wages and obtained little gratification to the places where they experienced some compensation, in terms of solidarity and excitement, for their efforts. As an observer noted, for Filipinos, a Garcia fight scheduled anywhere on the Pacific Coast "is a signal for a cavalcade of motor cars of various vintages to converge on the scene of action."[24] Robert Hilado, who fought in the boxing circuit as Little Dempsey, appreciated how some of his fans "would drive all night just to see the fight."[25] This routine was typical for many Filipinos. Sammy Escalona recalled how he and his friends drove overnight for more than 300 miles from their camp to attend a boxing match featuring Filipino pugilist Pablo Dano "because he's our boy. In those days, you do what you have to do to see your favorites."[26]

But the thrills of the matches were transitory, which in part explains why Filipinos attended bouts again and again. At daybreak after the Dano fight, Escalona and his friends were back at work in the fields of the San Fernando Valley. In efforts to sustain the intense experiences of the battle, Filipino workers sought to relive the action in the boxing arena through other ways. The avid reporting of bouts in their ethnic newspapers vividly delineates the community's desire to *read* about them. An examination of extant copies of the *Philippines Review* shows how faithfully Filipino journalists covered boxing matches. The exploits of Filipino pugilists like Ceferino Garcia, Small Montana, and Speedy Dado frequently made front-page news, alongside reports about the future of the Philippines. News about the financial negotiations between representatives of American banks and Miguel Cuaderno, vice president of the Philippine National Bank, shared front-page honors with the announcement of a grudge match between "Baby Face" Casanova, the featherweight champion of Mexico, and Speedy Dado, the Brown Doll of Manila. The news about the fight not only shared the front page, but also garnered more space than any other item. Apparently, Dado was the reigning champion until Cassanova knocked him out in Mexico City. The paper reported that the rematch was to take place on July 16 at the Olympic Stadium, where a "capacity crowd" was expected.[27]

In a similar vein, announcements about the fight between Garcia, "the knockout artist from across the Pacific," and welterweight champion Barney Ross shared the front page with news about Filipino repatriation.[28] The paper reported that two Filipinos had filed for repatriation, and it gave instructions on how to apply to the Immigration and Naturalization Service (INS) for this process. The front page also included a notice that tickets were still available for the upcoming bout between Robert "Little Dempsey" Hilado, "the rugged Filipino," and Wally Hally at the Olympic Boxing Arena. The article about the procedures for repatriation was continued on page 3, but complete on the front page was a step-by-step analysis of Garcia's "serious training siege," because "victory for Garcia will virtually clinch a championship fight with Ross later in the year. Chicago and New York promoters would be glad to stage a battle between the pair, if the knockout artist from across the Pacific can slash out a win over the Jewish boy." In addition, readers learned that "in the last 2 main events at Hollywood, Garcia easily outclassed the cagey Al Manfredo in ten rounds and gave Al Romero, the local Mexican puncher, a sound licking to capture a popular decision."[29]

For the Filipinos, reading about the fight was not a passive activity. They interpreted these events, and it formed part of a network wherein workers created meaning for their lives.[30] For laborers absent from the fight, the coverage served as more than a vicarious experience; it allowed them to participate in the stories of their compatriots who witnessed the event. For participants, reading about an experience once-removed became a tool for the remembering and reordering of that experience. Antonio Cabanag, who worked at the Thrifty Drug Store in Pasadena in the 1930s, went to every Garcia fight held in Los Angeles. Cabanag expressed his sentiments about the importance of these events and sports figures in the lives and narratives of many Filipino workers like himself, exclaiming, "Garcia! You know, that's all we Filipinos [had]. That's why when Filipino boxers fight, you see all the Filipinos come and see them."[31]

The fight directed their conversation; it became a collective experience and, win or lose, the potential of the brown body symbolized by the pugilists became part of the stories Filipinos told themselves about themselves and their experiences. Through the art of storytelling, Filipino workers produced tales and living heroes like Ceferino Garcia. They recalled that "when the going was rough for the [Filipinos], Ceferino was always there. There was a time when close to 50 armed men swooped down on him, gangland fashion, and you know what? He came out of it unscathed and triumphant."[32] Through these narratives, Filipino workers codified their ideals of Filipino masculinity: Garcia, outnumbered fifty to one, relying only on his wits and raw muscle, fought undaunted, and emerged victorious.

The theme of underdog heroes prevailing despite overwhelming odds is a universal pattern in myths, legends, and various forms of expressive cultures, notably in African American animal tales of B'rer Rabbit and B'rer Fox, in Filipino folk epics such as those of Agyu and Sandayo, in Mexican *corridos*, and in border ballads like "El Corrido de Gregorio Cortéz."[33] Because these stories are designed to be memorized and disseminated through oral communication, the narratives blend, as the historian Américo Paredes notes in his analysis of the border conflicts embedded in the ballad of Cortéz, "three kinds of ingredients: of straight fact, of fact exaggerated into fiction, and of pure folklore, found in easily recognizable motifs."[34] Fashioned from readily familiar texts and canted especially during stressful periods like warfare, mass migration, or invasion in a people's history, legends highlight the hero's journey toward spiritual and physical transformations. In Filipino folk epics, warriors like Agyu, Lam-ang, Banna, and Labaw Donggon embarked on voyages, endured strenuous tests to prove their courage and ability, and eventually conquered their enemies.[35]

To many Filipino immigrants of the 1920s and 1930s, Ceferino Garcia's rise to the middleweight crown exemplified these themes of heroic quest, validation, and metamorphosis. Garcia's conversion began when, as a novice boxer, he left the Philippines and migrated to the United States. In California, he faced numerous defeats in the ring, but he worked hard to perfect his skills and increase his strength. His sheer physical presence was significant in this transformation. While the vast majority of Filipino boxers competed in the lighter weight classes, Garcia was the exception, the only Filipino pugilist who fought, and won a championship title, in the middleweight division (up to 160 pounds). Garcia initially fought in the lighter weight ranks but qualified for the middleweight by undergoing a strict regimen that included building up bulk and muscle definition. His big athletic brown physique was a transgression against the dominant culture's perception of Filipinos as small agricultural workers whose bodies were especially suitable for the short hoe or meek domestics and service workers. Garcia's hard body represented the tenacity and potency of Filipinos, and he ultimately claimed his destined place as a champion in the boxing world and among his *kababayan* (countrymen).

Like other hero narratives, including the blossoming of "El Corrido de Gregorio Cortéz" during the Mexican–U.S. border conflicts, the story of Garcia besting fifty armed men developed as Filipino laborers faced brutalities from unemployed Anglo workers who claimed that Filipinos lowered the wage scales, and from the henchmen of business owners who routinely beat and shot Filipino union leaders and workers striking for equitable wages and safer working conditions. The Filipino American novelist Peter Bacho later captured the immigrants' pride and the importance of boxing idols and potential heroes during these turbulent times when he wrote that "from the champions to the obscure pugs perpetually scrapping for peanuts on undercards, the old men knew them. They knew their moves, shared their hopes, and basked in their bravado—from the glories of Garcia and Montana to the graceless, futile courage of fighters like Young Dempsey."[36]

This passion for boxing among Filipino immigrants in the United States can be traced to their experiences in the Philippines, where boxing had enjoyed widespread popularity since its introduction by the invading American armed forces during the Spanish-American War of 1898. A Filipino boxing trainer claimed that the sport found a home in the islands almost as soon as Commodore George Dewey's battleships landed in Manila Bay. A number of the ships' personnel were fans and former students of the legendary bare-knuckle prizefighter Boston Strongboy, the "Great John L." Sullivan. Initially, the soldiers held exhibition bouts only among themselves for their Filipino audience or gave private informal lessons to young Filipinos, until 1910 when boxing became legal in the colony. When several Filipino boxers began earning distinction in Manila and other Asian countries, American recruiters and trainers, including Frank Churchill, Joe Waterman, and Bill and Eddie Tate, went to the islands to coach the Filipino pugilists and to prepare them for export to the United States.[37]

While Filipinos first learned of prizefighting through soldiers, instruction in American sports, including boxing and baseball, became part of the U.S. policies of colonization and de-Filipinozation through education. In addition to the brutal repression of Filipino nationalist movements through military campaigns, the U.S. government established a public school system based on the American model and implemented English as the medium of instruction.[38] American teachers and missionaries went to the Philippines determined to eradicate what they considered the Filipinos' "reprehensible vices," especially gambling and cockfighting, through American institutions that they believed inculcated the "character building" values of democracy, industry, honesty, thrift, good sportsmanship, and patriotism.[39]

Protestant missionaries joined American teachers and officials in this venture. Some denominations, including Episcopalians and Baptists, established religious schools and dormitories for their Filipino students, despite vigorous protests from some parents. One U.S. official concluded that "once the dormitories were in operation, it soon became obvious that they offered an excellent *milieu* for the cultivation of behavior, attitudes and manners incorporating the values that the Americans, official and private, were seeking to inculcate. In the environment of the dormitory, a home away from home, it was possible to promote the dormitory managers' concepts of democracy, honesty, industry, responsibility, and punctuality."[40]

The Young Men's Christian Association (YMCA) was especially successful in organizing "wholesome" outdoor athletic activities, including boxing, baseball, swimming, tennis, and camping. The YMCA was one of the first organizations to establish facilities in the Philippines during the American occupation, initially accommodating only military personnel and American families. In November 1911, some Filipino businessmen initiated a fund-raising drive to build a Philippine YMCA. By January 1915, with donations from the Filipino elite, foreign business investors, various American officials, and the YMCA International Committee, the club opened in Manila. American administrators welcomed the athletic events, believing that organized recreational sports embodied "both a special exposure to the virtues, and an inoculation against the vices, which they were seeking either to instill in or to immunize against in the Filipinos."[41] E. Stanton Turner, chief executive of the Philippine YMCA, claimed that the physical workout not only improved the strength and moral fiber of young Filipinos but also facilitated the growth of the average Filipino male by more than three inches.[42]

Unlike the Spanish, who typically perceived the Philippines as the empire's outpost and concentrated their colonial reign almost exclusively in and around the capital city of Manila, Americans sought to permeate the mechanisms of "benevolent assimilation," especially through education and sports, throughout most of the archipelago. Severino Corpus, who grew up in the Ilocos region, relatively isolated agricultural provinces on the northwest coast of Luzon, recalled that in addition to studying "the same books in general literature that American students read[,] . . . our games during my [elementary and high] school days in the Philippines were [also] tennis, badminton, and the other American games, and horseback riding."[43] Through public education, Americans taught Filipinos English, U.S. history, and American sports, part of their training process on how to be "good" colonial subjects. As the Filipino historian Renato Constantino persuasively argues, "the most effective means of subjugating a people is to capture their minds. Military victory does not necessarily signify conquest."[44]

In his seminal *Beyond a Boundary*, the West Indian scholar and political activist C. L. R. James reflects on this relationship between colonialism and popular culture, analyzing how sports introduced by imperialist forces inevitably paralleled the racism and unequal power relations inherent in the politics of that enterprise. Writing about cricket in Trinidad in particular and the dynamics of colonialism in general, James argues that the game embodied British principles that conflicted with the social, political, and economic realities of colonized West Indian life. Cricket represented one of the ways that James and his friends learned the British "public-school code," which included honesty, loyalty to the academy, not questioning the umpire's decisions, and playing as a team member. More importantly, they learned the British ceremonies of winning graciously and keeping a stiff upper lip despite losses. But no matter how cricket was supposed to block out class and racial differences, inequalities implicit in imperialism were visible, especially when white cricket officials passed over gifted mulattoes and blacks in favor of less-skilled white players for the position of team captain. James recalls that the captains were always white, and there were "one or two others in reserve in case of accidents and as future candidates. They believed (or pretended to, it does not matter) that cricket would fall into chaos and anarchy if a black man were appointed captain." James challenges this blatant hypocrisy, writing that "the British tradition soaked deep into me was that when you entered the sporting arena you left behind the sordid compromises of everyday existence. Yet for us to do that we would have had to divest ourselves of our skins."[45]

The development of a Filipino boxing network in the Philippines and in the United States reflected many of James's observations about the relationship between colonialism and sport in the British West Indies. The principles of democracy, honesty, and patriotism that American officials and educators hoped to teach to their Filipino wards through sports sorely conflicted with the brutal repression of indigenous cultural production and expressions of Filipino nationalism.[46] In boxing, the principal positions, including trainers, managers, and promoters, were typically occupied by white men, some of whom also doubled as recruiters in the Philippines. Frank Churchill, for example, was responsible for the early training and eventual immigration of a number of Filipino fighters, most notably Pancho Villa, the Living Doll. In the United States, Churchill continued as Villa's manager, while Bill Miller worked as his press agent.[47] After Villa's death in 1925, and at the urging of some prominent Filipinos, Churchill took bantamweight Clever Sencio to the United States.[48] Joe Waterman, who initially coached Filipino amateurs in the Philippines, eventually returned to the United States to promote Benjamin "Small Montana" Gan, the Filipino Flash, who became the 1935 American flyweight champion.[49] Paddy Ryan, a former boxer, became Montana's manager.[50] In 1939, after Ceferino Garcia won the middleweight title, his manager, George Parnasus, went to the Philippines to scout for additional promising boxers.[51]

Other factors external to the Filipino and Filipino immigrant communities also played a part in influencing the course of ethnic sport enterprises.

Willie Orner, for example, owned the Main Street Gym in Los Angeles, which served as the training ground for the majority of Filipino boxers in the United States.[52] This dependence on sponsors outside the ethnic group can be partially explained by the recent arrival of Filipino immigrants in the 1920s and 1930s. But in many ways, it also delineated the very limited resources, including the weak economic infrastructure, of the Filipino community and the dearth of Filipino managers, trainers, and other boxing support personnel. Of the Filipino boxers in the United States, Garcia was one of the very few who had a Filipino trainer, Johnny Villaflores.[53]

African Americans, by contrast, had developed a relatively stronger economic base, although often through extralegal activities because of chronic discrimination by the dominant society in legitimate jobs, which accorded blacks some control over ghetto life as well as local politics. The social historian Mark H. Haller convincingly argues that the development of lotteries, bootlegging, and the black nightlife in and around Chicago's South Side beginning by the first decades of the twentieth century was important in the social and economic growth of urban black culture. Income generated through these underworld activities not only supported both legal and extralegal businesses in the ghetto but also financed black sports, including the segregated Negro baseball leagues and the careers of pugilists like Jack Johnson and Joe Louis.[54] The principal financial backers of the Brown Bomber were two of the most successful African American policy bankers: John Roxborough from Detroit and Julian Black from Chicago. Through Black's associations with local African American sports buffs in his speakeasy, Elite Number 2, the managers retained a retired lightweight boxer, Jack Blackburn, as Louis's manager.[55]

Despite the lack of tangible financial support and boxing staff from the ranks of their countrymen, Filipino pugilists and spectators at least did not have to contend with the disapproval of the small elite of the immigrant community. Unlike playing games of chance in Chinatown's gambling dens and dancing with Anglo women in the numerous taxi dance halls around Little Manila, the passion for the prizefight represented a common recreational activity enjoyed by the majority of Filipino workers, students, and self-appointed spokespersons. Indeed, Johnny Samson, one of two Filipino boxing trainers of the 1930s, was also the chairman of Los Angeles's Filipino Unity Council. As the organization's leader, Samson was one of the most vocal opponents of the taxi dance halls where Filipinos paid 10 cents a minute to dance with Anglo female partners. Samson urged his compatriots to refrain from patronizing these leisure centers. When this course failed, he appealed to the owners of the recreation halls to remain closed part of Sunday evenings in the hopes that Filipino workers would come instead to the council's planned socials and events. Some clubs like Danceland and the Hippodrome Dance Palace complied with the request, but Liberty Dance Hall opened early on Sundays, and with free admission to boot. Samson denounced owner Jack Goldberg, charging that "Goldberg is not a human being. He is only interested in what he gets from Filipinos—their MONEY, their hard earned MONEY!" But while Samson attacked dance halls, he was also busily engaged in promoting his boxing protégés, especially Young Tommy, recognized by the California State Athletic Commission as the world champion.[56]

Samson's charges, like other Filipino boxers, trained at the Main Street Gym, which also accommodated other would-be champion pugilists of many nationalities. This center of male culture established a competitive atmosphere that often transcended ethnicity. Athletes displayed their prowess for one another to scrutinize and, it was hoped, admire. The African American boxer "Hurricane" or "Hammerin'" Henry Armstrong, who eventually became the only fighter to hold three championship titles simultaneously, practiced at the facility in his early years. Armstrong recalled that "the gym was big inside, but bustling with activity. Fighters went through their paces—Mexican, Filipino, Negro, and white. There was plenty to look at."[57] In addition to this already diverse mix of ethnic pugilists, Los Angeles was home to the only Chinese heavyweight boxer in the world. Ah Wing "Frank" Dong, who lived in Chinatown, competed in the 1940 Golden Gloves Tournament. As a Los Angeles–based member of the Federal Writers Project maintained, this poly-ethnic nature of athletes led the city's sports enthusiasts to claim that "more nationalities compete in southern California boxing today than anywhere else in the world."[58]

Filipino boxers not only shared training grounds with other ethnic pugilists but also competed against them, principally in the categories up to, and including, the lightweight division.[59] At the time, the eight universally recognized classes in boxing were flyweight (up to 112 pounds), bantamweight (118 pounds), featherweight (126 pounds), lightweight (135 pounds), welterweight (147 pounds), middleweight (160 pounds), light-heavyweight (175 pounds), and heavyweight (more than 175 pounds). Filipinos fought against African Americans like Armstrong, but also "Baby Face" Casanova, the featherweight champion of Mexico, and Glen Lee, the Nebraskan Wildcat. When the Hollywood arena scheduled the main event between hometown heroes Garcia and Mexican pugilist Al Romero, for example, the *Knockout* projected that the fight "will pack the stadium to the rafters."[60] This diversity in both contestants and spectators can be explained because boxing continued to be dominated by a succession of different ethnic groups. Among white ethnics, Irish boxers like "Philadelphia Jack" O'Brien and the "Boxing Marvel" Jack Britton were prominent in prizefighting until around the 1920s, when Jewish pugilists like "Madcap Maxie" Baer and Al Singer became dominant. By the 1930s, Italian fighters like lightweight champ Tony Cansoneri ruled the boxing rosters. Concurrently, African Americans made their mark in the sport. Foremost among the early black boxers were 1902 World Lightweight champion Joe "Old Master" Gans and heavyweight great Jack Johnson, who, from 1908 to 1915, became the first African American to hold the title.[61] By the 1930s, now-legendary black pugilists, notably heavyweight champ Joe Louis, the Brown Bomber, and "Homicide Hank"/"Hurricane" Henry Armstrong—who held the featherweight, lightweight, and welterweight titles simultaneously— reigned over the boxing circuit.[62] Promoter Mike Jacobs's "four aces" of the 1930s in many ways exemplified the ethnic components of the boxing world. These fighters, under exclusive contract with Jacobs and whose names on the card drew top dollars, were African Americans Joe Louis (heavyweight) and Henry Armstrong (welterweight), Filipino Ceferino Garcia (middleweight), and Irish American Billy Conn (heavyweight).[63]

The immense popularity of boxing among ethnic groups becomes all the more significant when put into the context of the development of spectator sports. Organized sports events gained popularity beginning in the last third of the nineteenth century. Spontaneous play gave way to formalized game rules and institutionalized training programs for athletes. The beginning of the twentieth century witnessed a boom in the construction of stadiums and training facilities and the creation of businesses specializing in sports equipment. By the 1920s, spectator sports emerged as profitable commercial enterprises. Sports became professionalized, and patrons enthusiastically attended these events.[64] In downtown Los Angeles, former heavyweight champ Jack Dempsey, the Manassa Mauler, opened his Manhattan Athletic Club on Spring Street.[65] In 1925 a group of wealthy businessmen inaugurated the Olympic Auditorium, where scores of boxing fans, including Filipinos, paid to watch their heroes fight. Jack Root (Janos Ruthaly), the world's first light-heavyweight champion, was vice president and general manager of the stadium. Former boxing manager Joe Levy scheduled prizefights, while promoter Lou Daro handled the wrestling matches. The Olympic Auditorium, with a 10,000-seat capacity, became one of the most popular sports facilities in the United States.[66] By 1938, the 6,100-seat Hollywood American Legion Stadium rivaled the Olympic Auditorium, boasting to be "the safest ring in American boxing. Its base is covered with two inches of cork and this is topped by a thick horsehide mat."[67]

The rise and commercialization of organized sports also reflected the dynamics of gender, race, and class relations in the early decades of the twentieth century. Sporting events, largely promoted *by* men *for* men, typically neglected women's participation in athletics. In the 1930s the exploits of female great Babe Didrikson seldom received the coverage and adulation that followed men's achievements on the sports scene. Some columnists even ascribed women's capabilities to an unusually elevated amount of testosterone in the female athlete. As one journalist pointed out, "The same male sportswriters who called Babe Didrikson the greatest all-around athlete in the country were also quick to describe the down on her upper lip, the prominence of her Adam's apple and the angular contours of her 'boyish' body."[68]

In addition to largely ignoring female athletes, most professional sporting events practiced racial segregation. This policy became prevalent after the U.S. Supreme Court established the "separate but equal" criterion in the *Plessy v. Ferguson* ruling of 1896. By the turn of the century, African Americans and other people of color who had participated as athletes and as spectators in some integrated games were effectively excluded from certain events and arenas.[69] During the glory years of sports organizing, numerous encumbrances—including legislation, race riots, and the flat-out refusal of sports promoters to schedule black boxers specifically in the heavyweight division—prevented many African American pugilists from competing in that weight category. George L. "Tex" Rickard, one of boxing's leading promoters, adamantly refused to arrange interethnic, especially black-white matches, for heavyweight championship bouts after the reigning champion, African American Jack Johnson, clobbered Jim Jeffries, the so-called great white hope.[70] As the historian Jeffrey Sammons demonstrates in *Beyond the Ring*, this intense racism associated with black heavyweight titleholders grew largely from the controversies surrounding the performances of Arthur John "Jack" Johnson in and out of the ring. His command of the sport and his overt defiance of Jim Crow, which included openly dating white women, sent what Sammons described as "an odd alliance of racists, reformers, and public officials" scurrying for measures to preserve what they perceived as the "proper" social order by restricting black presence and participation in the sport.[71] They clamored that it was not possible for a symbol of American manhood, the boxing heavyweight title, to be held by a black man.[72] After Johnson, no serious African American contenders were scheduled for the heavyweight crown for almost twenty years, until the Brown Bomber captured the title in 1935.

The combination of racism, riots, fixed fights, and violence in and out of the ring made boxing, unlike some other spectator events, controversial, and the sport faced a harder struggle to attain some semblance of legitimacy in the larger society. Real and assumed scandals associated with the sport led to increasing calls for government regulation. By the turn of the twentieth century, some states, including New York and Louisiana, either banned the forty-five-round boxing matches or outlawed boxing altogether, while other states like California imposed stricter restrictions on the sport.[73] As early as 1905, Los Angeles city ordinances limited bouts to ten rounds, and by 1915, amid repeated allegations of fixed fights and the death of a heavyweight boxer in the ring, residents of the Golden State voted to prohibit professional prizefights and restrict amateur bouts to four rounds, with the maximum purse or medal worth $35. An election in 1924 repealed these mandates, but created a state athletic board to oversee boxing and wrestling.[74]

The California State Athletic Commission joined other organizations, notably the New York State Athletic Commission and the privately funded National Boxing Association (NBA), in attempting to regulate and clean up professional prizefighting. However, the organizations often competed with one another for sovereignty, and these conflicts tended to undermine the agencies' intended goals. One sportswriter called for a nationally unified administration, charging that "there can be no real, substantial progress—no big housecleaning in the ranks of boxers and promoters—no fully performed duty to the boxing devotees of America—unless all the commissions get together."[75]

Despite the attempts of the NBA and various state athletic councils to police boxing, a number of people, particularly the middle class and reformers, continued to associate the sport with gambling, fixed fights, and corruption, elements that they argued attracted crowds with "questionable" characters from the seedy underside of society. Reformers, boxing opponents, and even a few sportswriters were quick to point out that "Uncle Mike" Jacobs, the controversial but very influential boxing promoter in the 1930s, was friendly to some of the most powerful underworld mobsters, like Frankie Carbo, as well as certain political machine bosses.[76] In a series of exposés that focused on the life and career of Uncle Mike, writer Budd Schulberg illustrated how the young Jacobs learned his lessons in urban politics and sports promotion from the days when he worked as a waiter in Tammany Hall. Jacobs nurtured relationships with the Hall's dining-room patrons like Boss Richard Crocker, Police Chief William Devery, and, especially, Senator Timothy D. "Big Tim" Sullivan, whom Schulberg described as a man "who had a hand in almost everything and who held the boxing clubs of his day in the same single-handed control that Mike was to exert 40 years later." Schulberg concluded that from these men, especially Sullivan, Jacobs learned that "every man—except perhaps the hated reformers—has his price."[77]

Despite the corrupt practices associated with prizefighting, poor and working-class youths, frequently from ethnic communities, saw boxing as a viable ticket for socioeconomic mobility and celebrity status. Of the 196 men who applied for boxing licenses in California in 1935, the vast majority (75 percent) who listed their present occupation as other than "boxer" were unemployed or worked in unskilled or, to a lesser extent, semiskilled positions. The most typical listing other than "boxer" among those employed in this group was "common laborer." Furthermore, of the 194 applicants who specified their race, 43.2 percent were Filipinos, Mexicans, African Americans, and other ethnic minorities, with 26.8 percent falling into the nonwhite category.[78]

This affinity is in part due to the minimal capital investment required in learning the sport. Moreover, because of failures by both the state and the reformers to accomplish their objectives, boxing had fewer restrictions than other sports. Pugilists also faced fewer obstacles. Size, for example, was not a hindrance since there were various weight categories.[79] More to the point, most poor and working-class children initially learned the skills of self-defense by necessity. The majority of boxers started their careers in the rough streets of impoverished neighborhoods and ghettos, where they had to contend with racism, crime, and gangs. Some youths transferred these street-honed talents of survival into the ring when they faced limited opportunities for socioeconomic mobility.[80]

For many marginalized, working-class, and poor youths, sports served as a vehicle for advancement. Since its introduction in the United States, boxing aroused working-class passions and remained principally an ethnic enterprise, attracting athletes and patrons largely from marginalized groups and the laboring classes. As the social historian Kevin White has argued, boxing and the "alternative masculinity" that the sport embraced grew out of a largely immigrant, working-class rebellion against the repressive Victorian culture and its ideals of the "Christian gentleman" and the "self-made man."[81] Reform movements particularly targeted boxing, which the members viewed as a "potentially dangerous and barbaric activity," especially since the poor, immigrants, and working classes, as spectators and as pugilists, reveled in the game.[82]

By the first decades of the twentieth century, second-generation Jews, the majority of whom came from poor families and from ghettoes like New York's Lower East Side, made significant strides in prizefighting circles. Benny Leonard, the son of Russian Jewish immigrants, was among the first Jewish pugilists who made a name for himself in the ring. Leonard first learned the techniques of self-defense against the street gangs in his neighborhood and, at the age of fifteen, became an amateur boxer to supplement the family's earnings. Despite his mother's protests, Leonard turned professional and, in 1917, won the lightweight championship from British fighter Freddie Welsh.[83] By the 1920s, Jewish contenders dominated in all the weight categories.[84]

For Filipinos, boxing also proved a way to better their lives. Both Villa and Garcia, the two most-recognized Filipino champions during the American occupation, came from poor, landless families in sugar-producing regions of the Philippines. Because of the hacienda system imposed by the Spanish on the agricultural provinces of the islands, its perpetuation by American and other foreign capitalists, and the failure of indigenous peasant uprisings to force critical land reforms, internal migration to Manila and immigration to the United States, as workers or as athletes, were possible routes to socioeconomic mobility.[85]

While Filipinos learned the sport of self-defense from U.S. colonial administrators and American teachers who hoped to inculcate "proper" values to them as colonial subjects, some Filipinos used their acquired skills to fashion their own modes of cultural production. In arenas in the Philippines and in the United States, Filipino pugilists sought a legitimate place within organized sport by defying its assumptions about race and ability. In the tales of champions, Filipino boxers and spectators not only embedded their narratives with jabs at U.S. colonial policies in the islands and the nature of professional sports in the United States but also engaged the historical and cultural processes associated with the dynamics of masculinity in the United States and the way in which it was transported to the Philippines. As the historian

Kristin L. Hoganson argues, American gender politics in the late nineteenth century brings together the seemingly disparate social, economic, and political justifications for the Spanish-American and Philippine-American wars, campaigns that resulted in the invasion and subsequent colonization of the Philippines. By 1898, Hoganson posits, a number of politicians faced anxieties about what they perceived to be the deteriorating state of "manly" values, particularly the lack of opportunities to demonstrate courage and character through combat experience, among white, native-born middle-class and elite young men in America. As the century drew to a close, politicians who supported the wars looked to armed conflict as a means to revitalize their perception of American manhood through military service and the creation of a new generation of veterans as the memory of the American Civil War (1861–1865) faded and veterans who had served as models for heroes died.[86]

Unlike the Spanish-American War, which was justified as the liberation of Cuba and other Spanish possessions, the Philippine-American War raised controversies as it quickly turned into a bloody crusade for empire. Ardent imperialists supported the war, believing that acquiring colonies offered, among substantial economic benefits, an antidote to modern comforts that had rendered white, native-born rich young men morally weak, physically unfit, self-centered, and materialistic. These advocates, many of whom served in influential government positions in the United States and, eventually, in the colonial administration in the Philippines, had long emphasized physical activities as an essential component in the construction and maintenance of American manhood. Senator Henry Cabot Lodge, for example, who served as chairman of the U.S. Senate's Philippine committee, cited sports, particularly football, baseball, and hockey, as his "real education," during his boyhood. As an adult, he retained his veneration of athletes, including pugilists.[87]

These beliefs in sports and other extraneous physical activities as essential components of manhood among many of the middle class and elite in late-nineteenth-century America arguably found their way into the educational policies, which emphasized athletics, implemented by U.S. colonial administrators, teachers, and organizations in the Philippines. Indeed, a Chicago *Daily News* columnist remarked how sports became central in this effort to "civilize" the "savage" Filipinos.[88] But as C. L. R. James illustrates in *Beyond a Boundary*, skills imposed by, and learned from, the colonizers created the potential for colonized peoples to critique the status quo and to develop channels of resistance.[89] In the tales of champions like Ceferino Garcia, Filipino boxers and spectators embedded their narratives with jabs at American colonial policies in the islands, the nature of professional sports in the United States, and the meanings of heteromasculinity. Boxing arenas became important sites where Filipinos were regarded by men from the dominant society as virile men. This perception was particularly significant for Filipinos forced to work in traditionally feminized positions as domestics. Mainstream sportswriters imbued Filipino pugilists with the qualities of manhood prevalent by the 1930s, attributes that included ideals of aggressiveness, physical strength, and sexuality.[90] One author living in, and writing about, Los Angeles in the 1930s declared that while Filipinos "are not an appealing people," this sentiment did not extend to "the prize-fight ring, where they fight with courage and ferocity."[91] When Ceferino Garcia won the 1939 middleweight title after a bloody match, the *New York Times* observed admiringly that "Garcia embodies everything that goes to make a titleholder. . . . He is strong. He can box. He can punch. He can absorb punishment. He can adjust himself to ring situations as they develop, is resourceful, alert, cool under fire, a perfect fury when the tide swings his way."[92] Despite the marginalization of Filipinos, Filipino boxers proved to be formidable opponents, exemplified the Filipino spirit and strength in the face of battle, and won championships.

Basing their standards of male virility on prizefighting and boxing champions through their own narratives suggests that Filipinos viewed their masculinity as part of a continuing performance, whose principles are played out through shared rituals of physical confrontations in and out of the ring. As the historian George Chauncey argues, masculinity in bachelor subcultures is established through participation in male rites of solidarity and "demonstrated as well by his besting of other men in contests of strength and skill in all-male arenas. . . . Manliness in this world was confirmed by other men and in relation to other men."[93] Because validation by, and comparison with, other men is salient in defining potency, confronting challenges was crucial. Thus, when Small Montana refused to defend his American flyweight title against Oakland's Tuffy Pierpont, Filipinos derided their countryman. A Filipino journalist taunted that "in trying to side-step Pierpont, the Filipino champion [Montana] is not only jeopardizing his popularity with the fight fans, but is also endangering his fistic career. . . . Is it possible that Small Montana is afraid?" Due to this kind of pressure from his ethnic boxing community, Small Montana *did* meet the challenger and, using "some of his snake-like left hand punches[,] . . . kept Pierpont off-balance" for most of the ten rounds of fighting.[94] Some 9,000 fans, most of them Filipinos, cheered on Montana as he defended his title and, by extension, the community's bravery and worth as fighting men.

Young Filipino workers attended these boxing matches to support their equally youthful heroes but also because they *liked* the sport. In twentieth-century as well as nineteenth-century America, young, immigrant working-class men went to the fights to take part in "the fierce excitement of human battle—the blood, the bravos, the ambition, the dauntless courage and contempt for pain and danger, and even life, which make up the elements of the prize fight."[95] For both the pugilists and the spectators, the arena was an important component of a male youth culture that celebrated being male and being young. The overwhelming majority of the hundreds of potential contenders who applied for boxing licenses in California in the years 1935, 1936, and 1938 were between eighteen and twenty-four years old. During these three years, there were only thirty-one applicants in the twenty-five-and-older age group, but of these, only four were pushing thirty at twenty-nine years old. Further, there were only four aspirants who were thirty years old or older. Anton Pasich, a firefighter from San José, was, at age thirty-five in 1935, the oldest candidate for a boxing license during the three years.[96]

The physical confrontations that made boxing exhilarating, however, also made it dangerous. Doctors and members of the American Medical Association (AMA) were among the most outspoken opponents of pugilism and what they claimed to be the sport's greatest occupational risk: punch-drunkenness. In the late 1920s, Harrison S. Martland conducted one of the pioneering studies on *pugilistica dementia*. Based on his observations of more than 300 fighters, Martland argued that repeated blows to the head precipitated the disorder, generally characterized by progressively degenerative speech patterns, memory loss, fleeting attention span, sluggish walk, vision impairment, and delayed reaction to stimulation.[97] In a two-year study that followed up on Martland's findings, Edward J. Carroll watched matches, examined pugilists, and talked with trainers, promoters, and boxing commission physicians. Carroll concluded, much as Martland had, that every blow to the boxer's head jolted the brain against the skull, resulting in numerous minute lesions in the brain. Repeated head traumas in the ring, Carroll maintained, led to hemorrhages and irreparable damage to the tissues and nerve endings. He estimated that approximately 60 percent of boxers who stuck to the sport for five years would develop the punch-drunk syndrome.[98] Former lightweight champion

Ad Wolgast, the Michigan Wildcat, represented one of the most extreme cases of punch-drunkenness: insanity. In 1920, after fourteen years in the ring, Wolgast was committed to an asylum in Camarillo, California, where, until his death in 1955, he prepared daily for a bout scheduled for "tomorrow."[99]

To numerous pugilists, trainers, promoters, sports enthusiasts, and other physicians, however, Martland's and Carroll's studies remained solely a theory, largely because the doctors failed to perform laboratory tests, including postmortem examinations, on any athlete's brain.[100] Indeed, as one boxing opponent pointed out, aside from the physical symptoms for which trainers devised justifications, the difficulty with convincing boxing advocates of the dangers associated with the sport was that there were no psychological tests for punch-drunkenness. "Were such a test part of the fighter's [required physical] examination," he declared, "at least half of the current crop of boxers would be barred."[101] Jimmy Johnston, a promoter for New York's Madison Square Garden and a former manager, rejected the existence of punch-drunkenness, hotly declaring that "if a man ever left the ring mentally deficient, he was mentally deficient when he entered it." Johnston issued this denial despite the fact that two weeks earlier, he had offered to personally pay for the care of a former trainee, world light-heavyweight champion Mike McTigue, when the forty-three-year-old ex-boxer was committed to the Rockland State Hospital.[102]

While some AMA doctors mobilized around punch-drunk disorder and the fighter's eventual diminished mental and physical capacities as a rallying cry to abolish prizefights, other boxing opponents raised different dangers, including nasal and related facial injuries, and kidney and heart disorders. Some physicians asserted that too many punches to the chest could result in cardiovascular problems, including heart failure.[103] A sports columnist argued that kidney disease was a potential consequence of the "drying-out" period following the training sessions. Ostensibly, a fighter "dries out," abstaining from all liquids, so that when he weighs in for a bout, he carries no excess weight. Withholding liquids from the body, however, also desensitizes the stomach's gastric nerves, enabling a boxer to take more punches in the midsection area with relatively less pain. With this analysis of the drying-out process and the subsequent numbing of the boxer's midriff, the sportswriter concluded that "that's what a manager wants. What good is a fighter who backs up?"[104]

In addition to the protests of several doctors and sportscasters, some Roman Catholic priests questioned the morality of boxing. Father James Gillis repeatedly and vigorously condemned the sport because of its demoralizing effects on the athletes and spectators alike. In one of many editorials for the magazine *Catholic World*, Gillis argued that "it is difficult at best to lead men on towards a truly spiritual life. It simply cannot be done if from time to time they are encouraged to revert to savagery. It is therefore an amazing thing that we Americans—and I repeat especially we Catholics—tolerate this stupid and sordid business, and call it a sport."[105] Gillis was especially enraged that Christian organizations, particularly the YMCA, taught its young followers the mechanics of boxing and extolled its virtues as forms of play and self-defense. After detailing the blood, gore, and brutality characteristic of prizefighting, Gillis exclaimed, "Imagine! Christianity giving the sanction of the Supreme Gentle Man, Jesus Christ, to an encouragement of the savage in man."[106]

Despite the myriad criticisms ranging from physical deformities to moral transgressions, the majority of objections addressed the very real possibility of death, either in the ring or as the immediate or long-term result of a fight, as the foremost consideration for abolishing the sport. But for many poor, ethnic, and working-class boxers, the possibilities of dangers in the ring paled in comparison with the almost certain likelihood of serious job-related injuries and unhealthful working and living conditions that they faced if they remained in their occupations. For the majority of Filipino immigrants, their livelihood depended on performing physically demanding work that also exposed them to dangerous chemicals and fertilizers in California's fields and unsafe machines in Alaska's fish canneries. Filipinos who worked in the service-oriented sectors in Los Angeles and other urban areas faced relatively limited risks, but even they were not entirely exempt from unhealthy situations and the lack of safety equipment in the workplace. The historian Phyllis Palmer conveyed how domestics were prone to many chest, feet, and back injuries as a result of performing heavy labor around the middle-class home. Further, she noted that by the 1930s toxic substances such as lye, oxalic acid, and gasoline were routinely used for such household chores as cleaning and bleaching.[107]

Servants and other workers in the service industries, including Filipinos, routinely carried out strenuous manual labor and handled harmful chemicals with their bare hands in the course of doing their jobs. With no provisions for health, welfare, unemployment, or retirement benefits forthcoming from their employers or the state should they get injured, Filipinos could well reason that if they were boxers hurt in the ring, they could at least find solace in one of the three homes for athletes sponsored by the California State Athletic Commission. The agency had started gathering funds for these centers in 1932, collecting 1 percent of all gross receipts from fights to support "athletes injured in boxing and wrestling matches, for their temporary rest, for return transportation, for funeral expenses, and like purposes," and eventually expanding to include retirement benefits. One home was in San Francisco, but the other two were in Los Angeles: the Westmoreland House on 519 Westmoreland Avenue for "white" athletes and the Armstrong Cottage on 1830 West Jefferson for "colored" and other ethnic minorities.[108]

In addition to the potential assistance and benefits they could receive as injured or retired athletes, the opportunity for prominence in a society where there was little chance for people of color to achieve distinction or belong to a select group made boxing popular among young Filipinos. Nineteen-year-old Marino Guiang had embarked on his career as Young Marion in order to support himself through high school when he was unable to find a job in Seattle that fit into his class schedule. Guiang began attending the Friday boxing shows at the Austin and Bishop Gymnasium on Ninth and Olive Streets. He remembered that his opportunity "was a funny thing that came up. . . . One guy name[d] Ray Woods was beating everybody in his size, you know, one night I went over there and the men at the door shouted, 'Here's your opponent, Ray, he's coming.' And they asked me if I could fight. 'Sure, I could fight.' . . . So, they put the gloves on. . . . We fought over there but he got the decision." In spite of the loss in his first amateur outing, Young Marion was hooked. From 1926 to 1933, he boxed in feather- and bantamweight bouts in the Pacific Northwest, Canada, and Alaska, eventually attaining a title in Alaska.[109]

For other Filipinos, especially migratory laborers, boxing provided income and diversion during the off-season. In Stockton, Fred Pearl, a local boxing promoter and owner of the L Street Arena Club, organized Friday amateur nights for Filipinos, offering to pay $10 for the best bout of the evening.[110] The ring was a site where, at least for the moment, fans, professional fighters, and potential champions met on relatively equal terms. In the Main Street Gym in Los Angeles, Filipino workers fought as sparring partners, usually in four-round bouts, with some of the well-known Filipino boxers.[111] This practice was not restricted exclusively to Filipino fans and Filipino fighters. The African American fighter "Hurricane" Henry Armstrong recalled a particularly unforgettable day very early in his training period when, as an unknown boxer, he "worked out with [then Pacific Coast bantamweight champion, Filipino pugilist] Speedy Dado, the man whose success had inspired [me] to go in for boxing seriously."[112]

Armstrong's admiration of a Filipino champion suggests that sports presented possibilities for the creation of an array of ethnic heroes, especially in the 1920s and 1930s, when Anglo athletes and segregated professional games dominated the sports scene. Fighting largely amateur bouts as Melody Henry Jackson, the young Armstrong dreamed of duplicating the success of two of his boxing favorites: Eligio "Kid Chocolate" Sardinias, an Afro-Cuban fighter, and Speedy Dado, a Filipino champion. Lying in his bed one night in East St. Louis, Illinois, Armstrong resolved to go to California and triumph like Speedy Dado: "Why, Dado was drawing super-gates that netted him as much as $5,000 every two weeks! And on the ceiling over [my] staring eyes appeared a vision of Speedy Dado, just as he'd looked on the cover of the recent issue of *Knockout* . . . smiling, dressed in elegant, expensive clothes. A large diamond ring flashed insistently on one hand."[113]

The semiotician Roland Barthes suggested that unlike the spectacle and morality play associated with wrestling, boxing was a "story which is constructed before the eyes of the spectator."[114] Yet upon closer examination, Filipino audiences were not passive consumers of the action in the ring. They were passionately involved in the production of these stories. During boxing matches, Filipinos took control of a cultural space wherein rules that restricted their everyday lives were temporarily suspended. Bouts provided an opportunity to display passionate expressions of visceral anger at the daily indignities that they encountered and bore in silence. In addition, as consumers of organized sporting events, Filipinos possessed relatively more power than they had as workers. At the very least, they could refuse to participate, a route denied them as workers. Filipino laborers boycotted boxing matches in Watsonville, for example, to protest "white hogs" who, despite a notice that prohibited betting and profanity in the arena, swore throughout the matches and taunted Filipino fighters and fans with racial slurs.[115]

As spectators, Filipinos cheered for their "boy," booed the "enemy," and overtly challenged authority. Reports of numerous sideshow scrimmages routinely peppered Filipino newspapers. Once when a referee prematurely called a draw between an intense and much-anticipated bantamweight bout, the papers reported that "dissatisfaction with the decision was immediately evident from the spectators. . . . [A] little revolution" was diverted only after pleas for order from the referee.[116]

The referee in the 1932 match between "Hammerin'" Henry Armstrong and Filipino Kid Moro in Pismo Beach was not as successful in restoring peace. The event ended in a riot when referee Fred Gilmore declared Armstrong the winner after ten rounds of heavy fighting from both sides. Armstrong's recollection of the ensuing slugfest is illustrative of Filipino fight fans' defying an official ruling. He vividly described how the declaration of his victory brought "fierce cries of disagreement and rage . . . from Filipino fans in the audience. Scores of them crowded toward the ring, shouting their protest. The place was a bedlam. Moro himself was acting crazy, crying to Referee Gilmore that the victory belonged to him. He hopped up and down, waving his fists and pulling at the elastic ropes." While Moro raged, "one furious Filipino had pulled a knife and was creeping toward Gilmore. Someone jumped into the ring and tussled with him, twisting his wrist till the knife fell. Detectives and friends of Gilmore forced their way to the ring and escorted him in safety to the dressing rooms. The crowd, meanwhile, was going berserk."[117]

Armstrong and Kid Moro faced each other two more times in 1933, first in Stockton and then in Watsonville. Both bouts ended in draws. Armstrong later mused that he "thought he had a little [of] the best of each, but he figured that the large Filipino populations present in each of them influenced the referees to call the fights draws to avoid trouble."[118]

Crowd action among Filipinos was not restricted exclusively to interethnic matches. Chaos ensued in the Sacramento Civic Auditorium when the referee suddenly stopped a bantamweight bout between Filipino pugilists Pablo Dano and Young Tommy, giving what most of the Filipino audience declared was an unearned draw decision to Dano, who was the 2 to 1 favorite. Tommy had been leading in six of the ten rounds, and Dano, "begging no mercy . . . [but] with blood streaming down his eyes, was [such] a constant target of the ripping rights and lefts of Tommy that Referee [Jack] Kennedy intervened . . . giving Dano the benefit of a draw through his sheer grit and aggressiveness."[119] That the largely Filipino audience noisily exhibited their disagreement with a judgment that endorsed the crowd favorite suggests that the ring represented a site where Filipinos staked their sense of fair play. Even though the fans admired Dano's tenacity, they rioted when they felt that the decision was undeserved. The Filipinos' understanding of fair play was also evident when they boycotted a local Stockton arena when they suspected that the management engaged in fixing fights.[120]

In developing reputations as brave and daring fighting men, Filipino pugilists challenged both the dominant culture's stereotypes of Filipinos as "brown monkeys" in the United States and the colonizers' perception of "civilizing" the "natives" in the Philippines. At a time when American military personnel were still struggling to put down nationalist movements in parts of the islands, and growers and their henchmen were violently thwarting Filipino and multiethnic unionization efforts in the United States, the ring provided a stage where a "dangerous" or an "aggressive" Filipino was legitimate—indeed, desirable. Roberto "Little Dempsey" Hilado recalled that he fought harder to win a match when he heard a woman in the audience screaming for his opponent to "C'mon, c'mon, kill that monkey!"[121]

For Filipino immigrants, the most popular fights were often those involving their brown heroes and white boxers. As a local promoter in Stockton maintained, "Filipinos versus white fighters are . . . the favorite matches, and draw good houses, with good Filipino representation."[122] These Filipino–white matches were also popular in the Philippines. Pancho Villa recalled that in his bout with Michael Ballerino, an American soldier stationed in the islands, "the Olympic arena [in Manila] was packed like sardines with Filipinos, who had come to cheer for me, and hundreds of American soldiers [who] were there to root for Ballerino. He was their pride and joy."[123] When Ceferino Garcia defended his American middleweight title against Glen Lee in Manila's Rizal Stadium in 1939, Filipinos filled the open auditorium despite the pouring rain.[124] The Filipino American novelist Peter Bacho understood why Filipino–white contests occupied a special place among Filipino boxing fans in the Philippines and in the United States, writing that "in the ring, a Filipino could beat a white man with his fists and not be arrested."[125]

In the Little Manilas of cities like Los Angeles, Stockton, and Seattle, the achievements of Filipino boxers bolstered the spirits of Filipino immigrants, especially the workers. Triumphs, or even anticipated victories, of pugilists like the Bolo Puncher, Speedy Dado, and Pablo Dano were grounds for many Filipino laborers to declare a "holiday" from the fields, canneries, and service industries. A championship title, or at least a good showing of brown muscle in the ring, warranted pride and loud boasting, usually accompanied by all-day and all-night revelries in the streets, restaurants, and pool halls of their communities.[126] The noted African American author Maya Angelou eloquently captured the significance of a champion of color's success for a poor, marginalized community. Commemorating the Brown Bomber's win of the heavyweight title, Angelou wrote "champion of the world. A Black boy. Some Black mother's son. He was the strongest man in the world. People drank Coca-Colas like ambrosia and ate candy bars like Christmas. Some of the men went behind the Store and poured white lightning in their soft drink bottles."[127]

Commercialized boxing matches and the sporting life formed one stage in the cultural process that Filipino immigrants undertook to assemble a collective memory. The Filipinos' intense preoccupation with this sport provided compelling evidence that the struggle to create a working-class, ethnic identity occurred not only through mass movements associated with labor unions, but also through daily leisure activities, like sharing in the excitement of battle and swapping stories.

Reports and events surrounding the sudden death of Pancho Villa in 1925 reflect the significance of boxing heroes and their roles in shaping how Filipinos remember and reorder history. Standard descriptions and controversies pointed to Villa's demise ten days after a nontitle bout with Jimmy McLarnin in Oakland, California, as an example of the deadly consequences of boxing. It was widely believed around the sports world that the Living Doll had died from blood poisoning that was initially caused by infected teeth and was aggravated by the blows Villa sustained in the match.[128] Villa's press agent, Bill Miller, later charged that the flyweight champion did not die as a direct result of the fight. Villa died, he claimed, because the boxer had not followed the dentist's prescriptions for medication and rest to control the swelling in preparation for the extraction. Villa instead threw a party in his hotel room that lasted for several nights and days. In the meantime, the infection spread to his neck glands. By the tenth day, a few hours after checking into a hospital, the twenty-four-year-old Living Doll was dead of blood poisoning.[129]

While Villa gained renown for his skill and determination in the ring, in death he became larger than life. For countless Filipinos in the Philippines and in the United States, especially among the workers, he became the symbol of youth and exuberance, their hero who defied poverty and captured rightful glory through the grace and strength of the brown body. Filipino immigrants told and retold Villa's story and, in the process, created a vital countermemory to the official version of why Villa chose to fight that night, and why he died. Through their testimonies, Filipinos reclaimed the Living Doll from his non-Filipino fans and entourage. Villa was theirs; he was always theirs. He knew it as clearly as *they* knew it.

Filipinos' stories commemorated that hot Fourth of July evening when Villa, regardless of supposedly having had a wisdom tooth removed the day before, refused to cancel the scheduled bout. Their champion, they contend, did not want to disappoint his fellow Filipinos, for he knew that some of them had forfeited working hours and wages, while others had traveled great distances to watch the match. Inspired by the faithfulness of his supporters, the world flyweight champion fought for them, so they could bear witness to his undisputed talent in the ring and share in his splendor.[130] To the Filipinos, Villa knew each of them personally; he understood their hard lives and their individual and collective needs for his victory. To them, he was fighting for every Filipino in the audience, in the United States, and in the Philippines. When Villa's body arrived for burial in Manila, thousands of Filipinos paid respect to their fallen hero.

As members of an oppressed ethnic group, Filipinos celebrated their champions, in life as well as in death, with gusto. They invoked familiar themes from their native folk narratives to establish parallels between the lives of the great, indigenous warriors and Filipino boxers. The emergence of this subculture was also born out of conflict with the dominant society. Regarded as no more than cheap "stoop" labor and meek service workers by an insensitive host society, Filipinos engaged in strategies that offered the possibility of dignity and self-definition. These counterhegemonic maneuvers not only incorporated the Filipinos' understanding of their marginalized position in the United States but also celebrated the vibrant subculture of the Filipino immigrant community.

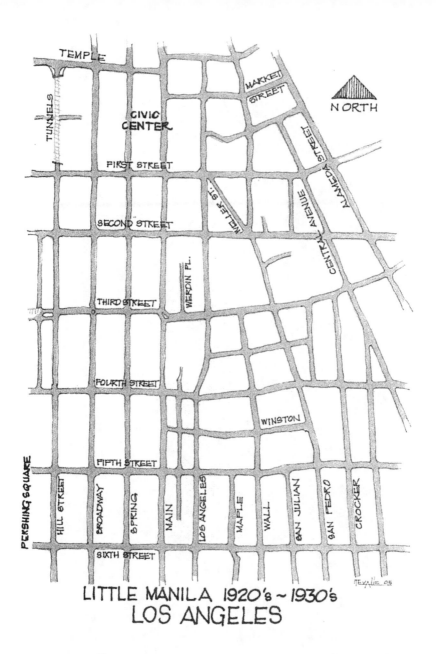

**LITTLE MANILA 1920's ~ 1930's
LOS ANGELES**

From the 1920s until World War II, the Filipino community of Los Angeles flourished in the downtown area, roughly demarcated by San Pedro Street on the east, Sixth Street on the south, Figueroa Avenue on the west, and Sunset Boulevard on the north. Weller Street was a major hub for both Little Manila and Little Tokyo. In the post–World War II years, Los Angeles's regentrification of the downtown area, demographic shifts among Filipino Angeleños, and reforms in U.S. immigration laws contributed to the demise of the community. (Tania Azores, "Filipinos in the Los Angeles Labor Force: Placemaking in Little Manila" [1983]; Rosemarie D. Ibañez, "'Birds of Passage': Filipino Immigrants in the 1920s and 1930s" [1990]. Map redrawn by Manolo Evalle)

☞ TAKE ONE SHEET

Home Sweet Home

Facts About This Home:

1. Centrally located; easily reached from anywhere in town.

2. One of the best residential districts in the city.

3. Equipped with nearly every facility of a good home.
   a. Furnished Rooms, Apartments and Cottage
   b. Garages and Parking Yard.
   c. With Social, Reading and Writing Room.
   d. With Tub and Shower Baths.
   e. With Kitchen Privileges.

4. In the midst of four great institutions:
   a. The Trade School.
   b. The Polytechnic High School.
   c. The National Automotive School.
   d. The University of Southern California.

PRICES: Only $2.00 a week
$7.00 a month

Take "J" or "M" car and get off on either Adams or 25th St. on Grand Ave. and you will surely find the

"FILIPINO HOME"

2507 S. Grand Ave.   Telephone ATlantic 5163
Los Angeles, Calif.

PRIMO E. QUEVEDO, Mgr.

PASS THE GOOD NEWS

"Filipino Home" on Grand Avenue, Los Angeles. Because most Filipino workers depended on mobility to earn a living, they created networks of portable communities. News items and advertisements for hotels, restaurants, and services along the migration circuit that routinely filled the pages of Filipino ethnic newspapers, as well as handbills like this one, attest to these systems of maintaining communal connections as Filipinos traversed between urban and rural spaces. (Courtesy of the Bancroft Library, University of California, Berkeley)

Top: Filipino Angeleños gather at First and Hope Streets, ca. 1930. (Photograph courtesy of the "Shades of L.A." Archives, Los Angeles Public Library)

Bottom: Camilo Serrano waiting on bridge players in Los Angeles, ca. 1938. Serrano, who moved to L.A. in 1928, attended the University of Southern California and served as the secretary-treasurer of the university's Philippine Trojan Club. In 1937 he earned his M.A. from USC. (Photograph courtesy of the "Shades of L.A." Archives, Los Angeles Public Library)

Romy Madrigal (*standing, second from right*), Dodo Zamorano (*standing, second from left*), Bonifacio Libre (*seated, center*), and townmates pose in their McIntosh suits in Los Angeles's harbor area during the 1930s. The men worked in the fish canneries on nearby Terminal Island. (Photograph courtesy of the "Shades of L.A." Archives, Los Angeles Public Library)

Clockwise, from far left: Ann Ferrer, Eddie Ferrer (*seated, fourth from left*), Joe Abrigo (*standing, second from left*), and Gene Aquino (*standing, fifth from left*) with friends at the L.V.M. Café, located at 113 East First Street in Little Manila. Filipino-owned establishments provided economic opportunities for entrepreneurs and contributed to the rich public life of Filipino Angeleños. To entice the bachelors who formed the majority of the community, restaurants invoked images of family and home life. (Photograph courtesy of the "Shades of L.A." Archives, Los Angeles Public Library)

Above: A gathering of champions: (*left to right*) Felix Santiago, 1931 Pacific Coast bantamweight and flyweight champion Speedy Dado, manager Jess Cortez, and future American middleweight champion Ceferino Garcia. (Photograph by Harry E. Winkler; reproduced from the original held by the Department of Special Collections of the University Libraries of Notre Dame)

Left: Ceferino Garcia perfecting his "bolo punch," a lethal combination of right uppercuts and half hooks. Garcia's manager in the Philippines, Jess Cortes, brought the nineteen-year-old amateur fighter to the United States around 1930. Two years later, Cortes left the still-unknown welterweight with a new manager, George Parnassus. By 1938, Garcia had fought and, more often than not, knocked out most fighters in his class division. (Photograph by Harry E. Winkler; reproduced from the original held by the Department of Special Collections of the University Libraries of Notre Dame)

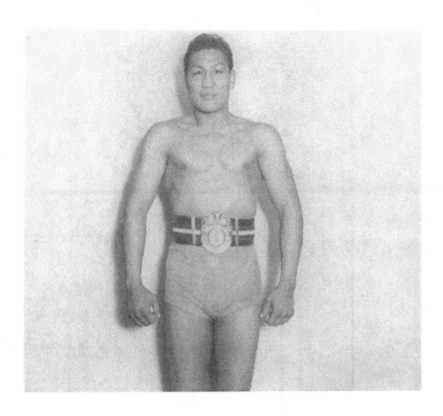

Ceferino Garcia, 1939 American middleweight champion. Garcia bulked up to 154 pounds to fight in the middleweight division, the only Filipino pugilist in the pre–World War II years to fight in this class. The Bolo Puncher became the twenty-fourth middleweight champion when he knocked out defender Fred Apostoli in seven rounds. Garcia was inducted into the *Ring*'s Boxing Hall of Fame in 1977. (Photograph by Harry E. Winkler; reproduced from the original held by the Department of Special Collections of the University Libraries of Notre Dame)

Company 1, First Filipino Infantry Regiment, Camp Roberts, California. This photo was taken immediately before the soldiers shipped out to help oust Japanese forces from the Philippines during World War II. In April 1942, the First Filipino Infantry Battalion of the U.S. Army was formed. Three months later, the First Filipino Infantry Regiment, comprising more than 3,000 soldiers under the command of Colonel Robert H. Offley, absorbed the initial company. Before the end of year, the Second Filipino Infantry Regiment was created. About 7,000 Filipinos served in these units. (Photograph courtesy of the "Shades of L.A." Archives, Los Angeles Public Library)

Severo Gubatan, technical sergeant, U.S. Army. In addition to the standard-issue U.S. Army and company insignias, soldiers in the First and Second Filipino Infantry Regiments wore a shoulder patch like the one above the sergeant's stripes on Gubatan's uniform. The embroidered yellow badge bore the silhouette of the Philippines' Mayon Volcano and three stars representing the major islands of Luzon, the Visayas, and Mindanao. Gubatan migrated to Los Angeles in 1928, and after his tour of duty in the Philippines and the Pacific Theater during World War II, he worked in the Long Beach Naval Shipyard. (Photograph courtesy of the "Shades of L.A." Archives, Los Angeles Public Library)

Left to right: Sam Reyes, Carmen Quinones, Kathy de la Rosa, Mrs. Quinones, Bonnie Quinones, Tim Reyes, and Ronnie Behasa pose on Jefferson and Normandie Streets in Los Angeles in the 1940s. (Photograph courtesy of the "Shades of L.A." Archives, Los Angeles Public Library)

4. "WHITE TRASH" AND "BROWN HORDES"

Taxi Dance Halls and the Policing of Working-Class Bodies

taxi dance	but my own
8 p.m.–2 a.m.	belonging to nobody
blondies	but you
seven days a week	if you want it
"I forgot	"they're all blondies
my labors	most of the women
for awhile	all mataba [plump] from the south"
at the taxi dance"	but the goddamn tickets
the hand around	for you
your waist	went so fast
feels good	into three minutes
is nothing	ten-cent squeezes

—al robles, "taxi dance"

In October 1935, the Los Angeles Police Department conducted a series of surprise raids on all the city's taxi dance halls for two consecutive Saturday nights. The police claimed to have received an anonymous tip that a murder was to take place in one of the recreation centers. Interrupting the busiest evening in the dance halls, the LAPD thoroughly searched the premises and the male patrons, confiscating a number of weapons, including knives, guns, and ice picks. Before the end of the week after the second raid, the police announced that patrons caught with lethal weapons in dance halls faced the possibility of deportation.[1]

Because immigration policies are under federal jurisdiction, the local police department did not have the authority to carry out the threat. But in the midst of the Great Depression, with repatriation campaigns directed against Mexicans and Filipinos in full swing, issuing such a decree suggests that the police sought to cloak a racist policy in the mantle of local "peacekeeping" tactics. Furthermore, the LAPD's full-scale response to a single anonymous tip and the consequences aimed specifically toward the immigrant male patrons of the taxi dance halls speak volumes about the relationship among the city's regulating agencies, marginalized populations, and commercialized recreation centers.

This chapter examines the leisure activity arguably most closely associated with Filipino immigrants of the 1920s and 1930s, the taxi dance halls where men paid to dance with women in timed, ritualized sequences. Some observers from the period decried these centers as nothing more than gathering places for working-class "brown hordes" and "white trash" women. The "hordes" included what one young woman described as the "sensuous, gaudily dressed, almost fierce-looking young Filipinos on the East Side of L.A."[2] White trash included the poor or working-class Anglo women who made their living by dancing with men who could pay for their time on the dance floor.[3] Of these women, the director of the U.S. Children's Bureau noted, "it is obvious that it is likely to be only the less respectable, more hardened type of taxi-dancer that signs up for work in a hall catering to men of another race."[4] But for the participants, these taxi dance halls became, especially during the 1930s, important sites for creating a vibrant subculture. Fueled by the intense nativism and racist and sexist legislation during the Great Depression and New Deal eras, these leisure centers provided opportunities for poor immigrant men and working women to create identities that allowed them to be something other than what their ethnicity, class, or national origin dictated.

Many working-class migrants called Los Angeles home by the 1930s. Attracted by social and economic factors like the ardent boosterism of the city's chamber of commerce in the past decades, the emergence and active recruitment of labor by agribusiness, and the lack of employment opportunities in their home areas, migrant Mexicans, Filipinos, African Americans, and southwestern farmers streamed into the state to work. The Filipino population in California increased from about 270 in the 1920s to more than 30,000 by 1930.[5] About 4,000 of these immigrants lived in Los Angeles on a year-round basis.[6]

This dramatic rise in the number of mostly poor people from rural areas coming to California alarmed many of the state's ruling Anglo elite, the majority of whom were migrants themselves. Two-thirds of Californians and three-quarters of the adult population in the 1930s had not been born in the state. Most came from other regions of the country, primarily the Midwest and the East Coast. Unlike the more recent migrants, however, the bulk of these earlier white settlers were affluent or at least middle class.[7] By the 1930s, the composition of Anglo migrants into California had changed dramatically: most were unemployed sharecroppers or agricultural laborers from the midwestern and southwestern states. Drought and other natural disasters, combined with massive unemployment because of the Great Depression and farm mechanization, convinced more than 500,000 residents of those regions that their future lay elsewhere. Annie Malbeuf, who left Oklahoma with her family in 1937, recalled "the swarms of grasshoppers and the swarms of dust. The dust would blow and drift . . . plumb up over the fence posts in the pastures. Then come another windstorm and it would take it down and blow it someplace else . . . [and] we had infestations of grasshoppers and locusts."[8] The Malbeufs, like many other families, packed their meager belongings and hit the road on Route 66. As one migrant put it, "The Arkies and Okies in thirty six, cranked up their flivvers and came west Sixty-six."[9]

Throughout the Depression years, between 300,000 and 400,000 of these migrants came to California. The squatters' growing presence alarmed many Californians, who considered them the state's "new" migrant problem. They were particularly concerned because, unlike Asian and Mexican immigrant workers who could be exploited through legislation or subjected to repatriation campaigns, midwestern and southwestern migrants were native-born, white, and Protestant. Further, the majority of these migrants came as families, and many Californians worried that this continued procession of poor citizens into the state would intensify problems in the already strained sectors dealing with unemployment relief, housing, education, and health care. One study estimated that in 1937 alone, of the 78,332 migrants who went to California, 68,429 individuals (87.3 percent) belonged to family units.[10]

Apprehensions related to the Dust Bowlers were prevalent especially among Los Angeles's power elite, and their response reflected some of the general attitudes in society regarding poor people. As the historian Richard Lowitt points out, to many Californians throughout the 1930s, "the term *migrant* came to be synonymous with *indigent* and *migratory worker*, and popular attitudes toward newcomers became at best unfriendly and at worst actively hostile."[11] In 1936 the city's police chief, James Davis, assigned 150 officers to "bum blockage" duties. These men set up and patrolled the state's border stations along Highways 91 and 66 in San Bernardino County, which served as the brigade's headquarters; Highway 395 in Inyo County; Highway 60 in Riverside County; and Highway 99 in Imperial County. These checkpoints were all less than 300 miles from Los Angeles, and the officers were supposedly there to deter criminals from coming into California and, more precisely, into Los Angeles. In practice, this blockade intimidated and turned away nonresidents and transients, particularly the migrants. Some observers noted that officers of the Riverside County border patrol "were interested in securing publicity so that undesirables might stay away from California. They said that they were being careful not to offend anyone who might be rich or have political influence."[12]

Within a few weeks, much to the chagrin of some Angeleños, controversies forced an end to the roadblock, and migrants continued to stream in unchecked. Some of them were unemployed professionals and skilled workers who had come to the Golden State out of desperation when friends, family, or former employers promised them work. More often than not, however, the jobs never came through and the migrants were left stranded. James M., a twenty-two-year-old pharmacist, came to California in 1935 after he lost his job in St. Louis, Missouri. His brother, a department store manager in the San Francisco Bay Area, had assured James of a job in the shop, but the position never materialized. James then hitchhiked to Los Angeles to try his luck, but nothing developed, and he eventually decided to return home by hopping freight trains.[13]

Around the Los Angeles area, the majority of men found work in the San Joaquin Valley only as underpaid itinerant laborers, and they and their families were forced to live in squalid conditions. A social worker estimated that more than 70,000 men, women, and children in the area were homeless.[14] As one historian notes, in California "their poverty in the shacktowns or ditch-bank settlements could not be ignored. By 1937, the Okies had become a local embarrassment, by 1938, a state concern, and by 1939, with the publication of *The Grapes of Wrath*, a national scandal."[15]

Despite the tremendous hardships associated with the cross-country trip, the mounting anger directed against them, and chronic poverty, migrants relocated in California and established communities in rural and urban areas. "Little Oklahomas" developed in Kern, Tulare, Kings, and other large farm counties. In Los Angeles, some migrants moved into the communities of Sawtelle and Bell Gardens.[16] Others settled in the downtown area, living and working with the city's ethnic populations. Jean Heff had moved to Los

Angeles with her husband and two children from Pryor, Oklahoma, in 1933. When she suddenly became a single parent, she found a job as a waitress, but her salary was not enough to pay the rent on their apartment. She eventually rented a room in the more affordable Majestic Hotel-Apartments on Fourth and Hope Streets, adjacent to Little Manila. There, with her bachelor Filipino neighbors and their girlfriends, she and her children celebrated birthdays and other holiday occasions.[17]

Heff's family as a female-headed, migrant household was not uncommon among the city's residents. In a study of female delinquency, Mary Odem found that as early as the 1920s, more than three-quarters of the single mothers who appealed to the Los Angeles Juvenile Court for help in raising their children were new to the neighborhood. Most of these cases involved conflicts between mothers and their adolescent daughters over the child's wages and leisure activities. These single-parent households depended on the daughters' income to make ends meet, but earning their own wages provided these young women with some level of autonomy from family and community constraints. By working in stores, offices, and factories and going to dance halls and movie theaters as part of their recreational activities, young working-class women resisted prescribed gender roles in the family.[18]

Looking at the appropriation of space by working-class youth is central to this chapter. Often these places represented hard fought–for locations where poor, working men and women could be themselves, where they were afforded some sense of dignity, away from the constant surveillance of the dominant society. In many ways, the public culture in the dance halls legitimized the creation of desire and sensuality denied them in their everyday lives. These sites opened up possibilities for the complex negotiations of viable individual and group identities. Because taxi dance halls functioned simultaneously as places of employment and as recreation centers, they became significant public arenas for an emerging working-class culture that fostered alternative presumptions associated with notions of work, leisure activities, and interethnic gender relations.

Conflicts emanating from issues related to the taxi dance halls indicate the effectiveness of popular culture practices as oppositional strategies among aggrieved populations. Within the Filipino community, issues related to taxi dance halls exposed the class distinctions between the self-described "adjusted group" of Filipino students, who claimed that they "cannot afford to waste much of their time in terms of the pleasures of their brothers," and the workers, whom they argued composed the "bewildered group, [whose] most outstanding characteristic . . . is the lack of any tangible aim in life."[19] On another level, the competition in the dance halls evinced the struggle among Filipino workers themselves, as they sought to develop individual and group identities. The controversies also elucidated tensions between the dance halls' working-class participants and the dominant society's policing agents. Reformers conducted campaigns against taxi dance halls in part because they presented a visible threat to the dominant culture's construction of youth, interethnic relations, and issues of "morality." In a broader sense, then, commercialized recreation centers populated by ethnic groups and the working class reflected struggles over issues of ethnicity, class, and popular culture not only within the Filipino community but within the larger U.S. society as well. In forging a collective sense of ethnicity and building a viable community, Filipino immigrants challenged the host society over the nature of "American" values. By displaying so-called improper behavior, they struggled to carve niches of autonomy, fought against imposed restrictions on space, and sought to expand the boundaries of alternative expressions.

Roughly 80 percent of the Filipino immigrants in the 1920s and 1930s became migratory laborers, routinely traveling among farms, canning industries, and cities. Earning meager wages for tedious, hard work often in closely supervised positions, Filipinos sought to create meaning in their lives by developing cultural practices that spoke to the connections between rural and urban experiences. The taxi dance halls and other recreation centers that dotted the migratory routes and were frequented by Filipinos became significant rendezvous points for calling the community into being, where Filipinos could cement and rejuvenate personal bonds, share food, swap stories, and surely gossip about the *kababayan* (countrymen) along the migration circuit. Through word of mouth and the ethnic press, Filipino migrant workers found out about the latest hangouts. As Miguel Lawagan points out, "You know how Filipinos are. . . . They scramble all around and talk to friends, some put advertising in the paper. 'The dance [hall] is open!', 'Come in!', 'Come one, come all!', [the ads] say . . . [but] everybody just *knows*."[20]

Sammy Escalona's recollections are typical of the experiences many Filipino workers faced and indicate the importance of popular culture practices in their lives. Escalona immigrated to California in 1928 and became a migrant laborer, commuting between the fields of central California to Alaska's fishing canneries in a car that he and two friends bought jointly. While he did not work in Los Angeles for any extended period, he knew where the recreation centers were located and regularly visited them. Escalona and his friends thought nothing of driving 300 miles round-trip, in the middle of a workweek, to watch a boxing match with fellow Filipinos. "Hey, if the action was in L.A.," he said, "you make it a point to be there."[21] His cousin Leo shared a kindred attitude. He would drive up to 200 miles to patronize certain taxi dance halls like the Hippodrome Dance Palace on Main and Third Streets in Los Angeles, saying that "it was no big deal. . . . I had a car and I wanted to go there, they knew me."[22] Still another Filipino fruit picker recalls driving more than fifty miles from a Stockton farm to Sacramento "just for a dance."[23]

Clearly, consumerism and the attraction of leisure activities provided an important link between urban and rural space. In their search for places that afforded them some sense of dignity and relative freedom of expression, Filipino workers flocked to taxi dance halls to tout young brown bodies not as exploited workers but as agents of enjoyment, style, and sensuality.[24] Living in a world where their work time was dictated by cycles of crops, migration patterns of fish, and demands of service-oriented industries, Filipinos found that dance halls provided the spaces for them to be what they also were: young men in search of the proverbial wine, women, and song.

Filipinos regularly attended taxi dance halls around Los Angeles's Little Manila, including Danceland and the Hippodrome Dance Palace on Main Street, the Liberty Dance Hall on Third, Roma Hall on Figueroa, and the Orpheum and the Red Mill Dance Hall on Broadway. Significantly, a large number of these recreation centers were within the borders of Little Manila. The dance halls were part of the vibrant street culture of the community, along with the various restaurants, cafés, barbershops, and pool halls frequented by the Filipino residents. Many of the dance halls were within easy walking distance, sometimes even next to each other or at least along the route of the red cars, the city's public transportation system in the 1930s.

In the dance halls, Filipino workers developed a dynamic alternative subculture where they celebrated the body attired in McIntosh suits, expensive formal attire with padded shoulders and wide lapels worn by some of Hollywood's most famous leading men, such as William Powell. In many ways, Filipinos regarded the possession and the donning of the double-breasted McIntosh as a measure of achievement in America. This point is poignantly demonstrated in *peregriNasyon* (Is America in the Heart?), a contemporary drama that focuses on the experiences of Filipinos in the Philippines and in the United States during the early decades of the twentieth century. Loosely based on Filipino author Carlos Bulosan's semiautobiographical *America Is in the Heart*, the play uses photographs and interviews with Filipino immigrants of the 1930s to explore such themes as violence and struggle, which influenced the creation of Filipino identities in a colonized homeland and in a racist adopted country.

peregriNasyon, which is about Filipino immigration to California, centers on two childhood friends, Mariano and Simeon, who grew up together in a rural farming village in the Philippines. As the drama opens, Simeon defies his father by refusing to stay and work the family's small plot. He makes plans to leave for the United States. As Simeon turns to go, his sobbing mother runs to kiss him good-bye. She makes him promise to contact Mariano, who had left some time before, as soon as he reaches California. Given the migratory nature of the immigrant Filipino's life, Simeon has a difficult time locating his townmate. In frustration, he cries, "How can you find a person when his address is a state?" One Saturday evening, Simeon and his townmates finally spot Mariano in a movie theater. Shouting his friend's name, Simeon runs toward him. Surprised, Mariano turns and broadly smiles at Simeon. Mariano then slowly twirls in front of Simeon, opens up his double-breasted jacket to reveal an immaculate, crisply ironed white shirt, puts his hands inside his pockets, and strikes a pose. As a way of greeting, Mariano asks Simeon, "How you like my McIntosh?"[25]

In the production, Mariano used the fashionably tailored suit as a symbol of an identity and status over his compatriots because the McIntosh separated him from the Filipino "FOBs," an acronym for "fresh off the *bangka* [boat]," denoting newer immigrants like Simeon. But for some workers, the garments eventually came to represent an investment. Filipinos bought McIntosh suits and used them for pleasure when their wages were relatively stable. But as the Depression deepened, several Filipinos sold their collections in order to obtain funds for necessities. In the late 1920s, when monthly wages for Filipino laborers in Los Angeles often ranged between $75 and $120, the biggest category of expenditure (between $50 and $80) was for car payments and, as one researcher put it, for "attempts to be 'the well attired man of good time.'"[26] But by the middle of the economic slump, when countless unemployed Filipino workers desperately pooled their meager resources in order to survive on a day-to-day basis, the McIntosh suits they had accumulated when times were better became commodities that could be exchanged for cash to buy food and pay rent. Romero Alin recalled that when he and his four compatriots exhausted their last $3.80, "some of those guys [said], 'well, I got four [McIntosh] suit[s,] maybe we can take [them] to the pawn shop . . . [for food money].'"[27]

The desire for a form-fitted McIntosh provided opportunities for entrepreneurs in Little Manila. When Vincent Bello tired of the migratory lifestyle, he opened the Bello Smart Tailor Shop on Main Street, where he made a living in custom-fitting, and sometimes designing, clothes for his compatriots. Bello never had to return to migrant labor.[28] Felix Pascua remembered that Bello "made the best McIntosh suit around town in those days."[29] Oscar F. Huck's tailor shop on 706 South Hill Street also thrived on a brisk business due to a "large Filipino clientele."[30] The Calderon Company on 105 East First Street, capitalizing on the appeal of the McIntosh suit to Filipinos, advertised that the shop specialized in "custom-built Hollywood clothes."[31] Farther north, in Stockton's Little Manila, A. V. Moscoso on 130 East Market Street sought to entice Filipinos into his shop by advertising that "the voice of Fashion is carefully heeded in the making of our custom-tailored clothes. . . . Every fabric is 100 percent wool, of course."[32]

Other sectors that offered services considered essential in nurturing the image of the well-groomed man-about-town and spaces for social interaction provided employment within Little Manila and thrived in the ethnic community. In 1933 three tailors, twelve restaurants, three pool halls, and seven barbershops catered to the demands of their Filipino clientele. The two concentrated areas of work among the 212 Filipinos employed by Filipino-owned businesses within the community were restaurants (67) and barbershops (47).[33] A contemporary researcher noted how in Los Angeles "on Thursdays, Saturdays, and Sundays there were enough Filipinos in all Filipino barber shops to keep the forty-seven Filipino barbers working till midnight," despite the fact that "their rate [50 cents a haircut] seems to be the only one that did not come down during the depression when everybody else in the country was cutting prices."[34] Barbershops were popular gathering places in part because Filipinos were unwelcome in white-owned establishments, but, more important, because of the activities that typically transcended the business of merely getting one's hair trimmed. A Filipino student indicated that it was typical to see "a group of Filipinos in one of the corners of the barbershop playing checkers, miniature ping pong, reading newspapers, magazines, or letters just received from the homeland, while in some parts of the shop one may be able to hear someone singing native songs, and American popular music as well; someone playing a mandolin, guitar, saxophone, or ukelele [sic]. These are usually played by the patrons though sometimes by the barbers themselves during their leisure hours."[35] By 1938, there was an increase in the number of these service-oriented establishments to four tailors, sixteen restaurants, seven pool halls, and twelve barbershops.[36]

Groomed to the hilt and impeccably dressed, Filipinos flocked to L.A. leisure halls to dance to music ranging from sentimental love songs to more rousing numbers like the swing, the jitterbug, and the fox-trot. Entrance fees for taxi dance halls usually ranged from 10 to 25 cents. Some, like the Red Mill, offered free admission up to a certain hour. Other halls charged $1 on entering, but patrons received tickets good for ten one-minute dances. Various establishments offered a spectrum of incentives, including the "lucky number" lottery where the owners hid numbers amid the decorations in the ceiling. At certain intervals, the house would call out a "lucky" number, and the patron standing under, or closest to, that numeral received free dance passes. The "lucky door ticket" was a variation of this scheme. Dance hall attendants deposited a portion of every ticket purchased by the patrons into a particular receptacle. In the course of the evening, an employee drew several ticket stubs from the box, which entitled the winning participants to cash prizes of up to $5 each.[37] For its special Christmas Eve drawing, the Liberty Dance Hall awarded radios to Andrin Perez, Frank Gonzales, and Ernesto Carlos.[38]

Other dance halls provided "free" entertainment like dance shows and musical recitals before or after the regular taxi dancing. The Hippodrome Dance Palace regularly sponsored a Sunday midnight program that featured an "all girl show" led by "Big" Rita Gaythorne. One such lineup included Spanish dances performed by Betty Bernard and a rumba number by Billie Wallace. But if "Big" Rita, Betty, and Billie were not enough for the patrons, the Hippodrome promised that all "other girls will be called on on demand."[39] A Filipino observer noted that during these shows, "the Filipino patrons cannot refrain from participation when watching the dancing or listening to the singing. When a dancing couple performs a 'blues' or a 'moonlight waltz,' voices from the crowd will be raised time and again. . . . Also, when there is a popular song, voices occasionally join in a wild exultant shout at certain intervals."[40] Social columns in Filipino newspapers routinely described the energy and enthusiasm of the Filipinos' night life. Reporters noted that in the

Hippodrome "fancy dancers in excellent pairs were . . . gliding jovially on the floor until the wee hours of the morning."[41]

The key to participating in the games and dances was the continual purchase of tickets. "If you wanted to dance you had to buy a roll of tickets in advance," a Filipino laborer recalled. "Then you would dance with a woman until all your tickets were gone. . . . Each ticket was 10 [cents] and you were lucky if your salary was even $5 a day then. So your whole salary might last for only an hour if you liked to dance."[42] For some Filipinos, this price was too high for one night's pastime. Johnny Garcia remarked that "if they [Filipino patrons] would work and save their money now instead of hanging around dance halls and going out with the girls they would be better off. I like to dance but I don't like to well enough to throw all my earnings on it."[43] Indeed, as Carey McWilliams quipped, taxi dancing "is about the costliest [entertainment] to be found in California: ten cents for a dance that lasts exactly one minute."[44] Still, most Filipinos bought rolls of tickets in the dance halls. Severely restricted by racism and segregation in other aspects of their lives, they reveled in the night clubs that accepted—indeed, encouraged—their participation. Felix Pascua recalled that Filipinos faced rejection in most social institutions and that "the only places that welcomed us with open arms were the gambling houses and dancing halls."[45]

While the tickets frequently represented the bulk of their wages, for some Filipinos, taxi dancing remained a popular diversion because it paid off in another way: it enhanced their prestige as "sporting men" among their compatriots. Frank Coloma bragged that "there were four main dancing cabarets in Los Angeles and I had a girlfriend in every hall."[46] Miguel Lawagan also frequented taxi dance halls in Los Angeles, going to the Hippodrome Dance Palace, the self-proclaimed "rendezvous of sportsmen," almost every night. For him, taxi dancing "is cheaper than a date—for one dollar you can have, say, ten different girls."[47]

While most dance halls remained open every evening, Saturday and Sunday were the busiest nights, when young, working-class immigrant men like Filipinos and Mexicans cruised these leisure centers in pursuit of some night moves.[48] Inside the crowded dance halls, one anxious observer described "dancing that was thoroughly immoral. Couples dance or whirl about the floor with their bodies pressed tightly together, shaking, moving, and rotating their lower portions to rouse their sex impulses. Some even engage in 'biting' one another on the lobes of the ears and upon the neck."[49] The sexual overtones in part reflected how workers took control of their own bodies and actions in these commercialized centers. Regarded by Anglo employers as no more than exploitable stoop labor in the fields, Filipino and Mexican men proclaimed their sensuality and virility in ways denied them as workers. Under the guise of performing modern dance movements, overworked brown bodies reveled in a charged atmosphere of raw sexuality. Through public displays of simulated sexual intercourse, workers seized moments of gratification absent from other aspects of their lives. Working for farm owners who pitted them against one another during often bitter labor disputes, these laborers found in taxi dance halls an interethnic working-class culture based on the body's ability to express, or at least effectively suggest, passion, arousal, and sexual bravado.

These dance halls no doubt sparked some genuine amicable interethnic relations among some of the patrons. Filipinos at times referred to other men of color as "cousins," creating a fictional familial network.[50] This practice of inventing kinship ties where none existed suggests that maintaining some semblance of the extensive family affiliations they had left behind continued to be important to Filipino immigrants. In the Philippines, both patrilineal and matrilineal lineages formed the essence of individual identity and communal memory through complex patterns of privileges and indebtedness among the relatives. As one anthropologist observed, these processes of interdependence, at times oppressive and at other times sources of security, prescribed that "kin members borrow money from each other and exchange food supplies with each other. In general, it is taboo to refuse any kin in need." While bloodlines and marriages as a rule defined membership in the group, kin alliances could also be forged through various channels, including the *compadrazgo* (godparent) system. Rites of passages, including births, baptisms, and weddings, further cemented consanguineous bonds and created new ones.[51]

While promoting a shared, decidedly heterosexual masculine experience, confrontations were also frequent enough among the Filipino and Mexican regulars and the Anglos who occasionally attended the dance halls to give the police a convenient reason to raid the clubs regularly.[52] Sammy R. Lopez, a migrant worker who came to the United States in 1929, recalled how "Filipinos, Americans, Mexicans . . . get jealous . . . [of] one another [because] they think somebody [is] fooling around with their sweetheart. . . . I see actually shooting, too, in Los Angeles in front of the [taxi dance hall]."[53] Rivalry over accoutrements and the affection, or at least the availability, of taxi dancers appears to have been the overwhelming cause of these skirmishes. One Mexican observer noted how a number of the Mexican immigrant men in the dance halls were "very poorly dressed . . . [and] many of them dance Mexican style."[54] This aspect of clothing and dancing style among Mexican patrons contributed to the competition with the customarily impeccably groomed, and periodically flashy, Filipinos who routinely frequented the same leisure centers on Main Street. Frank Coloma recalled that whenever he went out, "I always wore the very best suit—a McIntosh suit."[55] One novelist writing about Los Angeles's ethnic communities in the 1930s vividly described how "Main Street's Filipinos put Harlem to shame. They array themselves in brilliant-hued polo shirts out like pieces of pie. Their natty trousers, hiked up to armpits, may be mauve or apple green. Neckties make the rainbow weep."[56] Vicente Elequin remembered interethnic tensions also based on clothing in San Diego, where "the Mexican and Anglo guys did not like us [Filipinos] because we got all the girls at the dance halls. We wore the best clothes in the market and entertained the girls well."[57]

To the broader American culture and its policing agencies, the combination of youth, violence, and flagrant displays of sexuality between working-class brown men and white women in the taxi dance halls represented the close association they always assumed existed among vice, prostitution, and commercialized entertainment. But because of poverty, restrictive covenants, and brute force from neighboring Anglo residents, the establishment of ethnic communities was usually segregated in neighborhoods that were crime-ridden even before the arrival of immigrants or poor people of color in the area.[58] By the late nineteenth century, Los Angeles's first identifiable Chinatown was located near Main and Aliso Streets, east of the downtown business area. It overlapped an area of what racists called "nigger alley," a district that was already known for prostitute cribs on Alameda Street. As Chinatown developed, Chinese businesses, particularly laundries and curio shops, tried to provide jobs for the Chinese residents. However, Chinatown also housed extralegal activities, including prostitution, gambling halls, and drug trafficking, because, as in most cities, red-light districts were segregated in impoverished or marginalized neighborhoods.[59] Filipinos faced the same situation. As the Filipino immigrant author Carlos Bulosan recalled, he, his brother, and their friends lived on Hope Street, "where pimps and prostitutes were as numerous as the stars in the sky. It was a noisy and tragic street, where suicide and murders were a daily occurrence, but it was the only place in the city where we could find a room. There was no other district where we were allowed to reside."[60]

For numerous reasons, including recreation, employment, and varying degrees of protection from a hostile dominant society, immigrants often congregated in ethnic neighborhoods like Chinatown and Little Manila. Thus the police associated violence with the activities of people of color, despite the fact that arrest rates for Filipinos under twenty-five years old in Los Angeles during the Great Depression were lower than those for Anglo men of the comparable age group.[61] Further, these statistics were typical throughout California where Filipinos and Anglos worked and lived, including San Francisco and Stockton.[62] Manuel Buaken, who worked as a houseboy in Los Angeles in the 1930s, remembered how he and his friends constantly had to endure curbside questioning by police officers. Walking along one of Los Angeles's affluent residential streets during a break from his domestic duties one evening, he recalled, an officer ordered him to "move along, you appear like a questionable and suspicious character."[63]

A pervasive belief in the propensity of brown hordes toward violence was not the sole threat perceived by the dominant society and its other regulating agencies like middle-class reformers and various social welfare bureaus. Ever since the nineteenth century, crusaders had sought to eradicate "dance halls, gambling, spitting, and other recreational behavior" associated with the working class in order to impart middle-class notions of "morality" and "proper" values to immigrants, laborers, and their children.[64] Members of social institutions worried that the younger generation, especially young women from single-parent and working-class households, lacked suitable parental guidance, opportunities for "wholesome" recreation, and the chance to interact with suitable marriage partners. In Los Angeles, Paul Popenoe, director of the city's Institute of Family Relations, urged parents and teachers to encourage teenagers to regularly attend church services and school-sponsored club activities because they foster "a different scale of values, with increased emphasis on living a well-rounded life; a different attitude toward work and leisure; help young people in learning how to play; and intensive education for the wise use of leisure time."[65] Maria Ward Lambin, director of the Women's Recreation Committee, took a different route. Realizing that young people regularly went to dance halls without their parents' knowledge, she proposed to "place a supervisor in each of the halls to act, not as a kill-joy, nor as a harsh and unsympathetic critic, but as a friend to the boys and girls, an advisor in their many difficulties. Instead of attempting wholesale reform by edict, let us consider each individual as a separate problem and give these young people the help they need in practical, material ways."[66]

Aletha Gilbert, founder of the Los Angeles City Mother's Bureau, which eventually became a branch of the Los Angeles Police Department staffed by policewomen, worked with Angeleño families, particularly in assisting parents to protect their young daughters from the assumed "dangers" of "wild" parties and commercialized dance halls lurking in the city. Convinced that these centers were "immoral places where teenage girls and boys lost their inhibitions through liquor and unsupervised, sensual dancing," Gilbert and her associates organized and chaperoned "municipal dances" in downtown Los Angeles on Saturday nights as alternative venues for youths to participate in "proper, wholesome, refined" dances where dancing cheek-to-cheek, the "bunny hop," and "the shimmy" were banned for their "suggestive" content. To publicize the gatherings to the young working-class women who frequented the public dance halls and who the bureau therefore considered most susceptible to "moral dangers," Gilbert went to businesses like the telephone company and retail stores that employed significant numbers of these women.[67] These approaches represent some of the avenues reformers typically used to promote the regulation of commercialized dance halls, beginning with personal contacts with the participants and then calling for local ordinances, stricter licensing requirements, and more rigorous enforcement.

Determining exactly who needed protection in the taxi dance halls, however, was another matter altogether. Even some headlines in the conservative *Los Angeles Times* proclaimed "Taxi-Dance Girls Start Filipinos on Wrong Foot" and "Mercenary Women Influence Brown Man's Ego."[68] Nevertheless, campaigns for restrictive legislation regarding Filipino immigration became typical responses among associations like the Native Sons of the Golden West and the Commonwealth Club. Members aggressively lobbied for exclusionist policies based on the so-called unbridled sexual passions of Filipinos for Anglo women. David T. Barrows, a former president of the University of California, testified before the House Committee on Immigration and Naturalization that the Filipino "usually frequents the poorer quarters of our towns and spends the residue of his savings in brothels and dance halls, which in spite of our laws exist to minister to his lower nature."[69]

But reformers, social workers, and nativists preoccupied with "protecting" white women's "morality" failed to take into account that, for some women, working as taxi dancers provided a way of making a living. The same groups frequently referred to Anglo women working in the dance halls as white trash, because a number of them were daughters of poor southwestern migrants who came to California during the 1930s.[70] Nativists nevertheless conceded that these women were white and, by extension, had to be protected from the brown hordes because the dominant society's racial "purity" was at stake. Judge D. W. Rohrback of Watsonville, an ardent proponent of restriction on Filipino immigration, raged that "the worst part of his [the Filipino] being here is his mixing with young white girls from 13 to 17 . . . [and] keeping them out till all hours of the night. And some of these girls are carrying a Filipino's baby around inside them."[71]

Income and other benefits from taxi dance halls became crucial to single young women, especially during the Great Depression and the New Deal era. For many Americans, the New Deal of Franklin D. Roosevelt represented a fresh lease on life amid the financial and psychological hardships brought on by the economic downfall. Within the first hundred days of his presidency, FDR initiated a flood of emergency relief measures designed to ameliorate the massive problems of unemployment and homelessness. These early New Deal programs were controversial, and the U.S. Supreme Court eventually declared a number of them unconstitutional, but some nevertheless had far-reaching consequences because subsequent legislation absorbed several of the existing provisions. The National Labor Relations Act reaffirmed many of the principles, including the laborers' right to unionize and bargain collectively, of the earlier National Industrial Recovery Act (NIRA).[72]

Through legislation, regulation, and funding, the federal government sought to revitalize the economy, create jobs, and improve the living conditions of the poor. New Deal programs like the Agricultural Adjustment Act and the NIRA aimed to restore, respectively, the farming and business sectors of the economy. Government assistance procedures, beginning with the Federal Emergency Relief Administration (FERA) in 1933, sought to aid destitute families and jobless workers through increased financial support and work programs. Under the FERA (1933–1935), per-family relief packages for Anglos increased from a national average of $14.13 a month to $28.13.[73]

For many people, however, the New Deal did little or nothing to ease their particular situation. Federal assistance programs, including work relief and subsidized housing, ignored the needs of countless working women, female heads of households, agricultural laborers, and people of color who contributed to the nation's economy often by performing the most exploitative or dangerous jobs. Some New Deal officials decried these injustices. Eric H. Thomson of the Department of Agriculture's Resettlement Administration urged extending federal protection to agricultural and migrant workers, pointing out that while that "the Social Security Act protects millions of our people against unemployment and old age," it did nothing for agricultural workers, and that while "the Wagner Act guards millions of industrial workers against unfair labor practices," it ignored "the one-fourth of our rural population."[74]

Filipinos working in California's agribusiness were among the hardest hit of this rural populace during the Great Depression. But Filipinos in the urban areas also faced dire straits. One study estimated that in Los Angeles County, about 75 percent of the more than 12,000 Filipino laborers had lost their jobs.[75] As workers, Filipinos paid the taxes that supported the federal aid programs, but because of laws that rendered them aliens ineligible for citizenship and because of hostile public opinion that considered them as only temporary residents in the United States, the majority of Filipinos could not qualify for relief under the New Deal.[76]

The exclusion of segments of the population from government aid reveals how injustices based on race, class, and gender worked their way into some social welfare policies. New Deal legislation, through complex manipulations, rewarded select groups at the expense of less-powerful, marginalized populations. The emergence of the so-called welfare state in the 1930s gave Anglo men preferential treatment in federal programs like the Works Progress Administration on the assumption that men were the principal breadwinners. This policy squeezed not only single women from federally funded jobs but wives and female heads of households as well. In addition, the Social Security Act, one of the biggest and most enduring legacies of the New Deal, initially exempted domestic work and migrant labor, occupations in which the poor, women, and people of color were concentrated.[77]

For women working in factories, the first national recovery act contained paradoxical clauses. Requisites of the NIRA, including minimum wage laws and the standardization of production codes, aimed to provide jobs and improve conditions in the workplace. Contained in these mandatory provisions, however, were wage differentials, ranging from 14 to 30 percent, based on gender. In the garment industry, which employed the largest percentage of women in the workforce, women's hourly earnings were *legally* 10 cents less than men's for performing the same job. The miserly wages forced some women to take in piecework or home work after their regular factory shifts, which in many cases already included speedups and stretch-outs implemented by companies to increase productivity. Furthermore, the NIRA codes did not cover domestics and other household employees, the majority of whom were African American women, who worked long hours in deplorable conditions, with little or no privacy. In California, observers spotted domestics "sleeping on sofas or on cots set up at night, on back porches where wash tubs and garbage cans were kept, lying sometimes in the same bed with the children."[78]

Given the economic hardships of the Great Depression and the exclusionary clauses and sexist legislation of the New Deal, work as taxi dancers was a relatively profitable alternative job for some women. The wife of a business owner in the Stockton area recalled that "I know quite a nice girl who works [in a taxi dance hall] and makes enough money, dancing a few hours in the evening, to run a car, support her mother and herself."[79] As dance partners, these women typically earned one-half of the ticket price per dance plus whatever the patrons gave them as tips or gifts. One study estimated that taxi dancers could potentially earn between $35 and $40 a week, a figure representing two or even three times the salaries offered by factories and other light industry occupations.[80] Even in middle-class, white-collar "female jobs" in the manufacturing, retail, and clerical sectors, wages ranged only from $9 to $16 a week.[81] In Los Angeles, female operatives in the garment industry, which employed the highest percentage of working women, primarily immigrant Mexicanas, typically earned between $3 and $5 a week in the 1930s. Labor organizers, most notably Rose Pesotta, documented that women in the dress-manufacturing industry generally received $3 to $3.50 a week for forty-eight hours, while women in the millinery trade earned $9 a week for forty hours of work in the factory. But when combined with home work, the total labor time amounted to sixty or seventy hours a week. These income rates and work hours violated the state's minimum wage law for women, which specified $16 a week for forty-eight hours of labor.[82] Furthermore, because company policies typically relegated women to the least powerful and most vulnerable positions, female employees were routinely subjected to sexual harassment from male supervisors and bosses.[83] As one taxi dancer remarked, "As long as I have to put up with fresh guys no matter where I work, I might as well get $3.00 an hour for it."[84]

Employment as dance partners was demanding. Hall owners and operators required women to be ready for business as soon as the centers opened, generally between 7:00 and 8:00 P.M., and to keep dancing with patrons until closing time, around 1:00 A.M. on weekdays and later on weekends. Juana Martinez, who worked in one of the dance halls on Main Street, confided to an ethnographer that "it is true that at times I get a desire to look for another [job] because I get very tired. . . . One leaves almost dead on Saturdays because many Mexican people come from the nearby towns and they are dancing . . . with one all night."[85]

Musicians employed by these centers also had a hard time adjusting to the business cycle of taxi dancing. Because patrons paid for dances per minute, musicians had to be able to sequence entire songs into one-minute segments and pause for five seconds between intervals to allow for the exchange of dance tickets between clients and taxi dancers. Musicians had to maintain this routine for the duration of the evening's stint. One student who performed in taxi dance halls as part of an orchestra in order to gather data for his dissertation claimed that the management expected musicians to be familiar with a minimum of 500 songs "as well as read 'by sight' standard orchestrations or special arrangements. The same tunes are not repeated every night, nor the same tune twice, unless they happen to be on the current 'Hit Parade.' About three hundred tunes are played each night." Because of these requirements several musicians regarded the job as a "grind" and, if they could afford it, avoided taxi dance gigs.[86]

Despite the difficulties associated with timing musical arrangements to fit in with the business rhythm of the taxi dance halls, some unemployed musicians turned to these clubs to earn their livelihood. In a country locked in economic stagnation, recreation centers provided musicians with steady work and income. Ray Estabello and members of his Sampaguita Serenaders, for example, played nightly for a year in Maxwell, a nightclub on Third Street and Broadway in Los Angeles.[87] Frank Osias, another Filipino musician, sometimes played in and around Seattle's taxi dance halls with his band, Moonlight Serenaders, in the 1930s. He recalled that in addition to a weekly salary, the hall owners typically paid for the musicians' food and lodging.[88] In Los Angeles, an observer noted that African American musicians regularly performed in the city's dance halls.[89] A few Filipino musicians also made a living in these leisure centers. The Liberty Dance Hall on Third Street, the self-proclaimed club where "all Filipino boys dance," featured Larry Lang and His Manila Rhythm Boys, while Danceland on Main Street presented Festo G. Aspre and His Famous Manila Band.[90] In spite of the allusion to the Philippines by the use of the word "Manila" in their names, most of the bands played current American tunes. Carlos Malla, a member of the Manila Serenaders, an eighteen-piece traveling orchestra in the 1930s, remembered that the band usually played "ball room style. As usual, we just like blues, waltz and of course fox trot."[91] Vicente Galan, who came to the United States in 1927, played the saxophone in an orchestra that performed at the Orpheum on Los Angeles's Broadway from time to time. Galan's cousins came when his band played, and they recalled that the members usually "played American music, you know, like the jazz bands, the swing," even though the band knew how to play Filipino songs.[92]

Like these musicians, women came to the centers for employment, usually learning about the job through social contacts and informal networking, much as working women have always done. The Loren sisters eventually worked in the same dance hall when the older sister joined her sibling one week later.[93] Juana Martinez also landed a job after months of unemployment when her girlfriend recommended that she apply to one of the dance halls on Main Street. She accepted the position after discussing the job requirements with her mother and sisters. Taxi dancing became a vital source of income for Martinez because she had few marketable skills and a limited knowledge of English. She recalled that "at the beginning I didn't like this work because I had to dance with anyone but I have finally gotten used to it and now I don't care since I do it in order to earn my living."[94]

Still, for some women, taxi dancing offered a more stimulating line of work. One social worker related the story of "Wanda . . . [who] left the cigar factory because the work was monotonous. All day long she wrapped cigars until after a month she could endure it no longer. Through a friend in the factory she secured employment in the dance hall, dignified by the name of a 'dancing school for men.'"[95] Gloria Navas, a twenty-five-year-old immigrant from Sonora, Mexico, also found employment in the dance halls relatively more entertaining and enjoyable than her previous job as a waitress, at which she had to work for twelve hours a day. Navas said that as a waitress, "I was paid very little and I did not like that work. I would rather go to [work at] the dance hall. There I pass away the time happily, dancing and whiling away the time with my boy friends, and many times we go out on a spree."[96] Further, the sociability associated with their line of work also fostered a sense of cooperation among the women. Taxi dance hall veterans would sometimes mentor a newcomer: "Of all the goofy ideas of make-up—you have the world beat! You come over to my house tomorrow and I'll fix you up before we go to the dance. . . . And then we'll put a hem in your dress and make it tighter. You aren't such a bad looker. Your shape ain't bad, but you don't know how to show it."[97]

Amicable relations developed between some taxi dancers and their Filipino partners, suggesting that the attraction between brown men and white women was mutual. Alida C. Bowler, director of the Delinquency Unit of the U.S. Children's Bureau, noted that a number of Anglo taxi dancers preferred Filipino customers. When she worked as the LAPD's director of public relations, Bowler recalled that "from the Filipino youth, she [the taxi dancer] will tell you, she usually receives treatment greatly superior to that accorded her by the average American frequenter of the dance-hall. The Filipino is a natty fellow, almost always immaculately groomed, well garbed, with·a flair for that style of dress described by these girls as 'classy.' . . . And he has manners. His approach to the girl is habitually marked by a courtesy practically non-existent among the more or less uncouth American white men to whom she has already been or has become accustomed. The girls are by no means indifferent to these qualities."[98] An ethnographer in New York's dance halls echoed these same opinions, noting that "curiously enough however, one almost invariably observes that the conduct of these Chinese, Japanese, Filipino and African revelers is more restrained and orderly than that of the low white males with whom they rub elbows."[99]

Not all taxi dancers, however, shared these sentiments regarding Asian patrons of the leisure centers. Intense interethnic prejudices often had to be overcome before dancer and client ever stepped onto the dance floor. In some of Los Angeles's dance halls, "the majority of the Mexican [taxi dancers] do not like to dance with the Chinese, Japanese, or Filipinos who, for their part, generally prefer American or Mexican women who are very light-skinned and can easily pass as Americans."[100] Slang terms among Filipino workers reflected some of these pervasive racial tensions—for example, "staying white" referred to taxi dancers who danced with Filipinos but dated only Anglo men, while a "nigger lover" was a white taxi dancer who accepted dates with Filipinos.[101]

Thus the dance hall culture was neither inherently utopian nor even democratic. The only acceptable sexual mores were based on heterosexual desires. Further, hand in hand with the emergence of the male subculture was the patrons' objectification of women in the dance halls. The gendered arrangements of the public space underscored this principle. Unless working, all the taxi dancers were required to stand in a line, in full view of potential customers. While waiting in the queue, the women were strongly encouraged to attract the interests of male patrons. Slang expressions among Filipinos reflected the sexism within the largely male population. A number of them generally referred to taxi dancers and female Anglo companions, no matter how old, as *bata*, a Tagalog word for, literally, "baby" or "very young child," not a term of endearment.[102] These condescending attitudes may in part be what the taxi dancers perceived as "manners" among the Filipino patrons.

The predominance of young men paying to dance with women in these taxi dance halls nevertheless suggests how, on one level, the entertainment industries began to take seriously working-class youth, immigrant or not, as consumers.[103] Some of the most popular recreation centers, like the Orpheum and the Hippodrome, were originally built as luxurious theaters for quality vaudeville acts for the largely middle-class Midwesterners and their families who migrated to Los Angeles beginning at the turn of the century.[104] When vaudeville ceased to be profitable, a few theater owners sold their properties to entrepreneurs, some of whom catered to an emerging population of consumers, young working people with discretionary incomes. On another level, however, popular culture practices represented sites where workers, marginalized by class, race, age, or gender, took back what they felt was rightfully theirs: their bodies, their time, and the freedom to construct, affirm, or reject identities in their own fashion and among their peers. The historian Robin D. G. Kelley understands the urgency of this need within communities of exploited laborers. Writing about African Americans in the Jim Crow South, Kelley eloquently argues that the "search for the sonic, visceral pleasures of music and fellowship, for the sensual pleasures of food, drink, and dancing was not just about escaping the vicissitudes of southern life. They went with people who had a shared knowledge of cultural forms, people with whom they felt kinship, people with whom they shared stories about the day or the latest joke, people who shared a vernacular whose grammar and vocabulary struggled to articulate the beauty and burden of their lives."[105] Like these black workers, Filipinos went to dance halls because they not only liked to dance but also liked to share experiences and formulate a collective memory of more than just the workplace.

The competition over these spaces was rife with conflict, however. Divisions within the Filipino community illustrate the competing agendas and visions of what a Filipino ethnic identity should incorporate. Campaigns to regulate and "correct" the behavior of the Filipino workers came not only from the dominant society's policing institutions and reform associations but also from the small groups of self-appointed guardians of Filipino "morality" within the community. Controversies associated with the leisure activities of country-men reveal tensions, including interethnic class struggles and differences over the image of Filipinos in the United States, among the immigrants.

A small cadre of Filipino graduate students who studied with Emory Bog-ardus, a professor of sociology in the University of Southern California (USC), were among the most vocal critics of taxi dance halls and other Filipino work-ing-class leisure activities. Severino Corpus was a member of this elite crowd of Filipinos in Los Angeles. He was one of six children born to a farming family in a province along the northwest coast of the big island of Luzon. His parents approved of his education through the primary grades, but family tensions arose when he wanted to continue his studies through high school. His father had wanted him to help with the family's plot full time, but Corpus refused and finished high school. In 1929, still unwilling to farm but with no money and no other job prospects in the Philippines, Corpus immigrated to California to pursue a university degree. He eventually found employment and housing in Los Angeles, working as a housekeeper/cook for a small fam-ily and living at the Filipino Christian Fellowship Club on Winston Street. By saving what he could from his salary, Corpus attended Chapman College, where he eventually earned a bachelor's degree.[106]

By 1937, Corpus was finishing a master's degree in sociology at USC when a member of the Federal Writers Project (FWP) approached him for an inter-view as part of a survey of the city's ethnic population. In his narrative, Corpus orchestrated an image that blends what appeared to be desirable qualities in both Filipino immigrant and American societies, inadvertently providing cri-tiques of the Filipino laborers who appeared to waste their time and money on "worthless" pursuits. He presented himself as a Filipino Horatio Alger who came to California with no money but with a burning desire for advanced edu-cation. To fulfill this objective, he worked full time as a domestic servant and used his modest salary to pay for his tuition and books. Corpus told the FWP interviewer, "I think it is wonderful that a Filipino boy can come to this coun-try without funds and work his way to both an A.B. and M.A. degree."[107]

Corpus reveals a mentality stemming from a double dose of colonialism, from Spanish and then American occupation. In the earliest parts of his narrative, Corpus laid claim to a European heritage, stating that his native tongue, Ilocano, was a Spanish dialect. Some Filipino scholars acknowledge that Ilocano contains a few Spanish words (largely by way of Mexico), but Corpus's claim is an exaggeration.[108] Nevertheless, it served to distinguish him in terms of his racial lineage and class status from other Filipinos, especially the laborers. As one Filipino researcher has noted, Spanish or native dialect heavily influenced by Spanish did not fully take root in the northern regions of the Philippines, so that familiarity with Spanish marked the "elite class, those who had attended seminaries and colleges and the university established by the Spanish missionaries."[109]

Corpus's attitude reflects sentiments that Filipino historian Renato Constantino has described as the "miseducation of the Filipino" in the Philippines. Within months of the American conquest, Constantino states, the military personnel in the islands initiated a vast public school system as one way "to pacify a people whose hopes for independence were being frustrated by the presence of another conqueror. . . . The education of the Filipino under American sovereignty was an instrument of colonial policy. The Filipino had to be educated as a good colonial. Young minds had to be shaped to conform to American ideas."[110] The Filipino school system was closely patterned after the American model, with English as the medium of instruction and classes frequently taught with American textbooks.

While Corpus and his colleagues published numerous critiques of Filipino working-class life, some Filipino societies adopted the direct approach. They routinely organized dances for the "boys" as alternative recreational activities to commercialized dance halls, but these gatherings were generally not popular. The groups served no liquor, they kept the dance floor well lit, and the only female dance partners available were the wives of the organizers. As one young Filipino laborer explained, "I wouldn't want to go there and dance with them. They're married and they're too old and they don't dance very well."[111] Mutual-aid societies like the Filipino Federation of America aggressively renounced the workers' many "immoralities" and discouraged Filipinos from drinking, gambling, and dating white women, activities that its members argued contributed to disparaging stereotypes of Filipinos.[112] Still other Filipino organizations appealed to the business owners of nearby commercialized centers to close the dance halls part of Sunday evenings in the hopes that Filipino workers would come to community-based socials and events instead. Danceland and Hippodrome Dance Palace complied with the request, but Liberty Dance Hall remained open early on Sundays, and with free admission to boot. This issue evoked strong reaction among the small Filipino elite. Johnny Samson, chairman of the Filipino Unity Council, charged that Liberty Dance Hall's owner, "Jack Goldberg[,] is not a human being. He is only interested in what he gets from Filipinos—their MONEY, their hard earned MONEY!"[113]

Conflicts related to taxi dance halls were often intense among the Filipino workers themselves. Prejudices stemming from regional affiliations in the Philippines sometimes intensified these intraethnic tensions. Sigme Windam and his friends from the Visayas avoided the dance halls altogether because "there was just too much trouble there." Windam was born in Iloilo, one of a group of islands constituting the central part of the Philippines, and migrated to the United States in 1929 with the hope of continuing his education. He and a handful of townmates made up the smallest group of Filipino immigrants during the 1920s and 1930s. Windam explains that Visayans generally had good relations with police officers because they stayed clear of other Filipinos like the Ilocanos and the Tagalogs, who, in his opinion, "caused a lot of trouble by going to the [taxi dance halls]."[114]

A Filipino oldtimer recalled that tensions among the patrons occasionally ran high, and the "boys used to get jealous with each other because those girls would dance with anyone with ten cent ticket[s]. And some guys have more money than others and [the] boys think he's trying to outshine him. Naturally, the fight start[s]. . . . Filipinos are really hot-tempered when it comes to things of that sort. . . . It happened everywhere[,] . . . Los Angeles, Stockton, everywhere where they have [taxi] dances."[115] In part, these anxieties depict the importance of, and the urgency to maintain, an image of desirability among themselves. The competition, however, also evinced an internal code of behavior among Filipino workers that allowed them to define what was acceptable or unacceptable on their own terms. Living in a world that classified all their leisure activities as "deviant," the workers themselves formulated ways of discouraging conduct that threatened the community and communal experiences beyond a tolerable level. While they considered dressing in vogue for a night out proper behavior, monopolizing all the dances clearly was not.

The biggest and by far most turbulent confrontations at the taxi dance halls were between Filipino and Anglo laborers. On one occasion, an Anglo migrant worker complained about losing jobs to Filipinos because they worked longer hours and accepted lower wages. Included in this bitter complaint was that when Anglos went to the taxi dance halls, they found that "Filipino boys are good dancers. They can dance circles around these 'white' boys, and the 'white' boys don't like that—especially when the Filipinos dance with 'white' girls. It's no telling what these Filipinos will do if they keep comin'; and it's no tellin' what the 'white' man will do either. Something is liable to happen."[116]

In January 1930, something did, in what is arguably the largest and most vicious display of anti-Filipino sentiment in California. In Watsonville, crowds of white workers and residents stormed a new taxi dance hall in a nearby town because, as one participant declared, "taxi-dance halls where white girls dance with [Filipinos] may be all right in San Francisco or Los Angeles but not in our community. We won't stand for anything of the kind."[117] In the days that followed, the mob, at times numbering up to 700 men, roamed Watsonville's streets, beating or shooting all Filipinos on sight. A Filipino laborer recalled that "the mob came into the pool halls and with clubs bludgeoned all of us and followed us until we were out of the city. Then residences where Filipinos were quartered were ransacked and burned to the ground. Automobiles that contained Filipinos were fired upon, and many of the boys were wounded."[118]

In the following month, the Los Angeles correspondent for the *Baltimore Sun* explained that the ferocious attack on Filipinos occurred in part "because they [Filipinos] wore 'sheikier' clothes, danced better, and spent their money more lavishly than their Nordic fellow farmhands and, therefore, appealed more than some of the latter to the local girls."[119] This commentary underscores how the counterimage of Filipino workers created by the Filipino workers themselves unsettled the dominant culture's assumptions about the brown hordes. In sports quality, fashionable attire like McIntosh suits, and escorting white, working-class young women to dinners and dances, Filipinos disrupted the stereotypes of asexual laborers in the dirty, tattered overalls of the agricultural fields and the seemingly docile attendant in the uniforms issued by the service-oriented industries. In effect, Filipino laborers subverted the icons of white middle-class American masculinity, including the ability to dress stylishly, exhibit proper manners toward white women, and dance well.[120]

The combination of tensions based on economic competition and racial and gender relations that underscored these rivalries illustrate that the traditional "cheap labor" premise, even during the Great Depression, cannot wholly explain anti-Filipino sentiments among the white working class.[121] The reaction of the white migrant workers toward the Filipinos is akin to the volatile race relations between Irish immigrants and free blacks in the antebellum North chronicled by the historian David Roediger. Roediger expands on the African American scholar W. E. B. DuBois's observation that even if white workers "received a low wage [they were] compensated in part by a . . . public and psychological wage" in terms of tangible social rewards, including acceptance, because of their skin color.[122] Thus the competition between workers was not simply limited to economics—employment and wages—but extended to those benefits, including preferential treatment, secured by *whiteness*. Roediger recounts how white workers in blackface routinely concluded their participation in Christmas parades in Philadelphia "by engaging in the very traditional, white, male street activity of beating up free Blacks" and attacking African American street processions, churches, and places of interracial gatherings. Rejecting the notion that economic rivalry, no matter how dire, could fully explain the violent blackface attacks on blacks, Roediger instead effectively argues that "blacked-up Christmas maskers both admired what they imagined blackness to symbolize and hated themselves for doing so. In a backhanded way, the very insistence on excluding Blacks from a range of public celebrations may have reflected a perception that African-American style, music and dance would have dominated mixed celebrations."[123]

Roediger's perceptive analysis can be applied to the Watsonville and other race riots that occurred in California throughout the Depression. To numerous poor white migrant workers, principally those from the southwestern plains, the routine assaults on Filipinos because of their association with white women reflected anxieties felt by native-born Anglo Americans about their privileges. As one "Okie" descendant reminisced about the Dust Bowl refugees of the 1930s, "In the end, the only advantage for most has been the color of their skin and the white supremacy, particularly toward African Americans, that pervades the culture; what they are not (black, Asian, 'foreign') is as important as what they are (white, 'true' Americans) in their sense of propriety and self-esteem."[124]

Despite the intricate intra- and, especially, interethnic conflicts that at times erupted into violent confrontations, Filipino workers continued to frequent taxi dance halls. By the 1940s, however, reformers and church groups opposed to "our blondes dancing with Filipinos and Orientals" succeeded in getting legislation that barred all Asian men, including Filipinos, from taxi dance halls.[125] In Los Angeles, regulatory agencies, including the police commission, the fire department, and the health department, implemented this restriction by strict licensing requirements, expensive fees for infractions, and threats to suspend or revoke a license.

The guidelines to obtain permits shifted the internal regulation that had rested with the dance hall owners and dancers themselves to the police department, which assigned female officers to the newly formed Dance Hall Detail of the Juvenile Control Division under the administration of Lieutenant James Nelson. Among other things, this department supervised the hiring and work schedules of taxi dancers. These new procedures required women "to first report to the Dance Hall Detail . . . , fill out an identification card, be fingerprinted, and submit four photos."[126] Formal proceedings thus supplanted the more informal process of dancers bringing in their friends or siblings to the dance halls as potential co-workers, cutting off a vital link in the working women's network system.

Ironically, as the regulation of the taxi dance halls by the police department limited the conditions of working-class women's employment opportunities, the creation of a new division within the force expanded the possibilities of more professional positions and job mobility for women in the LAPD. The department had hired female "matrons" to staff its Juvenile Division beginning in 1909, but the women's role was geared more toward the prevention of "difficult" episodes in cases involving women and children in the home. Alice Wells, the LAPD's first official policewoman, secured her position in the force by arguing that women were better equipped to handle the tensions associated with the expanding role of commercialized leisure in the lives of, principally, adolescent daughters. In a speech detailing the urgency for more policewomen, Wells used gender to argue "that dance halls, skating rinks, picture shows, and the street, including the curfew law, could not properly be cared for by men officers [because] girls and women in trouble have a right to the sympathy and help of women officers."[127] But in addition to positioning gender as a requisite for the police to be more responsive to the needs of female constituents, Wells stressed that women officers could safeguard their male counterparts "from a forced and unnecessary association with those who, if resentful, may cast a cloud upon the reputation of the most exemplary."[128] A study of police departments and crime prevention conducted by the National Commission on Law Observance and Enforcement in 1931 echoed Wells's opinions, noting that female officers proved "more effective" in cases involving female juvenile delinquency and in "supervising dance halls and other recreational establishments."[129]

Despite the assumptions regarding the influential role of women in regulating youth and street culture, the new policies implemented by the LAPD's Dance Hall Detail suggest that the exclusion of Filipinos and other Asian men from the taxi dance halls did not accomplish what the reformers and pioneer policewomen hoped to fulfill: safeguarding young white working women's "morality." Simply put, the women just would not "behave." Although the guidelines specified that "if any taxi-dancer is found living with a man, as man and wife and not legally married ... [,] she shall be discharged and thereafter may not be permitted to work in any taxi dance hall in the city," these restrictions went unheeded.[130]

For Filipinos, exclusion from the taxi dance halls marked the cessation of one of their favorite leisure activities. This consequence, however, did not mean that Filipinos readily abandoned the rich alternative culture and community nurtured in the taxi dance halls. Some of these Filipinos shed their outdated McIntosh suits of the 1930s for the new craze: the zoot suit. Dressed in their drapes and the trousers with reet pleats, some Filipinos continued to frequent the black-and-tan cabarets in Los Angeles, dressing up and dancing to the rhythms of myriad sounds.

The persistence displayed by Filipinos in negotiating an identity in the context of complex race, class, and gender relations reveals the crucial role that popular culture practices played in the formulation of viable identities and coping strategies among an immigrant working class. Looking at the activities deeply embedded in the daily lives of members of aggrieved populations broadens our understanding of the effectiveness of resistance and complicates the questions associated with work, leisure, popular culture, and assimilation.

5. THE WAR YEARS

Identity Politics at the Crossroads
of Spectacle, Excess, and Combat

> Temple Street was so alive then, with clubs and music. What
> I remember most about the Filipinos was the way they'd walk
> down the street, so proudly, with these blond American girls.
> It was a common sight to see the Filipinos draped in their
> zoot suits, walking arm-in-arm with these tall blondes.
>
> —Lalo Guerréro

During the first two weeks of June 1943, throngs of U.S. servicemen stationed in and around Los Angeles descended on the city's downtown and east side neighborhoods on an assault mission directed against the city's zoot suiters. Claiming that gangs of drape-shaped youths had repeatedly ambushed fellow sailors enjoying shore leave, a caravan of seamen in cars and taxis cruised the city's streets, beating all zooters on sight. Other sailors patrolled on foot, raiding bars, dance halls, movie theaters, and even streetcars in search of zooted prey. When servicemen caught a zoot suiter, they beat the victim, stripped him of his prized drapes and reet pleats, and, time permitting, haphazardly clipped off the slicked-back "Argentine" ducktail. The political activist Carey McWilliams, who witnessed the episodes unfold in downtown Los Angeles, recalled how "street cars were halted while Mexicans, and some Filipinos and Negroes, were jerked out of their seats, pushed into the streets, and beaten with sadistic frenzy."[1] Servicemen usually left their targets naked and bleeding on the streets, with their garments shredded.

Toward the end of the second week, the fury of the so-called zoot suit riots had died down, except for a few isolated episodes in outlying areas. The respite ensued because commanders of the U.S. armed forces finally canceled shore leaves and declared Los Angeles out-of-bounds for its personnel, because most zooters kept lower profiles, and because the Los Angeles Police Department had rounded up and jailed a number of Mexicans and other youths of color as suspects, not victims, in the melee. In the meantime, Los Angeles city councilman Norris Nelson proposed jail sentences for those who insisted on wearing the "freak suit" within city limits.[2]

The disturbances during that summer in 1943 reflected the transformations in inter- and intraethnic relations brought on by the dramatic social, cultural, and economic shifts associated with the mobilization for war and the war itself. These changes—including the sudden availability of jobs because of the stunning growth in the defense industries, the massive immigration of workers and their families, and the forced evacuation of Japanese and Japanese Americans—effected changes not only in the city's infrastructure but also in the daily lives of ordinary Angeleños. These years ushered in conflicting messages emphasizing consumption and rationing, an abundance of jobs as well as discrimination in hiring and segregation in the workplace, and wartime unity alongside bursts of nationwide civil unrest.

For many Filipinos, World War II incorporated two disparate experiences: as zoot suiters in Los Angeles and as soldiers in the First and Second Filipino Regiments, segregated units of the U.S. Army sent to help liberate the Philippines from Japanese forces. As news spread about Filipinos fighting and dying with American soldiers in the defense of American bases on the islands, the image of Filipinos changed from working-class brown "hordes" to brave, loyal allies in an international conflict. Dress took on important meanings as Filipinos donned the uniform of the country whose policies made the Philippines a colony and whose racist ideology relegated the immigrant Filipinos to the lowest rungs of U.S. society. Because the Filipino regiments were part of the U.S. Army, the federal government extended the privilege of naturalization to the Filipino soldiers. That action created the possibility of divided loyalties within the community between those Filipinos who became American citizens and those committed to the creation of an independent Philippine nation. Filipino immigrants who had long campaigned for their rights to apply for naturalized U.S. citizenship now faced dilemmas about "home" and "homeland."

While some Filipinos enlisted in the military, other Filipinos, usually the more recent immigrants, became part of the zoot suit scene around Los Angeles. Given the controversies growing out of the servicemen's ritualized assaults and undressing of Los Angeles's zoot-suited ethnic youths, an analysis of the war years in the city's history must include how clothing and adorning the body became contested terrains associated with defining ethnicity, masculinity, and identity.

The drape shape attire—with its reet-pleat trousers, fingertip coats with heavily padded shoulders, long watch chain, pancake hats, and requisite ducktail do—was the craze among not only Mexican American youths but also scores of other young men who had been marginalized by race, class, and age.[3] As the cultural historian Stuart Cosgrove argues, the outfit with the "killer-diller coat" was "in the most direct and obvious way, an emblem of ethnicity and a way of negotiating an identity. The zoot-suit was a refusal: a subcultural gesture that refused to concede to the manners of subservience."[4] Cosgrove was writing about Mexican Americans and, particularly, African Americans who had long been associated with servitude, but his analysis is also applicable to Filipino Angeleños. These young immigrants had constituted a significant portion of employees in the service-oriented sectors, particularly in the hotel and restaurant industries and as domestics in private homes, since the mid-1920s. A proprietor echoed the attitude of many business owners who hired Filipino help when he told a researcher in the 1930s that "these Filipinos are always courteous and polite. They give the best of service even when there is no tip and give it to all alike. . . . The Filipino is a wonderful servant and far superior than the white."[5] Filipinos, in donning the zoot suit instead of the uniforms that marked them as servants, challenged stereotypes of being submissive, unassertive, and always eager to please.

The lifestyle that the zoot suit engendered further contradicted prevalent notions associated with the presumed obedience of Filipinos and other young men of color. For African American zooters, as the historian Robin D. G. Kelley points out, the "cool world of the hep cat," particularly its lively vernacular, "sharply contrasted with the passive stereotype of the stuttering, tongue-tied sambo; and in a world where whites commonly addressed them as 'boy,' zoot suiters made a fetish of calling each other 'man.'"[6] For Mexican American and Filipino zooters in Los Angeles, the drape shape presented an open challenge to the dominant society's perception of poverty-ridden "dirty" Mexicans and Filipinos. The Mexican American musician Lalo Guerréro, who performed regularly at the Bamba Club, a favorite rendezvous of these zooters in downtown Los Angeles, recalled that "what I liked about them was that they were clean and very neat. And the suits they would wear! Both the Mexicans and the Filipinos, they wore good quality clothes. They [looked] sharp! But what I remember most is that they were *so* neat. I mean, impeccable!"[7]

In a case study of the zoot suit as a gauge of the relationship among style, generational conflict, class struggle, and social change, Steve Chibnall suggests that the drape shape was one of the first battlegrounds between the dominant society and marginalized populations over who would control the urban fashion scene. Chibnall argues that because of this power struggle, "the zoot suit looms large in the tradition of Chicano and Afro-American cultural resistance. It was among the first fashionable costumes to be developed by the underprivileged and effectively to reverse the conventions of fashion diffusion—from top down to bottom up."[8] Filipino youths in Los Angeles also adopted the loose-fitting attire, donning brightly colored shirts and the punjab-style pants to stroll in Little Manila and around the city's downtown avenues and to jitterbug in nightclubs. Barred by legislation and poverty from buying homes and forced to rent small, shoddy rooms in the rundown sections of Los Angeles because of racism and de facto segregation, Filipinos invested instead in clothing and activities that created a vibrant public life. The streets became the stage where performances of spectacle during a period marked by war rationing were played out in the ethnic community. Filipino zooters strolled the streets in search of entertainment and, more important, to be seen. Lalo Guerréro, who frequently went to Little Manila to have his hair cut by Cris, a Filipino barber, remembered that it was typical to see Filipino zooters "parading up and down the streets, you know, in their sharp drapes and reet pleats, with their [long gold-plated watch] chains. . . . And they loved white women, and most of them had blonde women, and they would dress them to kill. . . . They [would] parade them up and down the street, real proud[ly]."[9]

Dressing up in the latest style was always important to Filipinos, in part because a snazzy ensemble transformed brown bodies from overworked, exploited laborers to symbols of sensuality, style, and pleasure. By the 1940s, the Filipino immigrant repertoire included a tradition, based largely on experiences in the United States, of using fashion to engineer an alternative image, negotiate a working-class ethnic identity, and celebrate the body in motion as learned from nights in the taxi dance halls during the Great Depression. For Filipino workers, stepping out in style with the zoot suit was nothing really new. Attired in the double-breasted McIntosh suit of the 1930s, they had cultivated a practice of using clothing as part of their oppositional strategies even *before* the zoot suit became the rage in the explosion of black-and-tan musical forms and nightclubs in wartime Los Angeles.[10] Unlike the McIntosh suit, however, which Filipinos appropriated from Hollywood actors and the upper and middle classes, the zoot suit was predominantly associated with the confrontational style of ethnic and youth cultures, which made it more controversial than the McIntosh. Nevertheless, the younger and relatively newer Filipino immigrants, who were the most likely to sport the drape shape, stepped into a usable collective memory assembled and once employed by some of the community's older members. Filipinos, as immigrants and as people of color who were pressured to assimilate while faced with institutional racism that prevented them from doing so, developed, as the cultural historian George Lipsitz argues, "a complicated cultural strategy designed to preserve the resources of the past by adapting them to the needs of the present."[11]

In using fashion as oppositional strategy, Filipino laborers imposed their own meanings on American-made products. In a case study of the impact of the consumer culture among Chicago's ethnic working class beginning in the 1920s, the historian Lizabeth Cohen argues that mass-produced goods enriched the existing collective life of the city's laborers. Phonographs and records, for example, enabled European immigrant workers to listen to recordings in their native tongues, while providing African Americans with channels of recognition otherwise denied them in society.[12] But this pattern of using standardized commodities for forging an ethnic American identity depended on several factors, including the availability of, and audiences for, foreign-language and race records that were absent in the Filipino community in part because the income and size of the immigrant population could not support these endeavors. In lieu of certain commodities available to other ethnic groups, Filipinos used their bodies to participate in the emerging consumer culture. They customized ready-to-wear clothing intended for American men to fit their own physiques. Suits manufactured according to the designers' representation of the "average" American male, who was generally taller than Filipinos, were tailored and refashioned to fit the shorter brown body. Living in a world where mass-produced, standardized items were fast becoming the norm, Filipino consumers subverted the perception of a "universal" man in adopting these tactics.

The drape shape was favored among members of the younger crowd, usually those between eighteen years old and their early twenties, which constituted only a small portion of the Filipino community by the war years.[13] Of the 3,925 Filipino men in Los Angeles in 1940, only 133 were between the ages of fifteen and twenty-four.[14] But when members of this group wore their reet-pleat togs, conflicts, even hostilities, frequently resulted between the newer immigrants and some of the older Filipinos, who in the 1930s had sported McIntosh suits, frequented taxi dance halls, and were themselves admonished by the elite of the community. These intraethnic conflicts suggest that communal self-regulation was moving from class to generational struggles. Some of the older, relatively more settled immigrants resented the recent arrivals for having a relatively easier time. The newcomers arrived in the United States when the national economy was becoming more prosperous because of mobilization for the war. In Los Angeles, these new immigrants filled jobs, especially skilled positions in the defense industries, that had been unavailable to the earlier group of Filipinos. These divisions in many ways point to the changing lifestyles, largely based on age, social relations, and economic opportunities, between Filipino immigrants who came in the 1920s and those who arrived in the first half of the 1930s. The earlier group had weathered the Great Depression, repatriation campaigns, race riots, and violent antiunionization tactics in their workplaces.

By World War II, most of the Filipinos in Los Angeles were approaching middle age. Data from the 1940 census reveal that among the 3,925 Filipinos living in the city at the time the figures were gathered, the largest age category (1,084) was filled by men between thirty and thirty-four years old, followed by those (824) between thirty-five and thirty-nine years old.[15] Some of these older, more-settled Filipinos had incurred additional financial and social responsibilities, particularly through marriage, that superseded obligations with kin in the homeland. These experiences also influenced their perceptions of the newer Filipino immigrants, especially those who sported the current fashion trend. Johnny Rallonza, who by the 1940s was married and a stepfather to two children but who as a single young man in the 1930s had gone to Los Angeles's taxi dance halls with his friends almost every night, bristled that "sure, there were some Filipino zoot suiters in the city during the war, but only the '*panggulo*' [copycats, troublemakers] wore them, because it was mostly the Mexicans and blacks who wore the suits."[16]

Rallonza's views about Filipino zoot suiters suggest that the life experiences of the newer immigrants and the ensuing intraethnic conflicts closely resembled the discords faced by their equally youthful Mexican American and African American counterparts in their respective communities. As men of color, these zoot suiters became the most visible targets of the dominant society's fears about the unsupervised activities of youths during the war years. Los Angeles's public officials and social agencies, alarmed at the number of youths roaming the city's streets at all hours, implemented restrictive measures, including curfews and organized recreational activities, to curb a perceived increase in juvenile "delinquency." Days before the outbreak of the zoot suit riots, the nearby city of Torrance revived and strictly enforced an abandoned 9:00 P.M. curfew. In supporting the measure, one police officer complained that "the kids are just taking the city apart."[17]

Tensions associated with the seeming escalation of crime principally among youths and ethnic minorities underscored the precipitous social, economic, and political transformations as the Depression gave way to the fervor of World War II. By most accounts, mobilization for the war and expansion of the defense industries in the West, particularly in the urban areas of California and the other Pacific Coast states, pulled the region out of the depths of the Great Depression. The historian Gerald Nash argues that the infusion of federal funds and military contracts made the region vital and productive, propelling its transformation from a "colonial" outpost to a major industrialized power. Whereas the West had been mainly a supplier of raw materials to the rest of the country, the defense industries provided the impetus for the diversification of western products like aluminum and timber. Because of massive industrialization and mobilization in preparation for World War II, these resources did not have to be shipped to other parts of the country for processing. The growth of the shipbuilding and airplane industries on the West Coast utilized the region's raw and finished materials. These locally produced commodities became more important as the federal government launched research and development projects in Western cities, like RAND in Santa Monica and the Jet Propulsion Lab in Pasadena.[18]

In Los Angeles, mobilization for the war and the subsequent flow of federal funds sped up the city's existing programs designed for sustained industrial growth and military contracts that had begun earlier in the twentieth century. The ports of San Pedro and Long Beach had been major headquarters for the Pacific Fleet of the U.S. Navy since World War I. In addition, several East Coast–based companies, including Firestone Tire and Bethlehem Steel, had recognized southern California's potential and built manufacturing plants and distribution centers by the 1930s. The advent of the war further accelerated the city's industrial growth, and, as the historian Arthur C. Verge argues, "the Second World War brought forth a new, substantially different, and much more economically powerful Los Angeles than the one that would have developed without the war." Expansion in the aircraft and shipbuilding industries, funded by substantial federal contracts, arguably best illustrates the city's coming of age. Acceleration in these sectors was nothing short of stunning: employment in aircraft manufacturing surged from 15,930 in 1938 to more than 120,000 by 1941, while employment in the shipbuilding industries rose from about 1,000 in 1939 to 22,000 by 1941.[19]

The explosive industrial recovery, the increasing demand for weapons, and the shortage of male laborers because of the military draft opened up jobs for numerous Angeleños, especially women and ethnic minorities, who entered the labor market in positions that had been closed to them. As more men left to join branches of the armed forces, women workers became the mainstay of the defense industries, at times comprising more than 50 percent of the workforce.[20] Among Asian immigrant and Asian American groups, Chinese Angeleños especially benefited from the process of mobilization. An analysis of census data between 1940 and 1950 suggests that Chinese and Chinese Americans secured jobs in sectors previously denied to them in the skilled and white-collar professional jobs as a result of World War II.[21]

The extensive opportunities for employment also convinced many residents from other parts of the country, including African Americans from the South, to seek their fortunes in the West, especially in the booming aircraft and shipbuilding industries. Euro-Americans had generally dominated the earliest stages of this "defense migration" to California, until President Franklin Delano Roosevelt, under pressure from A. Philip Randolph and the Brotherhood of Sleeping Car Porters, issued Executive Order 8802 in June 1941. This decree desegregated the defense industries.

African Americans had become a significant source of potential workers in California by the spring of 1942. Initially, they came as employees of the Southern Pacific Railroad Company. Letters home to friends and families, and desegregation of the booming defense industries, encouraged others to follow. Between 1940 and 1950, African American laborers and their families accounted for 9.2 percent of the state's population growth, with Los Angeles becoming the final destination for the majority of these migrants. One study estimated that African Americans made up more than 50 percent of the city's new inhabitants by the summer of 1943, when the cycle reached its peak: in June alone, between 10,200 and 12,000 African Americans entered the city. Subsequent arrivals in July and August almost equaled these numbers. Between 1942 and the end of World War II, 200,000 of the 340,000 African Americans who migrated to California settled in Los Angeles.[22]

In addition to the migration of Euro- and African Americans working in the defense industries, mobilization for World War II meant that California's military bases became home to the increasing number of sailors and soldiers, many of whom were Euro-Americans from southern states. Los Angeles became the preferred entertainment center for military personnel in southern California. The city attracted servicemen stationed in the vicinity, including guards in the Chavez Ravine Naval Armory, as well as sailors from San Diego, San Clemente, and San Pedro–Long Beach; marines from Camp Pendleton, Oceanside, and El Toro; soldiers from Fort MacArthur; and airmen from Muroc Air Base. An estimated 50,000 military personnel on passes swooped into the city each week, especially on their weekend furloughs. The downtown area, primarily along Main Street and Broadway, became the favorite haunt for these men.[23]

The mass internal migrations of workers, their families, and soldiers to Los Angeles during the war years exacerbated the already troubled race relations on the home front.[24] In the West Coast states, particularly California, the war in the Pacific had struck a volatile chord, particularly regarding interethnic relations because the majority of Asian immigrants and Asian Americans on the U.S. mainland lived in the region and constituted a significant segment of the workforce in agriculture, canning, and related industries. In Los Angeles, tensions erupted not only between Asians and members of the dominant society but also among the various Asian groups as well as the city's other ethnic communities. For most Asian Americans and Asian immigrants, the experiences of the war years were linked to changing socioeconomic fortunes and rights to naturalization and American citizenship as well as dilemmas about the "homeland." For Asians in the United States, World War II represented, depending on whether one was Korean, Chinese, Filipino, or Japanese, a period of revolutionary changes, mixed blessings, or abject denial of justice.[25]

The Japanese immigrant and Japanese American communities were no doubt the hardest hit in the tense, xenophobic atmosphere of wartime California. Long before World War II began, Japanese immigrants, as well as other Asians, were only grudgingly admitted to and tolerated in the United States because the country needed pools of cheap labor. Increasingly restrictive measures, beginning with the Chinese Exclusion Act in 1882, sought to curtail the immigration of Asian laborers. In 1907 a "Gentleman's Agreement" between the United States and Japan sharply reduced the number of Japanese laborers, but not their wives, coming to the continental United States. Despite additional racist measures, including alien land laws aimed specifically at preventing Japanese residents from buying real estate in the name of their American-born children, the issei and nisei thrived in California and acquired a reputation as dependable, hard workers. Anglo farm owners and others in California's agribusiness had generally preferred Japanese laborers over other Asian and ethnic groups before World War II. The perpetually simmering cauldron of anti-Japanese sentiments, however, boiled over with the Japanese attack on Pearl Harbor on 7 December 1941. Mass hysteria broke out as baseless allegations, publicized by the media, circulated that the nikkei were conspiring with Japan against the United States.

On 19 February 1942, two months after the Japanese strike, President Roosevelt issued Executive Order 9066, sentencing Japanese nationals and Americans of Japanese lineage on the U.S. mainland to internment "camps" as a matter of "military necessity."[26] Notification of the imminent relocation forced Angeleños of Japanese descent into quickly settling business affairs, transactions that proved economically disastrous for the nikkei. Japanese residents of Boyle Heights, a multiethnic neighborhood east of the Los Angeles River, were pressed into selling their homes, furnishings, and automobiles "dirt cheap" in light of the pending evacuation.[27] In Los Angeles, Leonard Christmas, an African American entrepreneur, bought a hotel in the vacated Little Tokyo neighborhood because "the property was practically being given away."[28]

The implementation of the president's injunction led to more than 100,000 Japanese and Japanese Americans, without any proof of their disloyalty, being uprooted from their homes and communities. Approximately 3,600 Japanese Angeleños were forcibly evacuated to the Santa Anita racetrack, where they joined another 18,719 evacuees before being relocated to "camps" established in desolate areas throughout the West.[29] A number of Los Angeles's Japanese residents were sent to Manzanar, a relocation camp about 200 miles north of the city.[30] For many nisei, the experience burst their hopes for and belief in the promise of U.S. democracy. Yuri Kochiyama, who was born and raised in San Pedro, recalled that "I was so red, white and blue, I couldn't believe this [evacuation and internment] was happening to us. Americans would never do a thing like this to us. This was the greatest country in the world."[31]

The forced evacuation of Japanese nationals and Japanese Americans elicited varying responses from members of Los Angeles's other communities. These reactions ranged from overt hostility to varying degrees of empathy and nascent interethnic solidarity to expressions of good will.[32] An African American newspaper attacked the unfairness of internment, while a rabbi drew a parallel between the "possible fate" of the Japanese in the United States with that of the Jews in Germany.[33] The Mexican American musician Lalo Guerréro remembered the chaos of the departure and regretted that he was not able do more to protest the government's unfair treatment of Japanese residents and citizens. Although Guerréro, who by 1942 was working in a defense plant in San Diego, did not have much contact with Los Angeles's Japanese community, he empathized with them because of their shared histories of discriminatory practices and legislation. "I really felt for them," Guerréro said. "A lot of them were American citizens, and even those who weren't, did nothing wrong. It was just like when Mexicans and Mexican Americans were unjustly rounded up in the repatriation campaigns during the Depression."[34] Other Angeleños also responded generously in light of the evacuation and internment. Yuri Kochiyama recalled that in San Pedro, "we were fortunate, in that our neighbors, who were white, were kind enough to look after our house, and they said they would find people to rent it, and look after it till we got back."[35] Korean immigrant Mary Paik Lee, whose family farmed in Whittier, about forty miles from Los Angeles, remembered that "our [Japanese] neighbors asked if we could look after their farms; they told us to take anything we wanted from their homes. They were our friends, so we couldn't do that, but we said we would look after their things as much as possible. One friend asked us to live on his property, rent-free, to keep out strangers who might be coming around to take whatever they could. We told all of them that we would do our best."[36]

While Executive Order 9066 primarily affected the lives and future of the Japanese and Japanese Americans, other Asian Angeleños also felt its repercussion. Mary Paik Lee, who lived in a Los Angeles suburb during the war, recalled how "even after all the Japanese were taken away to concentration camps, other Orientals were subjected to all kinds of violence. They were afraid to go out at night; many were beaten even during the day. Their cars were wrecked. The tires were slashed, the radios and batteries removed. Some friends driving on the highways were stopped and their cars were overturned. It was a bad time for all of us."[37] The particularly intense anti-Japanese sentiment after Pearl Harbor and the wholesale removal of the nikkei exacerbated a growing movement toward self-identification among the remaining Asian immigrants and Asian Americans as they repositioned themselves in the larger society as loyal, trustworthy Americans. Conflicts on the home front as well as across the Pacific propelled many Asians to distance themselves from the Japanese through public symbols that left no doubt as to their ethnic heritage and, by extension, to whom their loyalty belonged. Possibly out of patriotism but more probably because of fear of being mistaken for a "Jap," several Asians voluntarily began using identifying labels that proclaimed their nationality and allegiance.[38] A resolution by the Los Angeles Korean National Association, for example, mandated that "Koreans shall wear a badge identifying them as Koreans, for security purposes."[39] Chinese Angeleños began wearing buttons that announced "I am a loyal Chinese American, not a dirty Jap."[40]

Identification with a specific Asian group, however, posed a challenging problem for peoples of mixed ethnicity. In Los Angeles's Filipino immigrant community, the Reverend Felix Pascua recalled how he and his congregation, the Filipino Christian Church, complained to federal authorities when the Filipina-Japanese-American daughter of a church member was interned. The church vigorously campaigned for the child's release from the camps, arguing that she was Filipina American.[41]

Imperial Japan's attack on Pearl Harbor, the subsequent internment of the nikkei, intra-Asian attempts at self-identification, and declarations of war against Japan issued by China and the Commonwealth of the Philippines belatedly awoke the general public to the differences between Asian groups. Of course, racists had long made distinctions among the immigrants in various campaigns for restrictions. Paul Valdez, a Filipino laborer who immigrated in 1928, recalled that during the Depression, nativists "used to pass out leaflets saying that the Japanese were taking the lands from the Americans, the Chinese were taking the businesses, and the Filipinos were taking the women."[42]

Perceived collectively as the "other" by most of the dominant society in the prewar years, Asian immigrants in America were pigeonholed into new classifications because of domestic internment policies in the United States and untested alliances in Asia.[43] Popular magazines sought to "educate" readers on the finer points of differentiating between Chinese "friends" and Japanese "enemies." In its December 22 issue, *Time* emphasized the physical characteristics, noting that "virtually all Japanese are short. Japanese are likely to be stockier and broader-hipped than short Chinese. . . . Although both have the typical epicanthic fold of the upper eyelid, Japanese eyes are usually set closer together." Just in case readers found it difficult to detect the differences based on physical attributes, *Time* described alleged disparities in mannerisms, pointing out that "the Chinese expression is likely to be more placid, kindly, open; the Japanese more positive, dogmatic, arrogant. Japanese are hesitant, nervous in conversation, laugh loudly at the wrong time. Japanese walk stiffly erect, hard heeled. Chinese, more relaxed, have an easy gait, sometimes shuffle."[44] Indeed, for the Chinese community, the war years signaled a reversal of the cunning, "heathen Chinee" stereotype. By 1942, the immigrants once described as the epitome of a "yellow peril" were characterized in a Gallup Poll as "hardworking, honest, brave, religious, intelligent, and practical." [45]

The internment of Japanese Angeleños also affected the lives of other ethnic groups. For African American defense workers and their families, the vacated Little Tokyo area provided an answer to the chronic problem of inadequate housing. Because of de facto segregation and restrictive covenants, the city's new migrants had been forced to find accommodations in the communities earlier established by African American settlers. The most significant of these black neighborhoods was along Central Avenue, between Ninth and Twenty-fifth Streets. This stretch on "the Avenue" was the heart of black Los Angeles, an eclectic community where jazz nightclubs and black-owned businesses were concentrated and where the stately homes of the elite stood side by side with the shabby, substandard apartments hastily constructed for the new African American migrants. But the defense migration that began in 1942 brought in such unprecedented and unanticipated massive numbers that neither the black communities nor the city itself could accommodate all of them.[46]

Within weeks of the evacuation of Little Tokyo, Los Angeles's City Housing Authority refurbished the residences in the neighborhood to provide homes to as many as possible of the more than 12,000 African American migrants and their families. Little Tokyo was then renamed Bronzeville, and within months, agents from the City Housing Authority had assigned social workers to help the first ninety-three African American households move into the complex.[47] The rapid movement of African Americans desperate for homes quickly turned Bronzeville into one of Los Angeles's most congested slums by the summer of 1943. The City Housing Authority found numerous black families living in overcrowded, squalid sites, with no sanitation. In one such case, the agency reported that "in an abandoned store front and two nearly windowless storage rooms in Little Tokyo 21 people were found to be living—and paying approximately $50 a month for these quarters."[48]

The evacuation of the Japanese from Little Tokyo, while inadvertently providing one desperately needed remedy for the inadequate housing faced by African Americans, also created another source of interethnic tension in the city. For Filipino Angeleños, the wartime geographic relocation of African Americans, most of them southern migrants, into the vicinity necessitated new strategies for dealing with their neighbors. Because the traditional black community had been farther south on Central Avenue, Filipinos and African Americans had had limited relations with each other. Little Manila and Little Tokyo, however, shared close quarters, and, in some instances, the communities overlapped, especially along Weller, First, and San Pedro Streets. Weller Street was the hub of Little Manila, where Filipino restaurants, barbershops, and headquarters of the ethnic press and numerous mutual organizations were concentrated. But Weller Street also served as a major crossroads for Little Tokyo, housing a significant number of Japanese restaurants and small businesses.[49] With the arrival of African Americans into the neighborhood, as one contemporary observer noted, "now instead of the imperturbable Japanese who once streamed past their places of business and with whom relations at the worst had been merely a sullen indifference, [Filipinos] found their doorways filled with a new people."[50]

The tenuous, if not outright confrontational, relations that developed between the Filipinos and their new neighbors illustrate the limits of panethnic solidarity when minority groups are pitted against each other for day-to-day survival. Racial tensions ensued as both Filipinos and African Americans sought to escape poverty, ameliorate living conditions, and find jobs in the expanding economy. Some Filipinos, apprehensive about the development of a Little Harlem next door, left the Little Manila community and resettled in the Temple–Figueroa district. Filipinos who remained in Little Manila, however, complained incessantly about the "intolerable situation" created by their new African American neighbors. One Filipino reporter lamented that "there have been many instances in which many of our fellowmen have been stopped on [the] very doorsteps of their own houses by drunken Negroes and have had to practically fight their way into their own houses. . . . The Negroes seem to think that they run the town. When they are walking down town they seem to think that they are kings, pushing people. And in the streetcars they block traffic." The Filipinos' endless stream of criticism about their black neighbors and the exodus from Little Manila led one Filipino to comment that "although Filipinos have complained bitterly of white prejudices, unfortunately they too occasionally have a few of their own."[51]

The forced evacuation of the Japanese and Japanese Americans not only skewed interethnic relations in the Little Tokyo (Bronzeville)/Little Manila communities, but also recast the delicate balance of racial dynamics in the city itself by removing one of the minority groups that had buffered the attacks on other groups. As the political activist Carey McWilliams argued, economic and social issues, including racial tensions, that administrators had hoped would vanish with the internment not only persisted, but increased. To McWilliams, "It was a foregone conclusion that Mexicans would be substituted as the major scapegoat group once the Japanese were removed." Indeed, within days of the Japanese community's departure, the city's press began a heated anti-Mexican campaign, emphasizing Mexican American "juvenile delinquency" and "gang activity." The mounting animosity toward Mexican Americans culminated in the Sleepy Lagoon incident of 1942 when the Los Angeles Police Department seized twenty-four youths, alleged members of the Mexican American Thirty-eighth Street Gang. The district attorney's office charged them with the murder of José Diaz, whose bruised and beaten body had been found near a gravel pit, dubbed Sleepy Lagoon, in East L.A. In a sensational, highly prejudiced trial held in a city already antagonistic toward Mexican Americans, a jury convicted seventeen of the boys of Diaz's murder, the largest mass conviction in Los Angeles's history.[52]

Wartime hostilities directed against Mexican Americans, notably the Sleepy Lagoon case and the zoot suit riots in the following year, in many ways support McWilliams's assertion that Mexican Americans were destined to fill the breach of prejudice and discrimination in the absence of the Japanese. But McWilliams's analysis failed to take into account that there were more Mexicans and Mexican Americans than any other group of people of color in Los Angeles, which made them more visible. Further, as the image of minority groups that had historically been objects of animosity and violence underwent revolutionary changes during the war, Mexicans and Mexican Americans became more vulnerable to the full onslaught of racism. In the aftermath of the zoot suit riots, as the city council debated whether to outlaw the wearing of the outfit within city limits, a *Los Angeles Times* columnist implied that Mexican American zooters triggered the fracas. The writer argued that "it is silly to blame the whole trouble we've been having on the zoot suit itself. Filipinos by the thousand have worn zoot suits around this town for years without hurting their own reputation or that of their haberdasher."[53]

An international war, in which American soldiers from various ethnic groups were fighting and dying in their mission to defeat Japanese forces in Asia, created dramatic revisions in the perception of some Asian immigrant groups among the dominant society. In 1943, with thousands of Chinese Americans serving in the armed forces and with China as an ally, the United States lifted the Chinese Exclusion Act of 1882 and gave Chinese immigrants the right to file for naturalization. The transformation was just as dramatic for Filipinos, going from brown "hordes" to loyal allies, when news spread that American and Filipino soldiers were joining forces to defend Bataan and Corregidor, American strongholds in the Philippines. The positive depiction of Filipinos paralleled the extraordinary changes in the treatment of Filipino civilians during the war years. Lorenzo Pimentel, a Filipino laborer and later a soldier in the U.S. Army, remembered that "when the war was declared and [Americans] found out [that] those Filipinos [who] are in Bataan were fighting side by side with the Americans, that's the time when they respected the Filipinos."[54]

For Filipinos, World War II opened up opportunities but also dilemmas about their place in American society when the U.S. government granted Filipino soldiers, designated to be sent back to the Philippines, the chance to become naturalized citizens. Mass ceremonies became common when Filipino troops were sworn in as citizens as part of their induction into the U.S. armed forces. Private First Class Manuel Buaken of the First Filipino Infantry noted the solemnity of his own company's convocation, describing how "we, the twelve hundred candidates for citizenship, stood proud and silent in a V formation, [as] Colonel Cowley began the ceremony, saying in part, 'Officers who returned from Bataan have said there are no finer soldiers in the world than the Filipinos who fought and starved and died there shoulder to shoulder with our troops. I can well believe it as I look at the men before me. On those faces is quiet determination and a consciousness of training and discipline with a definite end in view. I congratulate them on their soldierly appearance and on their approaching citizenship.'"[55]

For many Filipino immigrants, this chance to be American citizens represented the culmination of a prolonged struggle regarding their legitimate status in the United States, as well as the meaning of that position in relation to the Philippines. This particular group of Filipinos, born during the American occupation of the islands, had existed in a state of liminality, citizens of neither the Philippines nor the United States. Because the archipelago became an American colony in 1898, their homeland could not grant them citizenship. They were, however, considered U.S. nationals. They traveled with U.S. passports and initially faced no quotas or restrictions in emigrating to America, although they were barred from applying for U.S. citizenship. As more immigrants came, racists, reformers, Anglo laborers, and unions campaigned to stop Filipino immigration. As nationals, however, Filipinos could not be easily restricted through routine exclusionary policies used to halt other Asian immigrants like the Chinese and Japanese. To solve the dilemma, the government passed the Tydings-McDuffie Act in 1934. The act, in promising the Philippines full independence in ten years, also reclassified Filipino immigrants as aliens. As such, immigration from the Philippines was restricted to fifty Filipinos annually, and Filipinos already in California were subjected to the tenets of the alien land law.

Less than a decade after this reclassification, when the United States faced a food shortage due to the military draft and the internment of Japanese farmers, the government reverted to recognizing Filipinos as U.S. nationals. In California the issue had come to a head when the Santa Clara County District Attorney's office issued a warrant for the arrest of a Filipino who had bought farm land. The state's attorney general, Robert W. Kenney, advised the department not to enforce the warrant because "our nation has been impressed with the heroism and the loyalty of the citizens of the Philippine Islands. We Americans do not—nor do our courts—regard them as 'aliens'— but as American nationals, who rose as one, unflinchingly, to make our fight their fight—they are adding their full strength and effort alongside that of this country for the total defeat of our enemies."[56] Freed from the restrictions against owning real estate, Filipino farmers were allowed—indeed, encouraged—to purchase or lease lands, especially those seized from the Japanese, and cultivate crops.

For many Filipinos, the opportunity to farm their own fields meant an alternative to the rigors of migratory labor as well as an entrance to truck farming, the business the Japanese had monopolized and had used to attain some measure of success. In the Los Angeles area, several Filipinos pooled their assets and ventured into truck farming or purchased farm lands in the San Fernando Valley and the Torrance–Gardena areas that were originally owned by Japanese farmers but had been appropriated by the government.[57] Toribio Castillo, after years of working as either a migrant laborer or a house-boy, finally became a farmer during the war years when he leased twenty-five acres of land in Gardena, on the outskirts of Los Angeles. He planted celery, cabbage, cauliflower, and radishes, and eventually branched out into truck farming. Castillo recalled that it "was a lucrative business. . . . I made a little money during the war years."[58]

Classified as U.S. nationals once more, Filipino farmers enjoyed privileges, particularly exemption from the alien land law, denied other Asian immigrants. But as Japanese forces invaded the Philippines, the status became an obstacle to the thousands of Filipinos in Hawaii and on the mainland who had rushed to recruitment centers to volunteer for military service. The prevailing regulation allowed only citizens and alien residents of the United States to join the armed forces. Filipinos, as U.S. nationals, were neither citizens nor aliens and were rejected. Moreover, the majority were middle-aged men whom the federal government considered too old to serve in the military. Aided by representatives of the Philippine commonwealth in Washington, D.C., Filipinos campaigned for legislation to lift the age restriction and approve Filipino enlistment in the army.[59]

On 3 January 1942, one day after Manila fell to Japanese forces, the National Headquarters of the Selective Services System formally announced congressional legislation permitting Filipinos, as volunteers and as draftees, to serve in the armed forces. In California, 16,000 Filipinos, almost half the immigrant community's population, enlisted.[60] In April 1942, at the height of the joint U.S.–Filipino defense of Bataan and Corregidor, the First Filipino Infantry Battalion, a segregated unit of the U.S. Army, was formed at Camp San Luis Obispo. As news spread about the destruction of the Philippine fortresses and the Japanese occupation of the islands, the number of Filipino recruits swelled. Three months later, the First Filipino Infantry Regiment and Band, under the command of Colonel Robert H. Offley and staffed by 143 commissioned officers, 6 warrant officers, and more than 3,000 soldiers, absorbed the initial, smaller Filipino company. Before the end of year, the Second Filipino Infantry Regiment was formed at Camp Cooke, California. About 7,000 Filipinos served in these units.[61] Vincent Mendoza, a migrant laborer who eventually joined one of the Filipino divisions, remembered how during their training "lots of Americans come and see us. One time we went down to have a parade in Los Angeles in the street and we ended down there in City Hall and the Chamber of Commerce. We fired our weapon[s]. . . . Oh boy, how the American[s] liked it."[62]

Issues associated with rights to U.S. naturalization were most controversial, and perhaps fittingly so, among these soldiers of the First and Second Filipino Regiments. Mariano Angeles, who enlisted in the First Filipino Infantry in Los Angeles, resented citizenship being offered initially only to Filipino soldiers who were preparing to be shipped off to the war in the Pacific. "Why now, major?" he asked his commanding officer, who had urged him to become a citizen. "[Why] that privilege now? When we were . . . private citizens [and] we ask[ed] . . . and they don't like us. In fact they brand us. Why now . . . are [citizenship rights] given . . . when we are soldiers? And at the same time why do they have to give [them] only to the soldiers rather than to all [Filipinos]?" The officer's reply—that Angeles and his fellow Filipinos in the service were extended the opportunity to become citizens because they were soldiers in the U.S. Army—infuriated Angeles even more. "So they mean to say that when my future is to die, that is the time when . . . they give me the privilege to become American, so [I said], 'Hell, no!'"[63]

While several soldiers felt as angry and as disillusioned as Angeles about the offer of citizenship, some Filipinos had no choice. A. B. Santos, who was drafted into the army in 1943, recalled that upon reporting to the Selective Service representatives in Los Angeles, "they swore me in as a U.S. citizen. I did not even have to file an application."[64] Others became citizens because of intense pressure and fear of retaliation from their officers. Private First Class Manuel Buaken recalled that his first sergeant told soldiers in the First Filipino Regiment that "if you [the company] don't want to be American citizens, you'll do K.P. [kitchen duty] the rest of your life. I personally guarantee that."[65] Many, like Miguel Lawagan, who joined the U.S. Army in Los Angeles in 1940 and was eventually assigned to the First Filipino Regiment, were proud to be a citizen in the U.S. armed forces. In the course of an interview, Lawagan repeatedly stressed that he was in the U.S. Army, *not* the Philippine Army: "The purpose of that [citizenship] is because we don't want to go there [the Philippines] as strangers; we came there to fight under the American flag and to protect the government under the American flag and protect the Philippines from the Japanese. That's the aim we got. Everybody knows that."[66]

Angeles's boiling anger and Lawagan's excessive pride represent two extremes of Filipino sentiments associated with the issue of citizenship. The feelings of most Filipino soldiers fell somewhere between these emotions, although all seemed unsure and anxious about what to expect from the United States should Filipinos accept its offer of citizenship in exchange for the Filipinos' primary allegiance. Private First Class Jose Trinidad perhaps most articulately expressed the Filipinos' dilemma when he told a fellow recruit, "I cannot give up my citizenship in the Philippines, it is in my heart. But America is also in my mind. I wish to have both loyalties."[67]

Even Filipinos who favored U.S. citizenship recognized the limits of the status because of pervasive racism and existing legislation, particularly anti-miscegenation laws, aimed at Filipinos. Private Buaken recalled that even in the heat of arguing the advantages of naturalization with his company, "I remembered that as a citizen I would still be denied the right legally to marry my American wife, my comrade and sweetheart for five years now. As far as marriage is concerned I still belong to an 'inferior race.'" Buaken surely stated the reservations of most of the Filipino soldiers when he wrote how "solemnly we took the oath of allegiance. We are prepared to shed our heart's blood to keep faith with you. We wonder if you will give us the same high-octane loyalty."[68]

Uniforms worn by soldiers in the First and Second Filipino Regiments of the U.S. Army best illustrate the mixed feelings and divided loyalties felt by the men. In the same way that Filipino zoot suiters altered the garment intended for taller American men to fit the shorter Filipino physique, enlisted men in the Filipino battalions modified their general-issue uniforms to convey their dual allegiances. In addition to standard army and company insignias, Filipino soldiers wore a yellow shoulder patch embroidered with a silhouette of the Philippines's Mount Mayon, the volcano with the world's most perfect cone. Three stars, representing the major islands of Luzon, Mindanao, and the Visayas, surrounded the smoldering peak.[69] The regiments' rallying cry, "Remember Bataan!" paralleled the emblems on their uniforms—a combination of American and Filipino icons—but each division selected exclusively Tagalog mottoes. The First Filipino Regiment adopted "Laging Una" (Always First), while the Second Filipino Regiment chose "Sulong" (Onward).[70]

For men in the Filipino divisions, wearing uniforms with emblems representing both the United States and the Philippines was an important aspect in negotiating political identities that reflected the Filipinos' binary obligations in the war. But for other Filipinos in branches of the armed forces that did not have all-Filipino units, military regalia and its trappings became objects of contention. When the U.S. Navy did not include what is arguably the most pervasive icon of the United States, the bald eagle, on the uniforms of chief stewards, stewards, chief cooks, and cooks—positions held by most Filipinos, African Americans, and Guamanians—protests broke out. Quentin A. Ramil, a chief steward in the navy, was especially angry because only the uniforms of the men who ran the officers' dining rooms lacked the emblem. The uniforms of men in all other branches of the navy, including those of the commissary steward and cooks who ran the enlisted men's mess hall, bore the eagle. Ramil's demand for the symbol offered a rare glimpse of panethnic consciousness: "If we [chief stewards and stewards, chief cooks and cooks] don't rate the Eagle on our arms, does this mean that we, who are deprived of this mark of respect, are less heroic? Is our death on the battlefield less honorable, merely because the color or our skin is different? If so, I am afraid our battle for democratic ideals abroad is being lost here at home, and our boys are fighting and dying in vain."[71]

In addition to concerns over military uniforms, Filipinos had to contend with discrimination inside their own camps and within their own companies. The situation was especially difficult for those not serving in all-Filipino units. A Filipino soldier on duty "somewhere in the South Pacific" described to the editor of a Filipino American newspaper how he and other soldiers of color were routinely denied privileges. "In the last camp [where] we stayed in the good U.S.A.," the soldier wrote, "we had the bitter experience of seeing Filipinos and Mexicans refused entrance to the Service Club."[72]

For some Filipinos, however, their status as personnel in the U.S. armed forces transformed how they perceived, and fought for, what they felt to be fair and just treatment as soldiers and sailors in Uncle Sam's service. Just as Filipino zoot suiters used the drape shape and the hepcat lifestyle as tokens of defiance against the presumed servitude associated with Filipinos, some Filipino GIs used their uniforms and status as fighting men as symbols of their refusal to tolerate inequitable practices that they had endured as poor, working-class civilians. As part of the military, Filipinos had powerful potential allies, particularly in the chain of command, whom they previously did not have. Private First Class Manuel Buaken of the First Filipino Infantry recounted how most businesses in Marysville, California, refused service to members of his unit stationed in nearby Camp Beale. When about 500 Filipino soldiers on weekend passes were denied service in all the city's restaurants, they informed their commander, Colonel Robert Offley, of the situation. For most of the Filipinos, especially those from California, being denied service outside ethnic communities was not a new experience. In cities like Los Angeles, Stockton, and San Francisco, de facto segregation and signs like "No Filipinos Allowed" and "No Dogs or Filipinos Allowed" were commonplace. What made the Marysville incident different for Filipinos, as Buaken pointed out, was that "we were in the army now. The army will go to bat for us." Indeed, the colonel and his assistants went to the Marysville Chamber of Commerce and "laid down the law of cooperation with the army—or else."[73]

Being men in uniform also affected how some Filipinos regarded their return home to the Philippines. Filipinos, as soldiers or as sailors in the U.S. armed forces, were more willing to return home, not only to prove their loyalty to the United States, but also, and primarily, to see their families. The majority of these Filipinos had not seen their families since they left the Philippines in the 1920s or 1930s. The U.S. government had sponsored a repatriation campaign for Filipinos in the middle of the Great Depression, offering free passage to the Philippines on condition that the returnees waive their right to come back to the United States. While many Filipinos seriously thought about taking up the government's proposal, only about 2,000 did so. The majority remained because they were ashamed to return to their families and hometowns financially broke, with nothing tangible to show for their hard work in the United States.[74]

As highly trained fighting men of Uncle Sam's forces, however, Filipino soldiers came home not as downtrodden, defeated expatriates, but as liberators of the commonwealth. Troops of the First and Second Filipino Regiments came into the Japanese-occupied Philippines as heroes, willing to give their lives, if necessary, to liberate their homeland. Lorenzo Pimentel was a tank destroyer with the Second Filipino Regiment when General Douglas MacArthur handpicked him to join eleven other Filipinos for a covert intelligence mission in the Philippines. The men were shipped to secret camps in San Francisco and Australia for additional rigorous training in clandestine operation techniques, telecommunications, and demolition. They then boarded a submarine headed for the Philippines. Pimental recalled being apprehensive as they neared the Japanese-occupied and well-fortified coast of the archipelago. He remembered that "before I [got] out [of] the submarine, my body felt like there was ice over my back. [But] when I hit the beach I felt strong. . . . I said to myself[,] this is my country, I am back."[75]

News about the bravery of Filipino soldiers and sailors with the American armed forces in the Philippines affected the lives of Filipino civilians in the United States. A Filipino porter for the Pullman Company in Chicago noted the favorable turnabout in the behavior of Anglo passengers toward him: "I am very much embarrassed. They treat me as if I have just arrived from Bataan."[76] Mainstream combat films reflected this shift to positive images of Filipinos during the war years. In the United States, with a once-again prosperous domestic economy based largely on federal assistance and the flourishing defense industry, most Americans earned discretionary income that they spent with gusto on commercialized entertainment. Feature films were by far the most popular form of leisure, with approximately 85 million people patronizing movie theaters weekly.[77] By 1944, this figure had escalated to almost 100 million, about two-thirds of the populace.[78] A study of the leisure activities favored by female employees in the defense industries in San Bernardino, California, in 1943 showed that going to the movies was the most popular recreational diversion. In a survey sponsored by the YWCA Committee for Business and Industrial Girls, 80.29 percent of the respondents rated watching feature films as their number-one pastime.[79]

Between 1942 and 1945, about one-third (500 out of 1,700) of all motion pictures released by Hollywood studios focused on the war.[80] At least eight of these combat feature films—*Manila Calling* (20th Century Fox, 1942), *Corregidor* (PRC, 1943), *Bataan* (MGM, 1943), *Cry Havoc!* (MGM, 1943), *So Proudly We Hail* (Paramount, 1943), *Air Force* (Warner Brothers, 1943), *Back to Bataan* (RKO, 1945), and *They Were Expendable* (MGM, 1945)—focus wholly or in part on the Philippines. Despite the lack of significant Filipino presence in most of these movies, they promoted an improved image of Filipinos as the United States' staunchest and bravest allies in the fight against Japan.[81] These sentiments became prevalent, especially after Filipino and American soldiers together fought, died, or endured the infamous death march in the bloody and unsuccessful defense of two of the best-known American strongholds in the Philippines: Bataan and "the rock," Corregidor.

Bataan was among the first films that depict the joint American–Filipino defense of the peninsula. Released by Metro-Goldwyn-Mayer in 1943, the movie focuses on the relationships forged among thirteen volunteers from various American patrol units and the Philippine Scouts who served as rear guards during the U.S. evacuation of Bataan. Their mission is to detain the advancing Japanese army by demolishing an important bridge, thereby securing more time for General Douglas MacArthur and his forces to regroup and retake the fortress. Initially, tension and internal fighting beleaguer the motley crew, but as they work toward their objective, they develop affection and mutual respect for one another. These feelings become especially meaningful when the men realize that they are doomed, destined to die for the sake of protecting American interests in the war effort.[82]

While the impact of film on audiences is difficult to gauge, efforts to portray Filipinos and other ethnic minorities (except Japanese) in a positive light certainly reflects conscious efforts on the part of screenwriters, producers, and filmmakers to cooperate with the federal government. At the urging of the Office of War Information, the producers and director of *Bataan* added Filipino characters who evince "an invincible determination to drive out the invader."[83] The result was two fairly important Filipino characters, Corporal Juan Katigbak (played by Roque Espiritu) of the Philippine Scouts and Private "Yankee" Salazar (played by J. Alex Havier), who join the American rear guard in its last mission. But the characterization of Filipinos is conflicting: while portrayed as a people enthusiastic about, and capable of, banishing the Japanese from the Philippines, they are also depicted as dependent on, and loyal to, the United States.[84] In *Bataan*, as starvation, disease, and Japanese snipers begin killing the men one by one, Private Salazar slips into the enemy-infested jungles in the middle of the night in a doomed attempt to obtain help from General MacArthur and the United States rather than the Filipino guerrillas who patrol the immediate area.

Bataan concludes with the prophecy that the dead American and Filipino heroes' sacrifices and courageous "spirit will lead us back to Bataan." In 1945 RKO Pictures fulfilled that prediction in film, releasing the only motion picture during the war years that focuses principally on Filipinos and their role in the liberation of the Philippines. *Back to Bataan* (originally called *Invisible Army*) depicts the desperate, last-ditch efforts of Filipinos and Americans to defend the doomed peninsula. Like its predecessor, the movie cloaks the crushing defeat of the joint forces within the mantle of future victory, set to the tune of "California, Here I Come." Like many of the combat films that exemplify a war-affirmative message, *Back to Bataan* uses what the film scholar Dana Polan describes as "a narrative of nontemporality. Narrative here is not an opening up of beginnings into the ambiguities of an unwritten future, but the controlled deployment of all temporalities according to one overarching schema."[85] For World War II films, that single purpose was imminent, total victory.

Back to Bataan is revealed in flashbacks, beginning with the successful rescue of American and Filipino prisoners of war from the Japanese at Cabanatuan and ending with the triumphant return to the islands of General Douglas MacArthur and Allied forces. The voice-over narration in the prologue ("Americans had been freed—hundreds of them. This was a promise of what was to come. Soon the whole world would be free.") and in the epilogue ("The blood, sweat, and tears have not been in vain. Freedom is on the march again.") emphasize the American fighting spirit and complete victory over the Japanese.[86]

After the triumphant rescue of the prisoners of war, Colonel Joseph Madden (John Wayne), returns to organizing and training Filipino guerrillas in the Luzon hills. Despite the film's claim that "the characters are based on real people," Madden's second-in-command is the fictional Captain Andres Bonifacio (Anthony Quinn), supposedly the namesake and grandson of the legendary Filipino revolutionary. Bonifacio, however, is bitter about the war and reluctant to lead the guerrilla forces because his sweetheart, Dalisay Delgado (Fely Franquelli), has seemingly become a Japanese ally, broadcasting anti-American and antiwar messages. Despite Bonifacio's obvious reservations about fighting in, much less winning, the war, Madden has to leave Bonifacio in charge of the guerrillas and Philippine Scouts when Corregidor requires his presence.[87]

Madden returns to the Luzon hills with orders to blow up a gasoline dump on a Japanese airfield to create a diversion so that General MacArthur's forces can land safely. But Bataan has fallen, and Bonifacio is a prisoner in the infamous death march. Madden's troops are tired and discouraged by the defeat, so the colonel urges the men to rescue Bonifacio, whom he hopes will provide the critical patriotic fervor. The freed Bonifacio, however, is as unwilling as ever to lead a campaign. Desperate to secure Bonifacio's assistance, Madden sends the unwilling hero to Manila, where he is sure to discover that his sweetheart is working undercover for the Philippine resistance movement. Strengthened by her faithfulness to the cause, Bonifacio turns his energies toward defeating the Japanese. He and Madden successfully organize Filipino guerrillas and Scouts to destroy the local Japanese camp in preparation for General MacArthur's promised return to Leyte.[88]

The narrative of *Back to Bataan* in many ways reflects the progressive attitudes of director Edward Dmytryk and screenwriter Ben Barzman, both of whom would be blacklisted in the Communist witch hunts of the 1950s.

Years later, Dmytryk reminisced about the film: "I am still proud that, at a time when . . . English-speaking heroes almost single-handedly won battles in which they were not only heavily outnumbered by the enemy, but somewhat handicapped by the presences of nonwhite allies, our film presented the Duke [John Wayne] primarily in the role of adviser and contact man, while the Filipinos themselves, led by [Anthony] Quinn (playing a Filipino) did most of the fighting and occasional dying."[89]

Nevertheless, colonial attitudes toward the Filipinos and the Philippines and reminders of the presumed superiority of Americans are embedded in the movie. Despite Dmytryk's pride that *Back to Bataan* shows Filipinos fighting and dying for the liberation of the Philippines, at least from would-be Japanese colonizers, the film never questions why Madden needs to organize the guerrillas. Filipino peasants had been effectively banding together in numerous uprisings against U.S. troops throughout the period of American occupation. The namesake and invented figure of Andres Bonifacio's grandson arguably epitomizes the colonial discourse of *Back to Bataan*. By fabricating an imagined progeny and making him fight *with* the American colonizers against the Japanese, the movie tames the image and nationalist message of self-determination promoted by the historical Bonifacio and his social movement, the Katipunan.[90] In a war where the loyalties of the Filipinos in the United States and particularly in the Philippines were crucial to American victory, the looming figure of an Andres Bonifacio and his rhetoric of self-determination and revolution against imperialism are tempered in the film.

Hollywood's war industry nevertheless provided numerous Filipinos with new avenues for relatively more lucrative employment. Of the hundreds of Filipino extras hired for *Back to Bataan*, the majority were agricultural laborers from the Salinas Valley area.[91] But in addition to bit parts, Pacific combat movies presented several Filipino and Filipina performers, notably J. Alex Havier (*Bataan* and *Back to Bataan*), Fely Franquelli (*Back to Bataan* and *Cry Havoc!*), and Pacita Todtod (*They Were Expendable*) with steady work in relatively significant roles. Working in motion pictures presented the ethnic actors, particularly the laborers, with opportunities to closely interact with some of the movie industry's most influential players.

The proliferation of Pacific combat films with a considerable number of parts for Filipino actors paved the way for the almost overnight success of the Filipino Screen Players Association (FSPA). In 1945 the union's more than 250 members called a strike on the set of RKO's *Invisible Army* (released as *Back*

to Bataan), demanding a raise from $10.50 to the $16.50 a day that the majority of players alleged the studio had guaranteed. The union scored a victory
when Mexican and Chinese actors, who were hired as replacements for the
striking Filipinos, proved inadequate.[92]

Despite the triumph of the FSPA, the good will toward Filipinos stopped
almost as soon as the Japanese surrendered to General MacArthur on the
USS *Missouri*. The end of the war in the Pacific also signaled the revival of
anti-Filipino sentiments throughout California. In Santa Maria, striking Filipino workers were warned that "at best, Filipinos are guests in the United
States . . . [and] if the Filipinos act as they have recently, they should be classified with the Japanese; denied renting of land and such, as the Japanese were
who also did not act properly as guests in America."[93]

While combat films provided Filipino actors with opportunities, for Filipino veterans, the military proved to be a conduit that had enabled at least a
few of them to finally capitalize on their college training, attain some degree
of prestige, and secure long-term benefits. Fabian Bergano, for example, had
earned a bachelor of science degree from an American university in 1936 but
was able to find work only as a migratory agricultural laborer until 1942,
when he was drafted into the U.S. Army. Bergano underwent basic training
in Texas and was eventually stationed in New Orleans for the duration of the
war. "I was never transferred [to the Filipino regiments]," he remembered,
"because I was in charge of a big hospital pharmacy in New Orleans. And
I stayed there until I was discharged in 1945. . . . When I was discharged I
worked in California . . . in a drugstore."[94]

For other veterans, benefits acquired through their tour of duty came from
the GI Bill. It enabled Private First Class Celestino Gloria, who had served
in the counterintelligence corps of the Second Filipino Regiment, to obtain
a college education. Gloria had had to leave school in the seventh grade to
help support his family, working for a steamship line carrying cargo and passengers between the Philippines and the United States. He was on shore leave
in New York when World War II broke out. A U.S. Army recruiter literally
grabbed the seaman from the street, asked him if he was Filipino, and then
signed him into the armed forces. When the Filipino regiments were dis-
solved after the war, Gloria remained in the Philippines and used part of the
money from the GI Bill to attend remedial courses at St. Paul's College. He
eventually transferred to the University of San Carlos, where he earned a
bachelor of arts and then a master's in education.[95]

While Fabian Bergano, Celestino Gloria, and other Filipinos acquired the means to achieve socioeconomic mobility through military service, most Filipino veterans do not appear to have done so. For many, the training in the armed forces resulted in skills not easily transferable to the civilian world. Sammy Escalona, for example, was a migrant laborer before being inducted into the U.S. Army in 1941; his job was in an army convoy unit in Alaska transporting munitions and soldiers, most of whom were African Americans, until he was honorably discharged in 1944. After his tour of duty, Escalona remained in Alaska for a while, working in the fish canneries, and then returned to migrant labor in California. His training in driving squadron trucks and transporting weapons and troops, while valuable in the army, was not particularly in demand outside the military.[96]

Financial provisions designed for education under the GI Bill were inadequate for many Filipino veterans. Miguel Lawagan, who served in the First Filipino Regiment, could not afford to go to school full time because the stipend "they give you [is] only a very small [amount], not enough, only $25 to $40 a month . . . then you have to go to school, [and] that's not enough to live on." In the postwar years, Lawagan lived with Filipino roommates on Cosmo Street in Los Angeles and worked as a "fountain boy," serving ice cream sodas and milkshakes in the Pig and Whistle Restaurant on Hollywood and Vine. He worked for forty hours a week and earned 75 cents an hour. But he also attended evening classes in a culinary school on Vermont and Hollywood as an investment in his future because, he said, "when I had worked as a dishwasher [during the Great Depression], I figured out that [in] learning something, you can get more pay."[97]

A researcher noted that by 1946, some Filipino Angeleños had become eligible for civil service jobs, while others were able to secure more stable and higher-paying positions, such as factory technician, in unionized industries.[98] The naturalization records of Filipino veterans of the U.S. armed forces, however, reflect the limited socioeconomic mobility in the immediate postwar period. In 1946, for example, 559 Filipino veterans applied for, and were granted, U.S. citizenship at the federal offices in Los Angeles. Excluding the 46 men who were still in the armed forces at the time of naturalization, data from the remaining 513 cases indicates that almost 80 percent (409) of the veterans listed an unskilled or a semiskilled job, such as busboy, cannery worker, or janitor, as their current position. Only 7.4 percent (38) had a skilled position, such as welder or mechanic, while a mere 3.7 percent reported holding a professional or managerial occupation.[99]

Since the applications do not indicate the veterans' prewar occupations, the data on Los Angeles naturalizations might be skewed in favor of applicants who had previous urban experiences. But even if the data are not skewed, they reveal what at best can be characterized as marginal mobility, since 367 (71.5 percent) of the Filipinos reported holding unskilled and semiskilled urban occupations. The jobs most commonly listed were cook, busboy, and domestic servant ("houseman"), positions in the service-oriented sectors that typified Filipino prewar urban employment.[100]

Only 42 (8.2 percent) of the 513 Filipinos naturalized in Los Angeles in 1946 reported rural jobs.[101] This figure represents a major shift in the occupation of Filipinos in the immediate postwar period. From the early 1920s until World War II, most Filipino immigrants were unskilled farmworkers. Hence, the data suggest that veterans who received citizenship moved out of the backbreaking grind of the fields and into the relatively more lucrative opportunities of the city. The age of the veterans further explains the Filipinos' exodus from the agricultural labor market. By the postwar years, the majority of Filipinos were more than forty years old, past their prime for performing the stoop labor required of them in the fields. Of the 46,101 Filipino men in the United States in 1950, the two highest categories were forty to forty-four (9,321) and forty-five to forty-nine years old (7,330), followed by those between thirty-five and thirty-nine (5,756) and from fifty to fifty-four years old (4,469). Discounting the male children to fourteen years old (7,807), Filipinos between thirty-five and fifty-four (26,876) constituted the greatest portion of the population.[102] In Los Angeles, of the 13,940 Filipino men, the two highest categories were for those forty-five to forty-nine years old (2,101) and forty to forty-four (2,014), followed by those between fifty and fifty-four (1,638). The next two categories were Filipinos between sixty and sixty-four years old (1,459) and those between the ages of sixty-five and sixty-nine (1,212). Taken together, these figures reveal that Filipinos in postwar Los Angeles composed an aging male population: men between forty-five and sixty-nine years old (8,484) constituted the majority of the Filipino community's adult male population.[103] In addition to the age factor, the U.S. government, as early as 1942, had contracted Mexican laborers to replace the farmworkers who were in the U.S. armed forces. By the end of the war, these younger *braceros* had largely displaced the aging Filipino and other non-Latino laborers.[104]

In the years following World War II, Filipinos who had not served in the U.S. armed forces began to grapple with the issues of citizenship that their compatriots in the military had wrestled with earlier in the decade. By 1946, the United States had granted the commonwealth its independence, and, as a sovereign nation, it could now offer its people, whether they lived in the archipelago or in the United States, citizenship. At the same time, the American government extended the privilege to apply for naturalized citizenship to Filipinos residing in the United States. Responses among Filipinos concerning their newly acquired rights to U.S. citizenship were mixed, ranging from ambivalence and indifference to questionable dividends. For some Filipinos, the once-elusive citizenship represented a prize with, at best, ambiguous rewards. Sam Figueras, for example, never applied for naturalization despite having lived and worked in the United States since 1926, when he was nineteen years old. Fifty years later, when an interviewer asked Figueras if he ever intended to apply for citizenship, he replied, "No, I don't believe in it."[105] Juan V. Mina, who immigrated in 1933 and became a naturalized citizen in 1947, felt that citizenship led to no significant changes in his life. "I've been here without any citizenship paper and I've been here with my citizenship paper," Mina stated. "I really didn't feel any different at all. When I was not a citizen, it didn't bother me anyway because I worked [on] a farm most of my life so it doesn't make a difference if I'm a citizen or not."[106]

Despite the heated intraethnic controversies associated with issues of citizenship, the pervasive stereotypes of Filipinos in the United States and in the Philippines as eager, loyal allies emerged as important cornerstones of wartime unity within the United States and its empire. Although the experiences of Filipinos during the war years affected economic mobility only marginally for both civilians and soldiers, the training and privileges experienced by some Filipinos in the military opened up new opportunities to question the status quo and challenge racial discrimination.

6. REFORMULATING COMMUNITIES
Filipino Los Angeles Since World War II

> The creation of "Historic Filipinotown" is definitely long over-
> due and its creation is due to all the hard work that has led up
> to it. Filipinos for decades worked toward its creation. This
> includes the former "Little Manila" in downtown L.A. and all
> the other places where Filipinos have resided. Filipinos have
> been successful in every way in Los Angeles, and it has been
> their success and spirit that has led to the designation.
>
> —George Villanueva, in Joey G. Alarilla,
> "L.A. Designates Official 'Historic Filipinotown'"

On 2 August 2002 Councilmember Eric Garcetti, Acting Los Angeles Consul General Ruth Prado, and Mayor James Hahn joined Filipino American residents, business leaders, and community activists in a ceremony designating the Temple–Beverly area of Los Angeles as Historic Filipinotown. Bounded by the 101 Freeway to the north, Glendale Boulevard on the east, Beverly Boulevard on the south, and Hoover Street on the west, the community includes a number of social service agencies, headquarters of several fraternal organizations, and Filipino-owned restaurants and other small businesses. The dedication ceremony was the culmination of decades of work among Filipino American Angeleños who had long campaigned for official recognition of the community's roots in the city. Councilmember Garcetti agreed, noting that "the contributions of Filipinos to American society are grand, wide and great and this is a long-overdue reward for them."[1]

Despite its designation as the "historic" district of Filipino American settlement in Los Angeles, however, the Temple–Beverly area is a relatively recent Filipino American community. Filipinos started moving into the district around the late 1960s, as the execution of several of the city's redevelopment and regentrification plans since World War II forced residents out of the original settlements around Weller Street and then the Bunker Hill area. Indeed, the only remnant of pre-1960s Filipino settlement in the historic district is the Filipino Christian Church, which was built in the 1920s to provide religious and other services to the immigrants of that period who were routinely denied entrance to Roman Catholic churches. The majority of the residents in the area, moreover, represent the more recent wave of immigrants who have come to the United States since 1965.[2] While a few Filipinos from the earlier wave of immigration still live in Historic Filipinotown, most have already passed away; others have returned to the Philippines, while still others have moved to areas in and around cities like Stockton, San Francisco, and Seattle, which had been part of the prewar migration route.

Los Angeles's gentrification programs, particularly when plans intensified in the immediate postwar years, resulted in the demolition of a number of the boarding houses and other remnants of Filipino settlements along Weller Street to make way for the construction of the Harbor Freeway. This manifestation of L.A.'s landmark concrete octopus freeway system followed the norm in displacing houses and businesses in the neighborhoods of the urban poor, such as the residents of Little Manila and the Mexican American district east of the Los Angeles River. As one scholar notes, "To keep right-of-way expenses under control, freeways were often routed through inexpensive property, with the result that a disproportionate number of those affected by relocation or disruption were poor, minority, or elderly—those least able to absorb uncompensated expense, and those least served by the projects."[3]

Some Filipinos, however, had begun leaving the old section in the late 1930s. Tensions with African Americans, who had moved into the neighboring Little Tokyo with the internment of Japanese and Japanese American residents during World War II, further escalated this trend. Filipinos began moving to the Bunker Hill area and to the vicinity of Temple and Figueroa, where, as one researcher observes, they "felt that they have undisputed claim."[4] By the 1940s, numerous Filipino restaurants, barbershops, newspapers, and headquarters of social organizations had relocated from First and Main Streets to Temple Street, between Figueroa and Fremont Avenues. While some established operations like the L.V.M. Café remained ensconced in the old quarters, the latest enterprises, including the Lucky Spot, Zamboanga Café, and Paco's Barber Shop, opened for business in the new neighborhood. In 1945 the Filipino Screen Players Association, fresh from its success in getting RKO Studios to raise the wage rates of Filipino actors and extras in *Back to Bataan*, set up its central office at 819 Temple Street. Manila Post 464 of the American Legion, located in the same building, boasted that the site was "fast becoming the center of all Filipino organization in all Southern California," noting the various services, conveniences, and facilities available in the structure.[5] But despite the hopes for and exultation about the new Filipino business district, the establishment of the ethnic community followed prewar patterns. The Temple–Figueroa district was already considered an unfavorable location, having "developed a rather sordid reputation because of a scattering of house of prostitution in that vicinity."[6]

Unlike the original Little Manila, the emerging Filipino neighborhood in the Temple–Figueroa site was predominantly a business, not a residential, district. Filipinos generally continued to rent cheap rooms around Bunker Hill and its vicinity. This neighborhood, once a fashionable middle- and upper-class development of Victorian houses, was, by the 1940s, a rundown area described by novelist Raymond Chandler as an "old town, lost town, shabby town, crook town. . . . In the tall rooms haggard landladies bicker with shift tenants. On the side cool front porches, reaching their cracked shoes into the sun, sit old men with faces like lost battles."[7] By the postwar years, as the demand for housing increased and freeways made downtown more accessible, the city's redevelopment agency declared Bunker Hill a blighted zone as a prelude to the demolition of its buildings, the majority of which were residential. Private developers were then encouraged to purchase the land and turn Bunker Hill into a high-rent district.[8]

In addition to the city's regentrification of the downtown area and the demographic shifts among Filipino Angeleños, reforms in U.S. immigration laws beginning in the postwar years effected modifications in the popular culture practices of what was once a predominantly young, bachelor, and highly mobile male-centered community. During the 1920s and 1930s, the policies of recruiters from American businesses, the attitudes and traditions of the home country, and the Tydings-McDuffie Act of 1934 limited the number of Filipinas in the United States. While some Filipinas immigrated, most, because of their parents' strong objections, did not leave the family homestead. In addition to this gender imbalance in the Filipino population, antimiscegenation laws, which forbade marriages between people of color and "whites," hampered the formation of conventional families. These statutes were inconsistent, varying from state to state, and enforcement largely depended on the marriage applicants' claim of ethnic heritages or the county clerk's judgment as to the "race" of the petitioners. In California, there were no specific injunctions against Filipino interethnic marriages until 1933, when the term "Malay," meaning "Filipinos," was added to section 60 of the state's civil code.[9] After World War II, the War Brides Act of 1945 (Public Law 271) allowed spouses, among them Filipinas, to join their husbands, who were either in active service or veterans of the armed forces, in the United States. In 1946 the Fiancées Act (Public Law 471) allowed other women, including Filipinas who had met Filipinos who had returned to the Philippines for vacations, family reunification, or wife-hunting trips in the postwar years, to join them in the United States.[10] Because of the Filipino tradition of wives managing the family's finances, Filipinos who married during the war or in the immediate postwar years now had less control of their wages, which they had spent in any way they saw fit when they were bachelors. As a contemporary graduate student put it, "The father is the breadwinner, and the mother the safe-keeper of the family's income."[11]

Despite the number of marriages and the gradual emergence of a second generation, the bulk of Filipino immigrants from the pre–World War II period remained unmarried and continued to socialize in the company of other men. Indeed, in 1940, Filipino Angeleños who lived on Temple Street, tired of being overshadowed by the exploits of their compatriots who lived along First and Main Streets in Little Manila, formed the Filipino Bachelors' Club to show that "social doings will be in full blast in that part of the Filipino colony."[12] And as World War II drew to a close and Filipino veterans began returning to California, the Bachelor's Club of Imperial Valley in Niland announced the revival of the organization there. Filipinos had formed the association during the 1930s, and it had enjoyed a large membership until the U.S. armed forces drafted almost all the club's members.[13]

But favorite gathering places, particularly taxi dance halls, had faced a steady decline beginning in the 1940s, and all these recreational centers were closed or razed by the postwar years. Shifts in Filipino business enterprises in Los Angeles between the Great Depression and the early 1950s in many ways also suggest the changes in the circumstances, needs, and life cycle of the community's residents. Throughout the 1930s, sectors that offered services considered essential in nurturing the image of the well-groomed man-about-town and spaces for social interaction thrived in Little Manila. In 1933 three tailors, twelve restaurants, three pool halls, and seven barbershops catered to the demands of their Filipino clientele. The two concentrated areas of work among the 212 Filipinos employed by Filipino-owned businesses within the ethnic community were restaurants (67) and barbershops (47).[14] In 1938 the number of these service-oriented establishments increased to four tailors, sixteen restaurants, seven pool halls, and twelve barbershops.[15] By 1952 the number of barbershops had grown to twenty, but only one tailor, twelve restaurants, and four pool halls remained.[16] The continued expansion of tonsorial businesses in the postwar years suggests that while Filipinos may have found substitutes, including wives and non-Filipino-owned establishments, to provide the services once furnished by tailors and restaurants, many Filipinos still desired the camaraderie and fellowship of men in a place run *by* men specifically *for* men.

Today, nothing remains of the Filipino settlements around Weller Street, Bunker Hill, or the Temple–Figueroa district.[17] They fell victims to Los Angeles's habit of forgetting the histories of its ethnic and poor communities in the downtown area.[18] But the historical significance of these spaces cannot be erased. When they *needed* to exist, they provided valuable sites for the vibrant and complex negotiations for viable ethnic identities and solidarity, however tenuous, through discursive practices and cultural processes. For Filipino immigrants of the 1920s and 1930s, the performance of brown bodies in the personal choices they made regarding their leisure time and the everyday acts of resistance they developed in the recreation centers became just as substantial as formal organizations in the struggles for autonomy and negotiations for self-definition.

NOTES

Introduction

1. A debate rages over which term, "Filipino" or "Pilipino," should be used to designate people from the Philippines. Some argue that the letter *f* and its sound should be eliminated from the Philippine national language because the Spanish conquistadores inserted them into the indigenous vocabulary and the American colonizers perpetuated their use. Indeed, the Spanish named the country itself after King Philip II of Spain, and "Filipino" was originally used to designate Spaniards born in the islands. While recognizing this sensitive issue, the terms "Filipino/Filipina" and "Filipino American/Filipina American" will be used in this study.

2. "Dahil Sa Iyo" was among the first and most successful recordings of Filipino music in the United States. See Fred Cordova, *Filipinos: Forgotten Asian Americans*, ed. Dorothy Cordova (Seattle: Demonstration Project for Asian Americans, 1983), 89–91.

3. Amparo S. Lardizabal, "Our Customs, Beliefs, and Superstitions," in *Readings on Philippine Culture and Social Life*, ed. Amparo S. Lardizabal and Felicitas Tensuan-Leogardo (Quezon City, Philippines: Rex Printing, 1976), 104–24.

4. Like the Filipino/Pilipino debate, controversy surrounds which spelling, "Ilocano" or "Ilokano," should be used to designate the inhabitants of the northern provinces of Luzon and their regional dialect. Again, while recognizing this sensitive issue, the term "Ilocano" will be used throughout this study to denote the speech and peoples of the Ilocos provinces.

5. George Lipsitz, *Time Passages: Collective Memory and American Popular Culture* (Minneapolis: University of Minnesota Press, 1990), 235.

6. U.S. Department of Commerce, Bureau of the Census, *Twenty-second Census of the United States, 2000* (available at: http://www.census.gov). See also Melany Dela Cruz

and Pauline Agbayani-Siewert, "Swimming With and Against the Tide," in *The New Face of Asian Pacific America: Numbers, Diversity and Change in the 21st Century*, ed. Eric Lai and Dennis Arguelles (Berkeley, Calif.: Consolidated Printers, 2003), 45–50.

7. Dela Cruz and Agbayani-Siewert, "Swimming With and Against the Tide." On post-1965 and contemporary Filipino immigration, see Rick Bonus, *Locating Filipino Americans: Ethnicity and the Cultural Politics of Space* (Philadelphia: Temple University Press, 2000); Catherine Ceniza Choy, *Empire of Care: Nursing and Migration in Filipino American History* (Durham, N.C.: Duke University Press, 2003); Martin F. Manalansan IV, *Global Divas: Filipino Gay Men in the Diaspora* (Durham, N.C.: Duke University Press, 2003), and "*Biyuti* in Everyday Life: Performance, Citizenship, and Survival Among Filipinos in the United States," in *Orientations: Mapping Studies in the Asian Diaspora*, ed. Kandice Chuh and Karen Shimakawa (Durham, N.C.: Duke University Press, 2001), 153–71; Benito M. Vergara Jr., "Betrayal, Class Fantasies, and the Filipino Nation in Daly City," in *Cultural Compass: Ethnographic Explorations of Asian America*, ed. Martin F. Manalansan IV (Philadelphia: Temple University Press, 2000), 139–58; Charlene Tung, "Caring Across Borders: Motherhood, Marriage, and Filipina Domestic Workers in California," in *Asian/Pacific Islander American Women: A Historical Anthology*, ed. Shirley Hune and Gail M. Nomura (New York: New York University Press, 2003), 301–15; Catherine Ceniza Choy, "Relocating the Struggle: Filipino Nurses Organize in the United States," in *Asian/Pacific Islander Women*, ed. Hune and Nomura, 335–49; Paul Ong and Tania Azores, "The Migration and Incorporation of Filipino Nurses," in *The New Asian Immigration in Los Angeles and Global Restructuring*, ed. Paul Ong, Edna Bonacich, and Lucie Cheng (Philadelphia: Temple University Press, 1994), 164–95; and Yen Le Espiritu, *Home Bound: Filipino American Lives Across Cultures, Communities, and Countries* (Berkeley: University of California Press, 2003). See also Timothy Fong, *The Contemporary Asian American Experience: Beyond the Model Minority* (Upper Saddle River, N.J.: Prentice Hall, 1998), and the following issues of *Amerasia Journal*, which focus on Filipinos: "Filipinos in American Life," 13, no. 1 (1986–1987); "Essays into American Empire in the Philippines: Legacies, Heroes, and Identity," 24, no. 2 (1998), and "Essays into American Empire in the Philippines: Culture, Community, and Capital," 24, no. 3 (1998).

8. On Filipino immigration to the Pacific Northwest during the 1920s until World War II, see Chris Friday, *Organizing Asian American Labor: The Pacific Coast Canned Salmon Industry* (Philadelphia: Temple University Press, 1994), and Dorothy Fujita Rony, *American Workers, Colonial Power: Philippine Seattle and the Transpacific West, 1919–1941* (Berkeley: University of California Press, 2003). On Filipinos in Chicago and the Midwest, see Kimberly Alidio, "Between Civilizing Mission and Ethnic Assimilation: Racial Discourse, U.S. Colonial Education and Filipino Ethnicity, 1901–1946" (Ph.D. diss., University of Michigan, 2001). On Filipinos in San Diego, see Adelaida Castillo-Tsuchida, "Filipino Migrants in San Diego, 1900–1946" (master's thesis, University of San Diego, 1979).

9. The Tydings-McDuffie Act of 1934 included provisions for the Philippines's independence within ten years, provided that the archipelago establish and maintain a

government acceptable to, and subject to the approval of, the United States. The act also stipulated that upon the commonwealth's independence, the U.S. government would cede all property, except for American military bases, in the islands. Further, while the act nullified the free trade agreement between the Philippines and the United States, it nevertheless imposed tariffs on Philippine products coming into the United States. American exports to the islands remained duty free. The passage of this act also restricted the immigration of Filipinos because it changed the status of Filipinos from U.S. "nationals" to "aliens." In light of the Great Depression, the act of 1934 thus satisfied the demands of a number of U.S. factions, including labor leaders, manufacturers, nativists, and isolationists. See Basil Rauch, *The History of the New Deal, 1933–1938*, 2d ed. (New York: Octagon Books, 1975).

10. H. Brett Melendy, *Asians in America: Filipinos, Koreans, and East Indians* (Boston: Hall, 1977); Sucheng Chan, *Asian Americans: An Interpretive History* (Boston: Twayne, 1991); Ronald Takaki, *Strangers from a Different Shore: A History of Asian Americans* (Boston: Little, Brown, 1989).

11. California Department of Industrial Relations, *Facts About Filipino Immigration*, (1930; reprint, San Francisco: R and E Research Associates, 1972), 16.

12. Harry H. L. Kitano and Roger Daniels, *Asian Americans: Emerging Minorities* (Englewood Cliffs, N.J.: Prentice Hall, 1988), 79–80.

13. Severino F. Corpus, "An Analysis of the Racial Adjustment Activities and Problems of the Filipino American Christian Fellowship in Los Angeles" (master's thesis, University of Southern California, 1938); Tania Azores, "Filipinos in the Los Angeles Labor Force: Placemaking in Little Manila" (1983, photocopy, in author's possession); Rosemarie D. Ibañez, "'Birds of Passage': Filipino Immigrants in the 1920s and 1930s" (1990, photocopy, in author's possession).

14. George Weiss, interview by Lundy, 16 February 1937, transcript, "Racial Minority Survey: Filipinos," Federal Writers Project, box 142, folder 1086, Charles E. Young Research Library, University of California, Los Angeles (hereafter cited as FWP). Weiss opened two other stores, in San Pedro and in Boyle Heights, but both failed.

15. Benecio T. Catapusan, "The Filipino Occupational and Recreational Activities in Los Angeles" (master's thesis, University of Southern California, 1934), 2.

16. Data gathered from advertisements in the *Philippines Review* (Los Angeles), 6 April 1935–6 March 1936. Other Filipino newspapers published in Los Angeles included the *Philippine Star Press*, *Little Manila Times*, and *Philippine Free Press*. Records of the *Philippines Review* were the most complete of these newspapers.

17. See, for example, Corpus, "Analysis of the Racial Adjustment Activities and Problems of the Filipino American Christian Fellowship," and Catapusan, "Filipino Occupational and Recreational Activities," and "The Social Adjustment of Filipinos in the United States" (Ph.D. diss., University of Southern California, 1940). Emory S. Bogardus also produced a number of studies on Filipino immigrants: "American Attitudes Towards Filipinos," *Sociology and Social Research* 14, no. 1 (1929): 59–69, and *Anti-Filipino Race Riots: A Report Made to the Ingram Institute of Social Science of San Diego* (San Diego, Calif., 15 May 1930).

18. Monographs by non-Filipinos that specifically examined the Filipinos' participation in taxi dance halls echoed the students' disparaging sentiments. See Paul Cressy, *The Taxi-Dance Hall: A Sociological Study in Commercialized Recreation and City Life* (New York: Greenwood Press, 1932), and Clyde Bennett Vedder, "An Analysis of the Taxi-Dance Hall as a Social Institution, with Special Reference to Los Angeles and Detroit" (Ph.D. diss., University of Southern California, 1947). For an analysis of Cressy's work, see Alidio, "Between Civilizing Mission and Ethnic Assimilation," chap. 4.

19. See, for example, Howard A. De Witt, *Anti-Filipino Movements in California* (San Francisco: R and E Research Associates, 1976), and *Violence in the Fields: California Farm Labor Unionization During the Great Depression* (San Francisco: R and E Research Associates, 1980); Arleen de Vera, "The Tapia-Saiki Incident: Interethnic Conflict and Filipino Responses to the Anti-Filipino Exclusion Movement," in *Over the Edge: Remapping the American West*, ed. Valerie J. Matsumoto and Blake Allmendinger (Berkeley: University of California Press, 1999), 201–14; Craig Scharlin and Lilia V. Villanueva, *Philip Vera Cruz: A Personal History of Filipino Immigrants and the Farmworkers Movement*, 3d ed. (Seattle: University of Washington Press, 2000); and Herminia Quimpo Meñez, *Folklore Communication Among Filipinos in California* (New York: Arno Press, 1980).

20. Melendy, *Asians in America*; Chan, *Asian Americans*; Takaki, *Strangers from a Different Shore*; Helen Zia, *Asian American Dreams: The Emergence of an American People* (New York: Farrar, Straus and Giroux, 2000); Robert G. Lee, *Orientals: Asian Americans in Popular Culture* (Philadelphia: Temple University Press, 1999). Some scholars have hailed Takaki's *Strangers from a Different Shore* as the definitive synthesis of Asian American studies, but the praise lavished on the book has also caused controversies in the field. See "Amerasia Forum: Strangers from a Different Shore," *Amerasia Journal* 16, no. 2 (1990): 63–154, and Gordon H. Chang, "Asian Americans and the Writing of Their History," *Radical History Review* 53, no. 1 (1992): 105–14.

21. Hune and Nomura, eds., *Asian/Pacific Islander American Women*; Chuh and Shimakawa, eds., *Orientations*; Manalansan, ed., *Cultural Compass*; Vicente L. Rafael, ed., *Discrepant Histories: Translocal Essays on Filipino Cultures* (Philadelphia: Temple University Press, 1995).

22. Gail Bederman, *Manliness and Civilization: A Cultural History of Gender and Race in the United States, 1880–1917* (Urbana: University of Illinois Press, 1996), 7.

23. Friday, *Organizing Asian American Labor*, 132.

24. George Lipsitz, "Con Safos: Can Cultural Studies Read the Writing on the Wall?" (1991, photocopy, in author's possession), 11–12. See also Lipsitz, "Listening to Learn and Learning to Listen: Popular Culture, Cultural Theory, and American Studies," *American Quarterly* 42, no. 4 (1990): 615–36; and Lipsitz, *Time Passages*, 3–20.

25. Antonio Gramsci, *An Antonio Gramsci Reader: Selected Writings, 1916–1935*, ed. David Forgacs (New York: Schocken Books, 1988), 300. On Gramsci's theories and ethnic studies, see, for example, George Lipsitz, "The Struggle for Hegemony," *Journal of American History* 75, no. 1 (1988): 146–50, and *Time Passages*, 133–60.

26. Lipsitz, "Struggle for Hegemony," 146–47.

27. Stuart Hall, "Notes on Deconstructing 'the Popular,'" in *People's History and Socialist Theory*, ed. Raphael Samuel (London: Routledge and Kegan Paul, 1981), 233. Work by prominent cultural historians include Hall, "The Rediscovery of 'Ideology': Return of the Repressed in Media Studies," in *Culture, Society, and the Media*, ed. Michael Gurevitch (London: Methuen, 1982), 56–90; Fredric Jameson, "Reification and Utopia in Mass Culture," *Social Text* 1, no. 1 (1979): 130–48; Raymond Williams, *Marxism and Literature* (Oxford: Oxford University Press, 1977); and Michel de Certeau, "On the Oppositional Practices of Everyday Life," *Social Text* 3 (1980): 3–43.

28. See, for example, Roy Rosenzweig, *Eight Hours for What We Will: Workers and Leisure in an Industrial City, 1879–1920* (New York: Cambridge University Press, 1983); Kathy Peiss, *Cheap Amusements: Working Women and Leisure in Turn-of-the-Century New York* (Philadelphia: Temple University Press, 1986); Robin D. G. Kelley, *Race Rebels: Culture, Politics, and the Black Working Class* (New York: Free Press, 1994); and Katrina Hazzard-Gordon, *Jookin': The Rise of Social Dance Formation in African-American Culture* (Philadelphia: Temple University Press, 1990).

29. Rosenzweig, *Eight Hours for What We Will*, 224–25.

30. Tamara K. Hareven and Randolph Lagenbach, *Amoskeag: Life and Work in an American Factory-City* (New York: Pantheon Books, 1978), 32.

31. David Brodsly, *L.A. Freeway* (Berkeley: University of California Press, 1981).

32. *Manong/manang*, inserted before a given name, are Ilocano words that express deference to, respectively, an older brother or sister. Generally, the titles are also used to show respect for a much older person. In contemporary usage, the terms *manongs* and "*manong* generation" also denote the Filipino immigrants of the 1920s and 1930s.

1. Making a Living

1. Manuel Fiores, interview by Lundy, 2 March 1937, transcript, "Racial Minority Survey: Filipinos," Federal Writers' Project, box 142, folder 1086, Charles E. Young Research Library, University of California, Los Angeles (hereafter cited as FWP).

2. Ibid.

3. Ibid.

4. The first big wave of Filipino immigrants were *pensionados*, government-sponsored students who came to the United States under the colonial administration in the Philippines of William Howard Taft. The first set of these students arrived in 1903, and by 1910, they had all returned to the Philippines. Subsequent groups of students arrived between 1903 and 1938 to study in American institutions, including Harvard, Stanford, Yale, and the University of Southern California. About 14,000 Filipinos were educated in American universities during these years. After completing their education, the vast majority of these students returned to the Philippines. See H. Brett Melendy, *Asians in America: Filipinos, Koreans, and East Indians* (Boston: Hall, 1977), and Fred Cordova, *Filipinos: Forgotten Asian Americans*, ed. Dorothy Cordova (Seattle: Demonstration Project for Asian Americans, 1983). On the *pensionado* program,

see Catherine Ceniza Pet, "Pioneers/Puppets: The Legacy of the *Pensionado* Program" (B.A. senior thesis, Pomona College, 1991).

5. Edwin B. Almirol, "Rights and Obligations in Filipino American Families," *Journal of Comparative Family Studies* 13, no. 3 (1982): 299.

6. The majority of Filipinos who stayed in California after their tour of duty in the U.S. armed forces, particularly the navy, settled in and around San Diego, which has historically served as a naval port for these sailors. See Adelaida Castillo-Tsuchida, "Filipino Migrants in San Diego, 1900–1946" (master's thesis, University of San Diego, 1979).

7. Chinese and Japanese laborers had worked in the agriculture fields in the late nineteenth and early twentieth centuries. However, the Chinese Exclusion Act of 1882 and the "Gentlemen's Agreement" between the United States and Japan in 1906 severely restricted the immigration of these groups. See Melendy, *Asians in America*, and Sucheng Chan, *Asian Americans: An Interpretive History* (Boston: Twayne, 1991).

8. See, for example, the collection of essays in Virginia Yans-McLaughlin, ed., *Immigration Reconsidered: History, Sociology, and Politics* (New York: Oxford University Press, 1990), especially Ewa Morawska, "The Sociology and Historiography of Immigration," 187–238.

9. Robert N. Anderson, Richard Coller, and Rebecca F. Pestano, *Filipinos in Rural Hawaii* (Honolulu: University of Hawaii Press, 1984).

10. Hermenegildo Cruz, "Problems of Filipino Emigration," in *Problems of the Pacific: Proceedings of the Fourth Conference of the Institute of Pacific Relations, 1931*, ed. Bruno Lasker (Chicago: University of Chicago Press, 1932), 433. Cruz was then director of labor in the Philippines.

11. Ibid., 432.

12. Chan, *Asian Americans*, 18.

13. Craig Scharlin and Lilia V. Villanueva, *Philip Vera Cruz: A Personal History of Filipino Immigrants and the Farmworkers Movement*, 3d ed. (Seattle: University of Washington Press, 2000), 7.

14. Marcelino A. Foronda Jr., "America Is in the Heart: Ilocano Immigration to the United States, 1906–1930," *Journal of Social History* (Manila, Philippines) 21, nos. 1–2 (1976): 24–37.

15. California Department of Industrial Relations, *Facts About Filipino Immigration* (1930; reprint, San Francisco: R and E Research Associates, 1972), 16–24.

16. Harry H. L. Kitano and Roger Daniels, *Asian Americans: Emerging Minorities* (Englewood Cliffs, N.J.: Prentice Hall, 1988), 79–80.

17. Chan, *Asian Americans*, 104. On Filipinas and interethnic tensions in Stockton, California, during the 1930, see Arleen de Vera, "The Tapia-Saiki Incident: Interethnic Conflict and Filipino Responses to the Anti-Filipino Exclusion Movement," in *Over the Edge: Remapping the American West*, ed. Valerie J. Matsumoto and Blake Allmendinger (Berkeley: University of California Press, 1999), 201–14. On waves of Filipina immigration to the United States, see Gail M. Nomura, "Filipina American Journal Writing: Recovering Women's History," in *Asian/Pacific Islander American Women: A Historical Anthology*, ed. Shirley Hune and Gail M. Nomura (New York:

New York University Press, 2003), 138–52, and Dorothy Cordova, "Voices from the Past: Why They Came," in *Making Waves: An Anthology of Writings by and About Asian American Women*, ed. Asian Women United of California (Boston: Beacon Press, 1989), 42–49.

18. Caridad Concepcion Vallangca, *The Second Wave: Pinay and Pinoy (1945–1960)* (San Francisco: Strawberry Hill Press, 1987), 212.

19. California Department of Industrial Relations, *Facts About Filipino Immigration*, 32.

20. Maria Garcia Cardoz, interview by Lundy, 9 February 1937, transcript, "Racial Minority Survey: Filipinos," FWP.

21. Kitano and Daniels, *Asian Americans*, 79–80.

22. Casiano Coloma, "A Study of the Filipino Repatriation Movement" (master's thesis, University of Southern California, 1939), 40. All figures related to Filipinos are estimates, since the vast majority of them were migratory laborers.

23. Severino F. Corpus, "An Analysis of the Racial Adjustment Activities and Problems of the Filipino-American Christian Fellowship in Los Angeles" (master's thesis, University of Southern California, 1938), 3.

24. Rex Ragan, "The Economic Effects on the Pacific Coast of Filipino Immigration to the United States" (M.B.A. thesis, University of Southern California, 1928), 35.

25. Howard A. De Witt, *Violence in the Fields: California Farm Labor Unionization During the Great Depression* (San Francisco: R and E Research Associates, 1980).

26. Chris Friday, *Organizing Asian American Labor: The Pacific Coast Canned Salmon Industry, 1870–1942* (Philadelphia: Temple University Press, 1994); Dorothy Fujita Rony, *American Workers, Colonial Power: Philippine Seattle and the Transpacific West, 1919–1941* (Berkeley: University of California Press, 2003).

27. Ragan, "Economic Effects on the Pacific Coast of Filipino Immigration to the United States," 35.

28. Scharlin and Villanueva, *Philip Vera Cruz*, 6.

29. Albert W. Palmer, *Orientals in American Life* (New York: Friendship Press, 1934), 79.

30. Quoted in Ronald Takaki, *Strangers from a Different Shore: A History of Asian Americans* (Boston: Little, Brown, 1989), 321.

31. Scharlin and Villanueva, *Philip Vera Cruz*, 5–6.

32. Friday, *Organizing Asian American Labor*, 125–32.

33. Scharlin and Villanueva, *Philip Vera Cruz*, 20.

34. Carey McWilliams, *Brothers Under the Skin* (1942; reprint, Boston: Little, Brown, 1964), 237.

35. Evelyn Nakano Glenn, "The Dialectics of Wage Work: Japanese American Women and Domestic Service, 1905–1940," in *Unequal Sisters: A Multi-Cultural Reader in U.S. Women's History*, ed. Ellen Carol DuBois and Vicki L. Ruiz (New York: Routledge, 1990), 345–72.

36. D. F. Gonzalo, "Social Adjustments of Filipinos in America," *Sociology and Social Research* 14, no. 2 (1929): 167.

37. Interview, in *Voices: A Filipino-American Oral History*, ed. Joan May T. Cordova and Alexis S. Canillo (Santa Rosa, Calif.: Northwestern Graphics, 1984).

38. Nakano Glenn, "Dialectics of Wage Work," 353.

39. Ibid. On Japanese gardeners, see Nobuya Tsuchida, "Japanese Gardeners in Southern California, 1900–1941," in *Labor Immigration Under Capitalism: Asian Workers in the United States Before World War II*, ed. Lucie Cheng and Edna Bonacich (Berkeley: University of California Press, 1984), 435–67.

40. Phyllis Palmer, *Domesticity and Dirt: Housewives and Domestic Servants in the United States, 1920–1945* (Philadelphia: Temple University Press, 1989), 9.

41. Eliot Grinnell Mears, *Resident Orientals on the American Pacific Coast: Their Legal and Economic Status* (Chicago: University of Chicago Press, 1928).

42. Ragan, "Economic Effects on the Pacific Coast of Filipino Immigration to the United States," 35.

43. Letter to the First Lady, August 1933, quoted in Palmer, *Domesticity and Dirt*, 72.

44. Evelyn Nakano Glenn, *Issei, Nisei, War Bride: Three Generations of Japanese American Women in Domestic Service* (Philadelphia: Temple University Press, 1986), 146.

45. Ibid. On narratives of African American domestics during the Great Depression, see Jacqueline Jones, *Labor of Love, Labor of Sorrow: Black Women, Work, and the Family from Slavery to the Present* (New York: Basic Books, 1985).

46. The figures did not include those Filipino students attending high school. See Corpus, "Analysis of the Racial Adjustment Activities and Problems of the Filipino-American Christian Fellowship in Los Angeles," 14.

47. Miguel Lawagan, interview by author, 26 June 1993, San Francisco, Calif. Lawagan never finished his studies, since he could not afford the tuition.

48. Severino Corpus, interview by Berkley Walker, 24 May 1937, transcript, "Racial Minority Survey: Filipinos," FWP. Corpus eventually earned his master's degree from the University of Southern California in 1938. See Corpus, "Analysis of the Racial Adjustment Activities and Problems of the Filipino-American Christian Fellowship in Los Angeles."

49. Johnny Garcia, interview by Lundy, 18 January 1937, transcript, "Racial Minority Survey: Filipinos," FWP.

50. E.W., interview by Madeline Lindsey, 8 October 1936, transcript, "Racial Minority Survey: Jamaicans," box 119, folder 1096, FWP.

51. Anonymous Filipino, interview by Lundy, 2 February 1937, transcript, "Racial Minority Survey: Filipinos," FWP. The interviewee declined to state his name for fear of retaliation for having killed the man who raped his fourteen-year-old girlfriend in the Philippines.

52. James Earl Wood, "Earning a Living," James Earl Wood Papers, box 1, folder 9, Bancroft Library, University of California, Berkeley.

53. Judith Rollins, *Between Women: Domestics and Their Employers* (Philadelphia: Temple University Press, 1985), 157. See also Nakano Glenn, "Dialectics of Wage Work," in which she calls the practice "benevolent maternalism."

54. Garcia interview, "Racial Minority Survey: Filipinos," FWP.

55. Eddie Manzoa, interview by Lundy, 10 February 1937, transcript, "Racial Minority Survey: Filipinos," FWP.

56. Shirley Lim, "Gender, Race, and Film in the West: Anna May Wong" (paper presented at the "American Dreams, Western Images" Conference, Part One: "Representation and Identity: The West and the Westerner," Los Angeles, 19–20 November 1993); Anthony B. Chan, *Perpetually Cool: The Many Lives of Anna May Wong (1905–1961)* (Lanham, Md.: Scarecrow Press, 2003). See also Donald Teruo Hata Jr. and Nadine Ishitani Hata, "Asian-Pacific Angelinos: Model Minorities and Indispensable Scapegoats," in *Twentieth-Century Los Angeles: Power, Promotion, and Social Conflict*, ed. Norman M. Klein and Martin J. Schiesl (Claremont, Calif.: Regina Books, 1991), 61–99. While MGM's production of *The Good Earth* provided thousands of jobs for Chinese and Chinese Americans, they were hired principally as extras. Euro-Americans Paul Muni, Luise Rainier, and Tilly Losch, made up in "yellow face," played the key roles.

57. Gina Marchetti, *Romance and the "Yellow Peril": Race, Sex, and Discursive Strategies in Hollywood Fiction* (Berkeley: University of California Press, 1993), 2. See also R. Lee, *Orientals: Asian Americans in Popular Culture* (Philadelphia: Temple University Press, 1999). For critiques on the stereotypes of Asian and Asian American women, see Renee E. Tajima, "Lotus Blossoms Don't Bleed: Images of Asian Women," in *Making Waves*, ed. Asian Women United of California, 308–17; and Jessica Hagedorn, "Asian Women in Film: No Joy, No Luck," in *Signs of Life in the USA: Readings on Popular Culture for Writers*, ed. Sonia Maasik and Jack Solomon, 2nd ed. (Boston: Bedford Books, 1997), 306–14. On Asian American cinema and film criticism, see Darrell Y. Hamamoto and Sandra Liu, eds., *Countervisions: Asian American Film Criticism* (Philadelphia: Temple University Press, 2000); Peter X. Feng, ed., *Screening Asian Americans* (New Brunswick, N.J.: Rutgers University Press, 2002); and Russell Leong, ed., *Moving the Image: Independent Asian Pacific American Media Arts* (Los Angeles: UCLA Asian American Studies Center and Visual Communications, 1991.

58. Mohammed, 1 June 1937, transcript, "Racial Minority Survey: Asiatic Indians," box 149, FWP.

59. Fatimah Tobing Rony, *The Third Eye: Race, Cinema, and Ethnographic Spectacle* (Durham, N.C.: Duke University Press, 1996), 8, 12.

60. Robert W. Rydell, *All the World's a Fair: Visions of Empire at American International Expositions, 1876–1916* (Chicago: University of Chicago Press, 1984); *A World on Display*, written and dir. Eric Breitbart, prod. Eric Breitbart and Mary Lance, 53 min., New Deal Films, 1996, videocassette; *Bontoc Eulogy*, written and dir. Marlon Fuentes, 57 min., videocassette.

61. Quoted in Cordova, *Filipinos*, 113.

62. In "Gender, Race, and Film in the West," Lim makes the same argument for Chinese and Chinese American extras, who could potentially earn between $5 and $25 a day. This sum is a substantial boost to a worker's income, given that the average monthly wage for jobs in Chinatown was between $30 and $50.

63. Leo Aliwanag, interview by Cynthia Mejia, 19 August 1976, interview FIL-KNG 76-50cm, transcript, Washington State Oral/Aural History Program, Olympia (hereafter cited as WSOAHP).

64. *Philippines Herald Tribune* (Los Angeles), 28 April 1936.

65. Agcaoili Sabino, interview in Roberto V. Vallangca, *Pinoy: The First Wave* (San Francisco: Strawberry Hill Press, 1977), 141.

66. Immanuel Tardez, interview by Lundy, 18 February 1937, transcript, "Racial Minority Survey: Filipinos," FWP.

67. Anonymous Filipino interview, "Racial Minority Survey: Filipinos," FWP.

68. Interview by James Earl Wood, n.d. (but definitely in the 1930s, when Wood conducted his fieldwork), Wood Papers, box 1, folder 9.

69. Leo Escalona, interview by author, 26 June 1993, San Francisco, Calif.

70. Ragan, "Economic Effects on the Pacific Coast of Filipino Immigration to the United States," 33.

71. Bruno Tapang, n.d., interview PNW 81-Fil-007, transcript, Pinoy Archives, Filipino National Historical Society, Seattle, Wash. (hereafter cited as FANHS).

72. Vincent Mendoza, interview by Cynthia Mejia, 13 January 1976, interview FIL-KNG 76-40cm, transcript, WSOAHP.

73. Manuel Buaken, *I Have Lived with the American People* (Caldwell, Idaho: Caxton Printers, 1948), 190.

74. Phil Riley, interview by James Earl Wood, n.d. (but definitely in the 1930s, when Wood conducted his fieldwork), Wood Papers, box 1, folder 10.

75. Sam Figueras, interview by Cynthia Mejia, 5 January 1976, interview FIL-KNG 76-39cm, transcript, WSOAHP.

76. Johnny Rallonza, interview by author, 23 April 1992, Downey, Calif.

77. Data on wages from Marcos P. Berbano, "The Social Status of the Filipino in Los Angeles County" (master's thesis, University of Southern California, 1930), 40–42. See also Ragan, "Economic Effects on the Pacific Coast of Filipino Immigration to the United States," 36.

78. Chris Mensalvas, interview by Carolina N. Koslosky, 10 and 11 February 1975, interview FIL-KNG 75-1ck, transcript, WSOAHP.

79. Mendoza interview, FIL-KNG 76-40cm, transcript, WSOAHP.

80. Friday, *Organizing Asian American Labor*, 134.

81. California Department of Industrial Relations, *Facts About Filipino Immigration*.

82. Chan, *Asian Americans*; Takaki, *Strangers from a Different Shore*; Cordova, *Filipinos*. The labor historian Howard De Witt charged that the Filipino immigration and wage rates published in the bulletin "reads like a time bomb ready to explode," which inadvertently fueled fears of a "third Asian invasion" and anti-Filipino attitudes in California (*Violence in the Fields*, 120).

83. James N. Gregory, *American Exodus: The Dust Bowl Migration and Okie Culture in California* (New York: Oxford University Press, 1989), 50.

84. Toribio Castillo, interview by author, 1 March 1992, Los Angeles, Calif.

85. Celedonio La Questa, Jacinto Sequig, and Florentino Mendoza, in *A Dollar*

a Day, Ten Cents a Dance: A Historic Portrait of Filipino Farm Workers in America, produced by George Ow Jr., Geoffrey Dunn, and Mark Schwartz, directed by Mark Schwartz, 40 min., Impact Productions, 1984, videocassette.

86. Frank Coloma, interview in Vallangca, *Pinoy*, 86–87. Employment patterns of Filipinos entering the civil service were different in Chicago, where the majority of Filipinos who passed the civil service exams were hired as postal clerks. During the 1920s and throughout the Great Depression, positions as civil servants and as employees of the Pullman Company ranked as "elite" jobs in the Filipino community. See Barbara M. Posadas, "Ethnic Life and Labor in Chicago's Pre–World War II Filipino Community," in *Labor Divided: Race and Ethnicity in United States Labor Struggles, 1835–1960*, ed. Robert Asher and Charles Stephenson (Albany: State University of New York Press, 1990), 63–80.

87. Castillo interview.

88. Mendoza interview, FIL-KNG 76-40cm, transcript, WSOAHP.

89. Interview by James Earl Wood, n.d. (but definitely in the 1930s, when Wood conducted his fieldwork), Wood Papers, box 1, folder 9.

90. Ibid.

91. Fiores interview, "Racial Minority Survey: Filipinos," transcript, FWP.

92. Tardez interview, "Racial Minority Survey: Filipinos," transcript, FWP.

93. Friday, *Organizing Asian American Labor*, 132.

94. Peter Quintero, interview by Dorothy Cordova, 8 June 1976, interview FIL-KNG 76-48dc, transcript, WSOAHP.

95. The references made to certain establishments and street addresses in this study of Little Manila are valid for only the 1920s and 1930s. Little Manila no longer exists. Most of the original buildings were demolished in the post–World War II period to make way for the gentrification of downtown, the expansion of Little Tokyo, and the construction of the Harbor Freeway (Interstate 110). Information on Little Manila came from advertisements in the *Philippines Review*; Corpus, "Analysis of the Racial Adjustment Activities and Problems of the Filipino-American Christian Fellowship in Los Angeles"; Tania Azores, "Filipinos in the Los Angeles Labor Force: Placemaking in Little Manila" (1983, photocopy, in author's possession); and Rosemarie D. Ibañez, "'Birds of Passage': Filipino Immigrants in the 1920s and 1930s" (1990, photocopy, in author's possession).

96. Takaki, *Strangers from a Different Shore*, 336. See also McWilliams, *Brothers Under the Skin*, 229–49, and Ibañez, "Birds of Passage."

97. Sally Miller, ed., *The Ethnic Press in America* (Westport, Conn.: Greenwood Press, 1987), xv–xvi.

98. Other Filipino newspapers published in Los Angeles included the *Philippine Star Press, Little Manila Times*, and *Philippine Free Press*. Records of the *Philippines Review* were the most complete of these newspapers.

99. When the islands became a colony in 1898, Americans established a public school system patterned after the U.S. model. They imported American teachers who used English as the language of instruction. Most of the Filipino immigrants had attended these schools and came to the United States reasonably literate in English.

100. *Philippines Review* (Los Angeles), 31 May 1935, 6 April 1935.

101. *Philippines Review* (Los Angeles), 23 February 1937.

102. *Philippine Examiner* (Stockton, Calif.), 23 February 1937.

103. *Philippines Review* (Los Angeles), 23 February 1937.

104. *Associated Filipino Press* (Los Angeles), 17 August 1939.

105. *Philippines Review* (Los Angeles), 6 April 1935.

106. *Philippine Examiner* (Stockton, Calif.), 30 July 1935–15 February 1937.

107. Aliwanag interview, FIL-KNG 76-50cm, transcript, WSOAHP.

108. Benecio T. Catapusan, "The Filipino Occupational and Recreational Activities in Los Angeles" (master's thesis, University of Southern California, 1934).

109. Benecio T. Catapusan, "The Social Adjustment of Filipinos in the United States" (Ph.D. diss., University of Southern California, 1940).

110. Ibid.; Catapusan, "Filipino Occupational and Recreational Activities."

111. On the significance of urban leisure spaces for immigrant, ethnic workers, see Roy Rosenzweig, *Eight Hours for What We Will: Workers and Leisure in an Industrial City, 1870–1920* (Cambridge: Cambridge University Press, 1983).

112. Wood Papers, box 1, folder 9.

113. Ragan, "Economic Effects on the Pacific Coast of Filipino Immigration to the United States," 36.

114. Aliwanag interview, FIL-KNG 76-50cm, transcript, WSOAHP.

115. Ibid.

116. *Philippines Review* (Los Angeles), 6 April 1935–6 March 1936.

117. The first of these land laws was passed in 1913, preventing "aliens ineligible to citizenship" from buying land. See Chan, *Asian Americans.*

118. Castillo interview; Rallonza interview.

119. Carlos Bulosan, *America Is in the Heart: A Personal History* (New York: Harcourt, Brace, 1946; reprint, Seattle: University of Washington Press, 1979), 112, 134.

120. *Philippines Review* (Los Angeles).

121. George J. Sánchez, *Becoming Mexican American: Ethnicity, Culture, and Identity in Chicano Los Angeles, 1900–1945* (New York: Oxford University Press, 1993).

122. Coloma, "Study of the Filipino Repatriation Movement."

123. Benecio T. Catapusan, "Filipino Immigrants and Public Relief in the United States," *Sociology and Social Research* 23, no. 4 (1939): 546–54.

124. Fabian Bergano, interview by Fredrick A. Cordova Jr., 15 April 1975, interview FIL-KNG 75-7jr, transcript, WSOAHP.

125. Alfonso Yasonia, interview in Vallangca, *Pinoy*, 77.

126. Rallonza interview. The Dorothy Chandler Pavilion now stands where the Majestic Hotel-Apartments once did.

127. Reverend James E. Dolan, Los Angeles, to J. E. Wood, Berkeley, 4 December 1930, Wood Papers, box 1, folder 17.

128. Weller Street contained one of the largest concentration of Filipino establishments during the 1930s. Today, Weller Street has been renamed Onizuka Street and is part of Little Tokyo.

129. Edwin B. Almirol, "Filipino Voluntary Associations: Balancing Social Pressures and Ethnic Images," *Ethnic Groups* 2 (1978): 65–92.

130. On the Filipino-American Christian Fellowship, see Corpus, "Analysis of the Racial Adjustment Activities and Problems of the Filipino-American Christian Fellowship in Los Angeles." On the Filipino Federation of America, see Steffi San Buenaventura, "Nativism and Ethnicity in a Filipino-American Experience" (Ph.D. diss., University of Hawaii, 1990).

131. Howard A. De Witt, *Anti-Filipino Movements in California* (San Francisco: R and E Research Associates, 1976).

132. De Witt, *Violence in the Fields*, 17. On post–World War II Filipino unionization, see Arleen Garcia de Vera, "An Unfinished Agenda: Filipino Immigrant Workers in the Era of McCarthyism: A Case Study of the Cannery Workers and Farm Laborers Union, 1948–1955" (master's thesis, University of California, Los Angeles, 1990).

133. De Witt, *Violence in the Fields*.

134. Ibid. See also Chan, *Asian Americans*. In 1936, Filipino and Mexican agricultural workers succeeded in getting a charter for a combined union from the American Federation of Labor. In 1937, the AFL-chartered Field Workers Union Local No. 30326, a Filipino agricultural workers' union. For unionization efforts among Filipinos as well as other Asian groups in Alaska's canning industry, see Friday, *Organizing Asian American Labor*.

135. Cruz, "Problems of Filipino Immigration," 436.

136. Juan (John) Castillo, interview by Frederic A. Cordova Jr., 29 July 1975, interview FIL-KNG 75-15jr, transcript, WSOAHP.

137. Jesus R. Yambao, interview by Carolina N. Koslosky, 10 and 11 February 1975, interview FIL-KNG 75-1ck, transcript, WSOAHP.

138. Buaken, *I Have Lived with the American People*, 60–62.

139. Charles Tilly, "Transplanted Networks," in *Immigration Reconsidered*, ed. Yans-McLaughlin, 92.

140. Mensalvas interview, FIL-KNG 75-1ck, transcript, WSOAHP.

141. Ibid. In 1952 the Immigration and Naturalization Service detained, and almost deported, Mensalvas to the Philippines for alleged "subversive" activities in a Communist union.

142. Mariano Angeles, interview by Cynthia Mejia, 6 November 1975, interview FIL-KNG 75-32cm, transcript, WSOAHP.

143. Berkley Walker, "Summary of Interviews," "Racial Minority Survey: Filipinos," FWP.

144. *Philippines Review* (Los Angeles), 23 February 1937.

145. Manzoa interview, transcript, "Racial Minority Survey: Filipinos," FWP.

146. Palmer, *Domesticity and Dirt*, 111–35.

147. Generoso Pacificar Provido, "Oriental Immigration from an American Dependency" (master's thesis, University of California, Los Angeles, 1931).

148. Mendoza interview, FIL-KNG 76-40cm, transcript, WSOAHP.

149. Robin D. G. Kelley, "'We Are Not What We Seem': Rethinking Black Working-

Class Opposition in the Jim Crow South," *Journal of American History* 80, no. 1 (1993): 75–112, esp. n. 43. See also Nakano Glenn, "Dialectics of Wage Work."

150. Corpus interview, transcript, "Racial Minority Survey: Filipinos," FWP.

151. Interview, in *Voices*, ed. Cordova and Canillo.

152. *Musicians Club Directory*, March 1926, Charles Leland Bagley Collection, box 15, Department of Special Collections, University of Southern California (hereafter cited as Bagley Collection).

153. *Overture* 18, no. 9 (1939), Bagley Collection.

2. Of Dice and Men

1. Vincent Mendoza, interview by Cynthia Mejia, 13 January 1976, interview FIL-KNG 76-40cm, transcript, Washington State Oral/Aural History Program, Olympia (hereafter cited as WSOAHP).

2. Ibid.

3. Thomas Allen McDannold, "Development of the Los Angeles Chinatown, 1850–1970" (master's thesis, California State University, Northridge, 1973), 26–45. See also Carey McWilliams, *Southern California: An Island on the Land* (New York: Duell, Sloan and Pearce, 1946; reprint, Salt Lake City: Peregrine Smith Books, 1988), 84–95, and Donald Teruo Hata Jr. and Nadine Ishitani Hata, "Asian-Pacific Angelinos: Model Minorities and Indispensable Scapegoats," in *Twentieth-Century Los Angeles: Power, Promotion, and Social Conflict*, ed. Norman M. Klein and Martin J. Schiesl (Claremont, Calif.: Regina Books, 1991), 61–99.

4. On the relationship among labor, racism, violence, and the anti-Chinese movement in California, see Alexander Saxton, *The Indispensable Enemy: Labor and the Anti-Chinese Movement in California* (Berkeley: University of California Press, 1971).

5. Hata and Hata, "Asian-Pacific Angelinos," 67.

6. Ibid., 74; McDannold, "Development of the Los Angeles Chinatown," 53–54.

7. On segregation, vice districts, and the regulation of "morality" in cities, see Neil Larry Shumsky, "Tacit Acceptance: Respectable Americans and Segregated Prostitution, 1870–1910," *Journal of Social History* 19, no. 4 (1986): 664–79.

8. On Chinese prostitution as an economic institution, see, for example, Lucie Cheng, "Free, Indentured, Enslaved: Chinese Prostitutes in Nineteenth Century America," in *Labor Immigration Under Capitalism: Asian Workers in the United States Before World War II*, ed. Lucie Cheng and Edna Bonacich (Berkeley: University of California Press, 1984), 402–30.

9. On the development of Los Angeles's African American community, see Douglas Flamming, *Bound for Freedom: Black Los Angeles in Jim Crow America* (Berkeley: University of California Press, 2005), and "Becoming Democrats: Liberal Politics and the African American Community in Los Angeles, 1930–1965," in *Seeking El Dorado: African Americans in California*, ed. Lawrence B. de Graaf, Kevin Mulroy, and Quintard Taylor (Los Angeles: Autry Museum of Western Heritage, 2001), 279–308; Lawrence Brooks de Graaf, "Negro Migration to Los Angeles, 1930–1950" (Ph.D. diss., University

of California, Los Angeles, 1962); Lonnie G. Bunch, "A Past Not Necessarily Prologue: The Afro-Americans in Los Angeles," in *Twentieth-Century Los Angeles*, ed. Klein and Schiesl, 100–130; and Kevin Allen Leonard, "'In the Interest of All Races': African Americans and Interracial Cooperation in Los Angeles During and After World War II" in *Seeking El Dorado*, ed. de Graaf, Mulroy, and Taylor, 309–40.

10. Joseph Gerald Woods, "The Progressives and the Police: Urban Reform and the Professionalization of the Los Angeles Police" (Ph.D. diss., University of California, Los Angeles, 1973), 86.

11. Ivan Light, "From Vice District to Tourist Attraction: The Moral Career of American Chinatowns, 1880–1940," *Pacific Historical Review* 43, no. 3 (1974): 368.

12. San Francisco Board of Health, *Annual Report, 1876–77*, quoted in Nayan Shah, *Contagious Divides: Epidemics and Race in San Francisco's Chinatown* (Berkeley: University of California Press, 2001), 17.

13. Shumsky, "Tacit Acceptance," 665.

14. Ronald Takaki, *Strangers from a Different Shore: A History of Asian Americans* (Boston: Little, Brown, 1989), 243. The Japanese immigrant communities had a more favorable gender ratio, in part because restrictions against Japanese immigration came in phases, allowing men relatively more time to decide whether or not to send for their wives. Even after the 1906 "Gentlemen's Agreement" between the United States and Japan, however, Japanese men already in the United States were still allowed to send for their spouses. Bachelors took advantage of this loophole by having their families in Japan arrange marriages for them through swapping pictures of the prospective bride and groom. The immigrants then sent money for their "picture brides" to join them in the United States. Although no more visas were issued to picture brides after 1920, there was already a substantial number of Japanese families in the United States, with almost 30,000 American-born children. See also Sucheng Chan, *Asian Americans: An Interpretive History* (Boston: Twayne, 1991), 107–9. On the development of Los Angeles's Japanese American community, see Lon Kurashige, *Japanese American Celebration and Conflict: A History of Ethnic Identity and Festival in Los Angeles, 1934–1990* (Berkeley: University of California Press, 2002), and John Modell, *The Economics and Politics of Racial Accommodation: The Japanese of Los Angeles, 1900–1942* (Urbana: University of Illinois Press, 1977).

15. On tensions between immigrant parents and their children, see, for example, Elizabeth Ewen, *Immigrant Women in the Land of Dollars: Life and Culture on the Lower East Side, 1880–1925* (New York: Monthly Review Press, 1985); Douglas Monroy, "'Our Children Get So Different Here': Film, Fashion, Popular Culture and the Process of Cultural Syncretization in Mexican Los Angeles, 1900–1935," *Aztlán* 19, no. 1 (1988–1990): 79–108; and Vicki Ruiz, "'Star Struck': Acculturation, Adolescence, and Mexican American Women, 1920–1950," in *Small Worlds: Children and Adolescents in America, 1850–1950*, ed. Elliott West and Paula Petrik (Lawrence: University Press of Kansas, 1992), 61–80.

16. John Mendoza, interview by Dorothy Cordova, 6 April 1976, Seattle, Wash., interview FIL-KNG 76-42dc, transcript, WSOAHP.

17. Ray Edralin Corpus, interview by Bob Antolin, 22 September 1981, Tacoma, Wash., interview PNW 81-Fil-028ba, transcript, Pinoy Archives, Filipino American National Historical Society (hereafter cited as FANHS).

18. James Earl Wood, "Field Notes," James Earl Wood Papers, box 1, folder 9, Bancroft Library, University of California, Berkeley.

19. Alfonso Yasonia, interview in Roberto V. Vallangca, *Pinoy: The First Wave* (San Francisco: Strawberry Hill Press, 1977), 78.

20. Wood, "Field Notes," Wood Papers.

21. Gregory Y. Mark, "Gambling in Oakland Chinatown: A Case of Constructive Crime?" in *Frontiers of Asian American Studies*, ed. Gail Nomura, Russell Endo, Stephen H. Sumida, and Russell C. Leong (Pullman: Washington State University Press, 1989), 14–24.

22. See, for example, Yasonia interview, in Vallangca, *Pinoy*.

23. Mark, "Gambling in Oakland Chinatown," 17, 23.

24. *Ang Bantay (The Guardian)* (Los Angeles), 7 December 1929.

25. Woods, "Progressives and the Police," 91.

26. Mark, "Gambling in Oakland Chinatown," 16–18. Vincent Mendoza, from the opening story of this chapter, won an "eight spot," matching the eight numbers on his lottery ticket with the numbers drawn by the house, playing this game. He bet 35 cents, and his winnings of $365 enabled him and his friends to continue on to Los Angeles.

27. John A. Larkin, "Philippine History Reconsidered: A Socioeconomic Perspective," *American Historical Review* 87, no. 3 (1982): 595–628; Edgar Wickberg, *The Chinese in Philippine Life* (New Haven, Conn.: Yale University Press, 1965); Renato Constantino, "Identity and Consciousness: The Philippine Experience" (Toronto: Eighth World Sociology Congress, 1974). On the role of the Chinese mestizo, see Edgar Wickberg, "The Chinese *Mestizo* in Philippine History," *Journal of Southeast Asian History* 5 (1964): 62–100. In contrast with the large Chinese and Chinese mestizo communities, there were few Japanese settlers, merchants, and small business operators in the Philippines.

28. Arturo Gonzales, interview by Lundy, 25 February 1937, transcript, "Racial Minority Survey: Filipinos," Federal Writers' Project, box 142, folder 1086, Charles E. Young Research Library, University of California, Los Angeles (hereafter cited as FWP).

29. Chan, *Asian Americans*, 41.

30. Severino F. Corpus, "An Analysis of the Racial Adjustment Activities and Problems of the Filipino-American Christian Fellowship in Los Angeles" (master's thesis, University of Southern California, 1938), 67.

31. Fabian Bergano, interview by Fredrick A. Cordova Jr., 15 April 1975, interview FIL-KNG 75-7jr, transcript, WSOAHP.

32. Bruno Lasker, *Filipino Immigration to the Continental United States and Hawaii* (Chicago: University of Chicago Press, 1931), 10.

33. Mark H. Haller, "Policy Gambling, Entertainment, and the Emergence of Black Politics: Chicago from 1900 to 1940," *Journal of Social History* 24, no. 3 (1991): 733.

34. Ivan Light, "Numbers Gambling Among Blacks: A Financial Institution" *American Sociological Review* 42, no. 6 (1977): 898. For a comparison between Chinese and

African American vice enterprises, see Light, "The Ethnic Vice Industry, 1880–1944," *American Sociological Review* 42, no. 3 (1977): 464–79.

35. Mark, "Gambling in Oakland Chinatown," 20–22.

36. Mariano Angeles, interview by Cynthia Mejia, 6 November 1975, interview FIL-KNG 75-32cm, transcript, WSOAHP.

37. Toribio Martin Sr., interview by Dorothy Cordova, 27 April 1976, interview FIL-KNG 76-44dc, transcript, WSOAHP.

38. Yasonia interview, in Vallangca, *Pinoy*, 80.

39. Other Asian groups also went to the Chinese gambling halls for this reason. See Chan, *Asian Americans*, 71.

40. Leo Aliwanag, interview by Cynthia Mejia, 19 August 1976, interview FIL-KNG 76-50cm, transcript, WSOAHP.

41. Yasonia interview, in Vallangca, *Pinoy*, 78.

42. Felipe G. Dumlao, interview by Cynthia Mejia, 21 November 1975, interview FIL-KNG 75-35cm, transcript, WSOAHP.

43. On "floating casinos," see Hank Messick and Burt Goldblatt, *The Only Game in Town: An Illustrated History of Gambling* (New York: Crowell , 1976). The SS *Rex* was arguably the most opulent of these gambling ships. Water taxis daily transported an average of 2,500 players and guests between Los Angeles's ports and the ocean liner every ten minutes.

44. Sidney L. Harring, *Policing a Class Society: The Experience of American Cities, 1865–1915* (New Brunswick, N.J.: Rutgers University Press, 1983), 191.

45. Ibid.

46. Ann Fabian, *Card Sharps, Dream Books, and Bucket Shops: Gambling in Nineteenth-Century America* (Ithaca, N.Y.: Cornell University Press, 1990), 39.

47. Calculated from data in Wood, "Field Notes," Wood Papers.

48. Calculated from data in Paul S. Taylor, "Crime and the Foreign Born: San Francisco," cited in U.S. National Commission on Law Observance and Enforcement, *Report on Crime and the Foreign Born* (Washington, D.C.: Government Printing Office, 1931), 361. The statistics provided in the report, however, did not distinguish between Chinese nationals and Chinese Americans.

49. Calculated from data in ibid., 352.

50. Felix Tapiz, interview by James Earl Wood, 22 February 1930, "Field Notes Relating to Filipinos in California," Wood Papers, folder 3.

51. Yasonia interview, in Vallangca, *Pinoy*, 78.

52. Woods, "Progressives and the Police," 91.

53. Kurashige, *Japanese American Celebration and Conflict*, 39–40.

54. While tongs are commonly associated with secret or semisecret societies in the Chinese underworld specializing in racketeering and other extralegal enterprises, the group was originally formed in southern China as a political organization, the Triad Society, to overthrow the Qing dynasty. Many Chinese immigrants in the United States belonged to tongs, but only a few of these organizations were actually engaged in illegal activities and fewer still were involved in the infamous tong wars in China-

towns. See June Mei, "Socioeconomic Developments Among the Chinese in San Francisco, 1848–1906," in *Labor Immigration Under Capitalism*, ed. Cheng and Bonacich, 387, and Light, "Ethnic Vice Industry," 472.

55. Light, "From Vice District to Tourist Attraction"; Mark, "Gambling in Oakland Chinatown."

56. Light, "From Vice Districts to Tourist Attraction," 379.

57. Ibid.

58. Sammy Escalona, interview by author, 2 January 1993, Stockton, Calif. Fines for cockfighting were steep. Escalona was caught twice, once in the San Fernando Valley and once in Stockton, and had to pay $50 for each offense.

59. Hermenegildo Cruz, "Problems of Filipino Emigration," in *Problems of the Pacific: Proceedings of the Fourth Conference of the Institute of Pacific Relations, 1931*, ed. Bruno Lasker (Chicago: University of Chicago Press, 1932), 436.

60. Adoracion Ordinario, interview by author, 23 April 1994, Altadena, Calif. Herman de los Santos was Ordinario's uncle.

61. Money Order Division, Bureau of Posts, Philippine Islands, cited in Lasker, *Filipino Immigration*.

62. "Filipinos in California," Wood Papers, box 1, folder 8.

63. Money Order Division, Bureau of Posts, Philippine Islands, cited in Lasker, *Filipino Immigration*, 252.

64. "Filipinos in California," Wood Papers, box 1, folder 8.

65. *Philippines Herald-Tribune* (Los Angeles), 28 April 1936.

66. Light, "Ethnic Vice Industry," 468.

67. Ibid.; Light, "From Vice District to Tourist Attraction"; Haller, "Tacit Acceptance," 666–67.

68. See, for example, Light, "From Vice District to Tourist Attraction," and Woods, "Progressives and the Police."

69. Woods, "Progressives and the Police," 109.

70. Richard Whitehall, "When the Mobsters Came West: Organized Crime in Los Angeles Since 1930," in *Twentieth-Century Los Angeles*, ed. Klein and Schiesl, 131–51.

71. Woods, "Progressives and the Police," 109.

72. Whitehall, "When the Mobsters Came West," 131.

73. Woods, "Progressives and the Police," 22–25.

74. Ibid., 84–112.

75. Ibid., 230, 57.

76. *Philippines Review* (Los Angeles), 31 October 1935.

77. Saxton, *Indispensable Enemy*; Elmer Clarence Sandmeyer, *The Anti-Chinese Movement in California* (Urbana: University of Illinois Press, 1939); McWilliams, *Southern California*; McDannold, "Development of the Los Angeles Chinatown"; Light, "From Vice Districts to Tourist Attraction."

78. California Commission on Immigration and Housing, *Second Annual Report* (Sacramento, 1916).

79. Christine Sterling, who was responsible for bringing the "charm" and "quaint-

ness" of Old Mexico to Los Angeles through the renovation of Olvera Street and the central plaza, is the person most associated with the design of China City, where she sought to bring the "drama" and the "mysteries of the Orient." In the 1950s, a fire ravaged the center of China City. The charred area was redeveloped as a parking lot that connected the New Chinatown and China City, resulting in the present-day geographic location and boundaries of Chinatown. See McDannold, "Development of the Los Angeles Chinatown."

80. Light, "From Vice District to Tourist Attraction."

81. Carl (Carlos) Miguel, interview by Lundy, 10 March 1937, transcript, "Racial Minority Survey: Filipinos," FWP.

82. Los Angeles Police Department, *Annual Report of the Los Angeles Police Department, 1936–37*, Los Angeles Public Library, Central Branch, Los Angeles, Calif.

83. W. L. Tambolero, "Fight for Title a Drawing Card Far Beyond Expectations of Match-Makers," *Philippines Review* (Los Angeles), 23 February 1937.

3. From the "Living Doll" to the "Bolo Puncher"

1. Like many championship bouts, the Apostoli–Garcia fight was scheduled in New York because Mike Jacobs, the most influential boxing promoter of the 1930s, held court at Madison Square Garden. For coverage of the Apostoli–Garcia Middleweight Championship event, see the *New York Times* and the *Los Angeles Times*, 3 October 1939. See also Cross Counter, "Garcia Thrills Again!" *Ring*, December 1939, 24–25, 42.

2. *New York Times*, 3 October 1939.

3. While there are some rare exceptions, these U.S. government–sponsored students tended to be from wealthy and influential Filipino families. See Renato Constantino, *The Miseducation of the Filipino*, 2d ed. (Quezon City, Philippines: Foundation for Nationalist Studies, 1983).

4. *New York Times*, 15 September 1922.

5. Quoted in Lester Bromberg, *Boxing's Unforgettable Fights* (New York: Ronald Press, 1962), 132.

6. Genaro received recognition as the American flyweight champion only after Villa's death in 1925. See Alexander Johnston, *Ten—And Out! The Complete Story of the Prize Ring in America*, 3d ed. (New York: Ives Washburn, 1947), 347.

7. Quoted in Bromberg, *Boxing's Unforgettable Fights*, 134.

8. *New York Times*, 19 June 1923.

9. *New York Times*, 31 May 1924. The following year, Villa died in Oakland from blood poisoning caused by an infected tooth. In 1961 the Hall of Fame posthumously awarded him a place in its gallery of boxing greats. See Bob Burrill, *Who's Who in Boxing* (New Rochelle, N.Y.: Arlington House, 1974), 193–94. A majority of Filipino oldtimers continue to regard Pancho Villa as the greatest Filipino boxer of all time. See, for example, Cornelio Pasquil, "Filipino Boxers Make History in America," *Los Angeles Filipino Bulletin*, 21 April–20 May 1992.

10. "Tex" Rickard, "Boxers of World Ranked in 1924," *Ring*, February 1925.

11. Quoted in Bromberg, *Boxing's Unforgettable Fights*, 132–33.

12. *New York Times*, 19 June 1923.

13. Norris C. Mills, "Filipino Boxing Invasion Coming," *Ring*, September 1925, 17.

14. Bill Van, "'Speedy' Dado Is a Pancho Villa," *Knockout*, 21 February 1931.

15. Harry B. Smith, "California's Classy Fighters," *Ring*, April 1939, 24.

16. *Philippines Review* (Los Angeles), 28 September 1935.

17. *Associated Filipino Press* (Los Angeles), 9 December 1939.

18. Garcia's statistics are in Burrill, *Who's Who in Boxing*, 78.

19. H. A. Elumba, "Sports Slants," *Filipino Pioneer* (Stockton, Calif.), 16 December 1938.

20. Bill Henry, "Ceferino Garcia Loses Game Fight to Ross," *Los Angeles Times*, 24 October 1937.

21. For coverage of the Apostoli–Garcia championship match, see the *Los Angeles Times* and the *New York Times*, 3 October 1939. In 1940 Garcia defended his title against Henry Armstrong in Los Angeles.

22. Nat Fleischer, "Louis Tops for 1939," *Ring*, February 1940, 3–8.

23. Toribio Castillo, interview by author, 1 March 1992, Los Angeles, Calif.

24. Gene Vinassa, "Brown Bomber in Miniature," *Ring*, September 1939, 25.

25. Robert Hilado, in *The Great Pinoy Boxing Era: Three Decades of Filipino-American Boxers*, prod. Corky Pasquil, ed. Bernard Espinosa, n.d., videocassette.

26. Sammy Escalona, interview by author, 2 January 1993, Stockton, Calif.

27. *Philippines Review* (Los Angeles), 1 July 1935.

28. Ibid. In 1935 the United States passed the Filipino Repatriation Act in an effort to reduce the number of Filipino workers during the Great Depression. The act offered Filipinos free passage back to the Philippines, and in exchange they forfeited applying for reentry to the United States. Few Filipinos, however, returned to the Philippines under this act. Upon the declaration of the act as unconstitutional by 1940, only 2,190 Filipinos had voluntarily returned to the Philippines.

29. *Philippines Review* (Los Angeles), 31 August 1935.

30. On the act of reading and formulaic literature, see Janice Radway, *Reading the Romance: Women, Patriarchy, and Popular Literature* (Chapel Hill: University of North Carolina Press, 1984). See also Michael Denning, *Mechanic Accents: Dime Novels and Working-Class Culture in America* (New York: Verso Press, 1987).

31. Antonio Cabanag, interview by author, 26 June 1993, San Francisco, Calif.

32. Interview, in Alfredo N. Muñoz, *The Filipinos in America* (Los Angeles: Mountainview, 1972), 96.

33. The literature on folklore is extensive. On African American expressive cultures, see, for example, Lawrence W. Levine, *Black Culture and Black Consciousness: Afro-American Folk Thought from Slavery to Freedom* (Oxford: Oxford University Press, 1977); on Philippine folk tales, see Herminia Quimpo Meñez, "Agyu and the Skyworld: The Philippine Folk Epic and Multicultural Education," *Amerasia Journal* 13, no. 1 (1986–1987): 135–49, and Francisco R. Demetrio, "Themes in Philippine Folk

Tales," *Asian Studies* 10, no. 1 (1972): 6–17; on gender and the Mexican *corrido*, see Maria Herrera-Sobek, *The Mexican Corrido: A Feminist Analysis* (Bloomington: Indiana University Press, 1990); on the evolution of the *corrido* along the Mexican-U.S. border, see Américo Paredes, *"With His Pistol in His Hand": A Border Ballad and Its Hero* (Austin: University of Texas Press, 1958), and Maria Herrera-Sobek, "The Corrido as Hypertext: Undocumented Mexican Immigrant Films and the Mexican/Chicano Ballad," in *Culture Across Borders: Mexican Immigration and Popular Culture*, ed. David R. Maciel and Maria Herrera-Sobek (Tucson: University of Arizona Press, 1998), 227–58.

34. Paredes, *"With His Pistol in His Hand,"* 114. On Paredes and anti-imperialist literature, see, for example, José David Saldívar, "Américo Paredes and Decolonization," in *Border Matters: Remapping American Cultural Studies* (Berkeley: University of California Press, 1997), 36–56. See also José E. Limón, *Mexican Ballads, Chicano Poems: History and Influence in Mexican-American Social Poetry* (Berkeley: University of California Press, 1992).

35. Meñez, "Agyu and the Skyworld," 137–46.

36. Peter Bacho, "A Manong's Heart," in *Dark Blue Suit and Other Stories* (Seattle: University of Washington Press, 1997), 111.

37. Johnny Samson, "History of Boxing in the Philippines," in DeWitt Van Court, *The Making of Champions in California* (Los Angeles: Premier Printing, 1926), 146–47. John Lawrence Sullivan is generally considered the first "modern" American prizefighter. On the "Great John L.," see Elliott J. Gorn, *The Manly Art: Bare-Knuckle Prize Fighting in America* (Ithaca, N.Y.: Cornell University Press, 1986), and Jeffrey T. Sammons, *Beyond the Ring: The Role of Boxing in American Society* (Urbana: University of Illinois Press, 1998), chaps. 1 and 2.

38. Renato Constantino, *The Philippines: A Past Revisited*, vol. 1, 14th ed. (Quezon City, Philippines: Foundation for Nationalist Studies, 1993), and "The Miseducation of the Filipino," *Weekly Graphic*, 8 June 1966. See also Barbara S. Gaerlan, "The Pursuit of Modernity: Trinidad H. Pardo de Tavera and the Educational Legacy of the Philippines Revolution," *Amerasia Journal* 24, no. 2 (1998): 87–108, and Kimberly Alidio, "'When I Get Home I Want to Forget': Memory and Amnesia in the Occupied Philippines, 1901–1904," *Social Text* 17, no. 2 (1999): 145–60. On American repression of Filipino nationalist production, see, for example, Vicente L. Rafael, "White Love: Surveillance and Nationalist Resistance in the U.S. Colonization of the Philippines," in *Cultures of United States Imperialism*, ed. Amy Kaplan and Donald E. Pease (Durham, N.C.: Duke University Press, 1993), 185–218. On colonial and neocolonial writings by Filipino Americans, see Oscar V. Campomanes, "Filipinos in the United States and Their Literature of Exile," in *Reading the Literatures of Asian America*, ed. Shirley Geok-lin Lim and Amy Ling (Philadelphia: Temple University Press, 1992), 49–78.

39. Lewis E. Gleeck Jr., *American Institutions in the Philippines (1898–1941)* (Quezon City, Philippines: Garcia, 1976).

40. Ibid., 36.

41. Ibid., 39.

42. Quoted in ibid., 76.

43. Severino Corpus, interview by Berkeley Walker, 24 May 1937, transcript, "Racial Minority Survey," Federal Writers Project, box 142, folder 1086, Charles E. Young Research Library, University of California, Los Angeles (hereafter cited as FWP).

44. Constantino, "Miseducation of the Filipino," 2.

45. C. L. R. James, *Beyond a Boundary* (London: Paul, 1963; reprint, Durham, N.C.: Duke University Press, 1993), 70, 66.

46. See, for example, Rafael, "White Love."

47. Bromberg, *Boxing's Unforgettable Fights*, 132.

48. Mills, "Filipino Boxing Invasion Coming," 17.

49. *Philippines Review* (Los Angeles), 31 October 1935.

50. *Philippines Herald Tribune* (Los Angeles), 28 April 1936.

51. *Associated Filipino Press* (Los Angeles), 9 December 1939.

52. *Philippines Review* (Los Angeles), 28 September 1935.

53. Vinassa, "Brown Bomber in Miniature," 24–25.

54. Mark H. Haller, "Policy Gambling, Entertainment, and the Emergence of Black Politics: Chicago from 1900 to 1940," *Journal of Social History* 24, no. 3 (1991): 719–39. See also Ivan Light, "Numbers Gambling Among Blacks: A Financial Institution," *American Sociological Review* 42, no. 6 (1977): 892–904. On support from numbers businessmen for the Negro Leagues, see Rob Ruck, *Sandlot Seasons: Sport in Black Pittsburgh* (Urbana: University of Illinois Press, 1987).

55. A manslaughter conviction resulting from a barroom fight cut Blackburn's career in 1909. Before working for Roxborough and Black, he trained boxers for Max Hoff, a prominent Philadelphia gambling hall owner and bootlegger. See Gerald Astor, "... And a Credit to His Race": The Hard Life and Times of Joseph Louis Barrow, a.k.a. Joe Louis* (New York: Saturday Review Press/Dutton, 1974), esp. 32–42. See also Haller, "Policy Gambling."

56. *Associated Filipino Press* (Los Angeles), 15 February 1939 (emphasis in original), 9 December 1939.

57. Henry Armstrong, *Gloves, Glory, and God: An Autobiography* (Westwood, N.J.: Revell , 1956), 119.

58. Guido L. Geilfuss, "Sports and Recreation," folder 722, folio no. 3 (April 1940–March 1941), FWP. On boxing and the negotiation of Mexican and Mexican American ethnic identity in Los Angeles, see Gregory S. Rodríguez, "'Palaces of Pain'—Arenas of Mexican-American Dreams: Boxing and the Formation of Ethnic Mexican Identities in Twentieth-Century Los Angeles" (Ph.D. diss., University of California, San Diego, 1999). On Japanese pugilists, including those in Los Angeles, see Joseph R. Svinth, "Combative Sports and Muscular Theater: Judo, Boxing, and Freestyle Wrestling," in *More than a Game: Sport in the Japanese American Community*, ed. Brian Niiya (Los Angeles: Japanese American National Museum, 2000), 124–37.

59. While the vast majority of Filipino boxers fought in the lighter weight classes, Ceferino Garcia was the exception, winning his title in the middleweight division. He initially fought in the lighter weight divisions, and to qualify for the middleweight rating, he had to undergo a strict regimen that included building up bulk.

60. *Knockout*, 22 April 1939.

61. On the succession of ethnic groups, see S. Kirson Weinberg and Henry Avond, "The Occupational Culture of the Boxer," *American Journal of Sociology* 57, no. 4 (1952): 460–69. See also Steven A. Riess, "Sport and the American Dream: A Review Essay," *Journal of Social History* 14, no. 2 (1980): 294–303. On the life and career of Jack Johnson, see *Unforgivable Blackness: The Rise and Fall of Jack Johnson*, dir. Ken Burns, 4 hours, Florentine Films/PBS, 2004, DVD.

62. Wally Jones and Jim Washington, *Black Champions Challenge American Sports* (New York: McKay, 1972). On Joe Louis, see his autobiography, *My Life Story*, 2d ed. (New York: Duell, Sloan and Pearce, 1947), and Astor, *". . . And a Credit to His Race."* On Henry Armstrong, see his autobiography, *Gloves, Glory, and God*.

63. Fleischer, "Louis Tops for 1939." Garcia was inducted into the Ring Magazine Hall of Fame in 1977 and into the World Boxing Hall of Fame in 1981.

64. Baseball had emerged as the "national pastime" by the early twentieth century. The tremendous surge in professional sports developed between 1909 and 1929, when attendance in baseball games grew by 330 percent and its profit margin increased by 1,130 percent, while attendance at boxing matches rose by 1,750 percent and its profitability by 6,645 percent. See Jack Kofoed, "A Dirge for Baseball," *North American Review*, July 1929, 107.

65. *Ring*, April 1925, 41.

66. Van Court, *Making of Champions in California*, 153.

67. Geilfuss, "Sports and Recreation," FWP.

68. Robert Lipsyte, *SportsWorld: An American Dreamland* (New York: Quadrangle Books, 1975), 217.

69. Sammons, *Beyond the Ring*; Ruck, *Sandlot Seasons*.

70. Astor, *". . . And a Credit to His Race,"* 55–57.

71. Sammons, *Beyond the Ring*, 40, esp. chap. 2.

72. Burns, *Unforgivable Blackness*. On Jack Johnson and issues of masculinity in Victorian culture, see Gail Bederman, *Manliness and Civilization: A Cultural History of Gender and Race in the United States, 1880–1917* (Urbana: University of Illinois Press, 1996), esp. chap. 2.

73. Sammons, *Beyond the Ring*.

74. Van Court, *Making of Champions in California*, 5–16; Geilfuss, "Sport and Recreation," FWP.

75. A. D. Phillips, "Boxing Commissions at Fault, Failure to Set Aside Jealousies and Respect Each Other's Ruling a Tremendous Detriment to the Game," *Ring*, January 1925, 21.

76. On gamblers and organized crime in prizefighting, see Steven A. Riess, "Only the Ring Was Square: Frankie Carbo and the Underworld Control of American Boxing," *International Journal of the History of Sport* 5, no. 1 (1988): 29–52.

77. Budd Schulberg, "Champions for Sale: The Mike Jacobs Story," *Collier's*, 22 April 1950, 84. For an alternate appraisal of the career of "Big Tim" Sullivan and his support of human rights issues for the poor, working class, immigrants, and women, see Dan-

iel Czitrom, "Underworld and Underdogs: Tim Sullivan and Metropolitan Politics in New York, 1889–1913," *Journal of American History* 78, no. 2 (1991): 536–58.

78. The categories were established by the author. Calculated from data in "Application for [Boxing] Licenses, 1935," Records of the California State Athletic Commission, California State Archives, Sacramento.

79. Riess, "Sport and the American Dream," 295–96.

80. Louis, *My Life Story*; Armstrong, *Gloves, Glory, and God*.

81. Kevin White, *The First Sexual Revolution: The Emergence of Male Heterosexuality in Modern America* (New York: New York University Press, 1993). On sport and middle-class masculinity, see Steven A. Riess, "Sport and the Redefinition of American Masculinity," *International Journal of the History of Sport* 8, no. 1 (1991): 5–27.

82. Sammons, *Beyond the Ring*, 45.

83. Leonard defended his title fourteen times before joining the U.S. Merchant Marine in 1917. See Lionel Koppman and Bernard Postal, *Guess Who's Jewish in American History*, 2d ed. (New York: Steimatzky, 1986), 242–43.

84. Peter Levine, *Ellis Island to Ebbets Field: Sport and the American Jewish Experience* (New York: Oxford University Press, 1992).

85. On Pancho Villa, see Bromberg, *Boxing's Unforgettable Fights*, 132–34; "Villa's Rise Meteoric," *New York Times*, 19 June 1923; John L. (Ike) Dorgan, "Grim Reaper Removes Two Fistic Stars," *Ring*, September 1925, 8–9; and Ed Hughes, "We Mourn His Loss," *Ring*, September 1925. On Ceferino Garcia, see Vinassa, "Brown Bomber in Miniature." On peasant uprisings over land beginning in the Spanish period of colonization, see Reynaldo C. Ileto, *Pasyon and Revolution: Popular Movements in the Philippines, 1840–1910*, 3d ed. (Quezon City, Philippines: Ateneo de Manila University Press, 1989).

86. Kristin L. Hoganson, *Fighting for American Manhood: How Gender Politics Provoked the Spanish-American and Philippine-American Wars* (New Haven, Conn.: Yale University Press, 1998).

87. Ibid., 148.

88. Quoted in Stanley Karnow, *In Our Image: America's Empire in the Philippines* (New York: Ballantine Books, 1989), 204.

89. James, *Beyond a Boundary*. See also Robert Lipsyte, "Introduction to the American Edition," in James, *Beyond a Boundary*, xiii.

90. Bederman, *Manliness and Civilization*, 19.

91. Harry Carr, *Los Angeles: City of Dreams* (New York: Appleton-Century, 1935), 244.

92. *New York Times*, 3 October 1939.

93. George Chauncey, *Gay New York: Gender, Urban Culture, and the Making of the Gay Male World, 1890–1940* (New York: Basic Books, 1994), 80. On sexuality and performance among contemporary Filipino immigrants in New York, see Martin F. Manalansan IV, *Global Divas: Filipino Gay Men in the Diaspora* (Durham, N.C.: Duke University Press, 2003).

94. *Philippine Enterprise* (Sacramento, Calif.), 6 December 1935, 23 December 1935.

95. George Foster, *New York in Slices* (New York, 1849), 47, quoted in Richard B. Stott, *Workers in the Metropolis: Class, Ethnicity, and Youth in Antebellum New York City* (Ithaca, N.Y.: Cornell University Press, 1990), 234.

96. Calculated from data in "Application for [Boxing] Licenses, 1935," "Application for [Boxing] Licenses, 1936," and "Application for [Boxing] Licenses, 1938," Records of the California State Athletic Commission, California State Archives, Sacramento.

97. Harrison Martland, "Punch-Drunk," *Journal of the American Medical Association* 91 (1928): 1103–7.

98. Edward J. Carroll Jr., "Punch-Drunk," *American Journal of the Medical Sciences*, May 1936, 706–12.

99. "Punchy: Prize-Fighters Walk on Their Heels After Getting Numerous Hooks to Chin," *Literary Digest*, 10 April 1937, 40; Burrill, *Who's Who in Boxing*, 203.

100. Sammons, *Beyond the Ring*.

101. Arthur Mann, "The Prize-Fighting Racket," *American Mercury*, August 1934, 412.

102. Jimmy Johnston, quoted in "Punchy," 40.

103. See, for example, J. S. Butterworth and Charles A. Poindexter, "An Electrocardiographic Study of the Effects of Boxing," *American Heart Journal* 23 (1942).

104. Mann, "Prize-Fighting Racket," 414. For a more comprehensive description of the "drying out" process and other strategies for boxers to qualify in the desired weight category, see, for example, Jimmy De Forest, "How to Control Weight," *Ring*, February 1925.

105. James Gillis, in *Catholic World*, September 1927, 837.

106. James Gillis, "Prize Fighting," *Catholic World*, July 1924, 553.

107. Phyllis Palmer, *Domesticity and Dirt: Housewives and Domestic Servants in the United States, 1920–1945* (Philadelphia: Temple University Press, 1989), 82.

108. Works Progress Administration, "Southern California Factbook," box 24, folder 722, FWP.

109. Marino F. Guiang, interview by Dorothy Cordova, 24 September 1976, interview FIL-KNG 76-52d, transcript, Washington State Oral/Aural History Program, Olympia.

110. *Philippine Enterprise* (Sacramento, Calif.), 18 November 1935.

111. Felix Pascua, Johnny Rallonza, and Toribio Castillo, group interview by author, 12 April 1992, Los Angeles, Calif.

112. Armstrong, *Gloves, Glory, and God*, 139.

113. Ibid., 78.

114. Roland Barthes, "The World of Wrestling," in *Mythologies*, trans. Annette Lavers (New York: Hill and Wang, 1976), 16.

115. *Three Stars* (Stockton, Calif.), 1 July 1929.

116. *Philippine Examiner* (Stockton, Calif.), 30 July 1935.

117. Armstrong, *Gloves, Glory, and God*, 154.

118. Ibid., 155.

119. *Philippine Examiner* (Stockton, Calif.), 30 July 1935.

120. *Philippine Examiner* (Stockton, Calif.), 30 July 1937.

121. Hilado, in *Great Pinoy Boxing Era*.

122. Interview by James Earl Wood, n.d. (but definitely in the 1930s, when Wood conducted his fieldwork), James Earl Wood Papers, Bancroft Library, University of California, Berkeley.

123. Pancho Villa, "My Hardest Fight" *Ring* (April 1925): 16.

124. *New York Times*, 24 December 1939.

125. Bacho, "Manong's Heart," 110.

126. Sammy Escalona, interview by author, 3 January 1993, Stockton, Calif.

127. Maya Angelou, *I Know Why the Caged Bird Sings* (New York: Bantam Books, 1971).

128. See, for example, Burrill, *Who's Who in Boxing*, 194, and Johnston, *Ten—And Out!* 374.

129. Bromberg, *Boxing's Unforgettable Fights*, 133; Dorgan, "Grim Reaper Removes Two Fistic Stars."

130. Pasquil, "Filipino Boxers Make History in America."

4. "White Trash" and "Brown Hordes"

1. *Philippines Review* (Los Angeles), 31 October 1935.

2. R. K., an "American girl," interview by Emory S. Bogardus, in "American Attitudes Towards Filipinos," *Sociology and Social Research* 14, no. 1 (1929): 68.

3. Paul Cressy, *The Taxi-Dance Hall: A Sociological Study in Commercialized Recreation and City Life* (New York: Greenwood Press, 1932). For an analysis of Cressy's work on taxi dance halls and Filipino ethnic identity in Chicago in the 1920s and 1930s, see Kimberly Alidio, "Between Civilizing Mission and Ethnic Assimilation: Racial Discourse, U.S. Colonial Education and Filipino Ethnicity, 1901–1946" (Ph.D. diss., University of Michigan, 2001), chap. 4. On the term "white trash" and how Californians applied it to southwestern migrants streaming in to the state, especially during the 1930s, see James N. Gregory, *American Exodus: The Bowl Migration and Okie Culture in California* (New York: Oxford University Press, 1989).

4. Alida C. Bowler, "Social Hygiene in Racial Problems—The Filipino," *Journal of Social Hygiene* 18, no. 8 (1932): 454.

5. California Department of Industrial Relations, *Facts About Filipino Immigration* (1930; reprint, San Francisco: R and E Research Associates, 1972).

6. Severino F. Corpus, "An Analysis of the Racial Adjustment Activities and Problems of the Filipino-American Christian Fellowship in Los Angeles" (master's thesis, University of Southern California, 1938), 3. All figures related to Filipinos are estimates, since the vast majority of them were migratory laborers.

7. Gregory, *American Exodus*, 39–40.

8. Annie Malbeuf, interview by Garnette Malbeuf Long, in "A Dust Bowl Perspective," *American Papers* 12 (1992): 7.

9. Quoted in Walter J. Stein, *California and the Dust Bowl Migration* (Westport,

Conn.: Greenwood Press, 1973), 19. On the drought and other disasters in Oklahoma and Kansas, see also Donald Worster, *Dust Bowl: The Southern Plains in the 1930s* (New York: Oxford University Press, 1979).

10. United States Farm Placement Services, "Report of People Who Have Entered California from Drought States Seeking Employment," Federal Writers' Project, Bancroft Library, University of California, Berkeley.

11. Richard Lowitt, *The New Deal and the West* (Bloomington: Indiana University Press, 1984), 179.

12. State Relief Administration of California, Division of Special Surveys and Studies, *Transients in California* (Sacramento: State of California, 1936), 249–56.

13. John N. Webb, *The Transient Unemployed*, Publication of Works Progress Administration, Division of Social Research (Washington, D.C.: Government Printing Office, 1935), 124.

14. *New York Times*, 9 July 1937.

15. Stein, *California and the Dust Bowl Migration*, 44, chap. 3.

16. Ibid., 151–52.

17. Jean Heff Rallonza, interview by author, 23 April 1992, Downey, Calif.

18. Mary Odem, "Single Mothers, Delinquent Daughters, and the Juvenile Court in Early 20th Century Los Angeles," *Journal of Social History* 25, no. 1 (1991): 27–43. See also Janis Appier, *Policing Women: The Sexual Politics of Law Enforcement and the LAPD* (Philadelphia: Temple University Press, 1998), and Kathy Peiss, *Cheap Amusements: Working Women and Leisure in Turn-of-the-Century New York* (Philadelphia: Temple University Press, 1986).

19. D. F. Gonzalo, "Social Adjustment of Filipinos," *Sociology and Social Research* 14, no. 2 (1929): 171–72.

20. Miguel Lawagan, interview by author, 26 June 1993, San Francisco, Calif.

21. Sammy Escalona, interview by author, 2 January 1993, Stockton, Calif.

22. Leo Escalona, interview by author, 26 June 1993, San Francisco, Calif.

23. Interview by James Earl Wood, n.d. (but definitely in the 1930s, when Wood conducted his fieldwork), James Earl Wood Papers, Bancroft Library, University of California, Berkeley.

24. Robin D. G. Kelley touches on these themes in relation to leisure activities of African Americans in "'We Are Not What We Seem': Rethinking Black Working-Class Opposition in the Jim Crow South," *Journal of American History* 80, no. 1 (1993): 75–112.

25. Chris B. Millado, *peregriNasyon* (Is America in the Heart?) (performance at the Center for the Arts Forum, San Francisco, 27 August 1994).

26. Marcos P. Berbano, "The Social Status of the Filipino in Los Angeles County" (master's thesis, University of Southern California, 1930), 46.

27. Romero Alin, interview by Dorothy Cordova and Fred Cordova, 12 May 1976, Seattle, Wash., interview FIL-KNG 76-46dc, transcript, Washington State Oral/Aural History Program, Olympia (hereafter cited as WSOAHP).

28. Toribio Castillo, interview by author, 1 March 1992, Los Angeles, Calif. By 1938,

the Vincent Bello Smart Tailoring Shop had moved to 238 East Second Street. See Corpus, "Analysis of the Racial Adjustment Activities and Problems of the Filipino-American Christian Fellowship in Los Angeles," 67.

29. Felix Pascua, interview by author, 21 May 1995, Los Angeles, Calif.

30. *Philippines Review* (Los Angeles), 6 April 1935.

31. *Ang Bantay (The Guardian)* (Los Angeles), 7 December 1929.

32. *Three Stars* (Stockton, Calif.), 1 August 1929.

33. Benecio T. Catapusan, "The Filipino Occupational and Recreational Activities in Los Angeles" (master's thesis, University of Southern California, 1934), 13.

34. Ibid., 18.

35. Ibid., 67.

36. Benecio T. Catapusan, "The Social Adjustment of Filipinos in the United States" (Ph.D. diss., University of Southern California, 1940).

37. On the "lucky number" and "lucky door ticket," see Benecio T. Catapusan, "Leisure Time Problems of Filipino Immigrants," *Sociology and Social Research* 24, no. 2 (1940): 548.

38. *Philippines Review* (Los Angeles), 31 December 1936.

39. *Philippines Review* (Los Angeles), 13 November 1935.

40. Catapusan, "Leisure Time Problems," 548.

41. *Associated Filipino Press* (Los Angeles), 24 April 1938, 8.

42. Interview, in *Voices: A Filipino-American Oral History*, ed. Joan May T. Cordova and Alexis S. Canillo (Santa Rosa, Calif.: Northwestern Graphics, 1984).

43. Johnny Garcia, interview by Lundy, 18 January 1937, transcript, "Racial Minority Survey: Filipinos," Federal Writers' Project, box 142, folder 1086, Charles E. Young Research Library, University of California, Los Angeles (hereafter cited as FWP).

44. Carey McWilliams, *Brothers Under the Skin* (1942; reprint, Boston: Little, Brown, 1964), 238.

45. Felix Pascua, interview in Dante Ochoa, "Little Manila Revisited," *Philippine Beat Magazine*, January–February 1989, 15.

46. Frank Coloma, interview in Roberto V. Vallangca, *Pinoy: The First Wave* (San Francisco: Strawberry Hill Press, 1977), 96.

47. Lawagan interview.

48. On Mexican immigrants and dance halls in La Placita, see George J. Sánchez, *Becoming Mexican American: Ethnicity, Culture, and Identity in Chicano Los Angeles, 1900–1945* (New York: Oxford University Press, 1993), esp. chap. 8.

49. Clyde Bennett Vedder, "An Analysis of the Taxi-Dance Hall as a Social Institution, with Special Reference to Los Angeles and Detroit" (Ph.D. diss., University of Southern California, 1947), 183.

50. Stanley Garribay and Severino F. Corpus collected the slang terms among Filipinos in Los Angeles in the 1930s. See the list in Corpus, "Analysis of the Racial Adjustment Activities and Problems of the Filipino-American Christian Fellowship in Los Angeles," 26–27.

51. Edwin B. Almirol, "Rights and Obligations in Filipino American Families" *Journal of Comparative Family Studies* 13, no. 3 (1982): 297–98.

52. Conflicts were also common between Filipino and white ethnic patrons of Chicago's taxi dance halls. See Cressy, *Taxi-Dance Hall*, esp. chap. 10.

53. Sammy R. Lopez, interview by Cynthia Mejia, 24 November 1975, interview FIL-KNG 75-36cm, transcript, WSOAHP.

54. Luis Felipe Recinos, "Observaciones—Los Salones de Baile," Los Angeles, 15 April 1927, Manuel Gamio Papers, Bancroft Library, University of California, Berkeley. See also Sánchez, *Becoming Mexican American*, 171–72.

55. Coloma interview, in Vallangca, *Pinoy*, 87.

56. Richard Hallburton, "Half a Mile of History," *Readers Digest*, October 1937, 70–75.

57. Quoted in Adelaida Castillo-Tsuchida, "Filipino Migrants in San Diego, 1900–1946" (master's thesis, University of San Diego, 1979), 52.

58. See, for example, Neil Larry Shumsky, "Tacit Acceptance: Respectable Americans and Segregated Prostitution, 1870–1910," *Journal of Social History* 19, no. 4 (1986): 664–79.

59. Thomas Allen McDannold, "Development of the Los Angeles Chinatown, 1850–1970" (master's thesis, California State University, Northridge, 1973). See also Donald Teruo Hata Jr. and Nadine Ishitani Hata, "Asian-Pacific Angelinos: Model Minorities and Indispensable Scapegoats," in *Twentieth-Century Los Angeles: Power, Promotion, and Social Conflict*, ed. Norman M. Klein and Martin J. Schiesl (Claremont, Calif.: Regina Books, 1991), 61–99, and Shumsky, "Tacit Acceptance."

60. Carlos Bulosan, *America Is in the Heart: A Personal History* (New York: Harcourt, Brace, 1946; reprint, Seattle: University of Washington Press, 1973), 134.

61. Los Angeles Police Department, *Annual Report of the Los Angeles Police Department, 1936–37*, and *Annual Report of the Los Angeles Police Department, 1937–38*, Los Angeles Public Library, Central Branch, Los Angeles, Calif.

62. Honorante Mariano, "The Filipino Immigrants in the U.S." (master's thesis, University of Oregon, 1933).

63. Manuel Buaken, *I Have Lived with the American People* (Caldwell, Idaho: Caxton Printers, 1948), 89.

64. The phrase comes from Sidney L. Harring, *Policing a Class Society: The Experience of American Cities, 1865–1915* (New Brunswick, N.J.: Rutgers University Press, 1983), chap. 8. The literature on nineteenth-century reform organizations and the working class is extensive. Some useful references to consult before delving into the subject include Karen J. Blair, *The History of American Women's Voluntary Organizations, 1810–1960* (Boston: Hall, 1989), and Ronald G. Walters, *American Reformers, 1815–1860* (New York: Hill and Wang, 1978).

65. Paul Popenoe, "How Can Young People Get Acquainted?" *Journal of Social Hygiene* 18, no. 4 (1932): 218–19.

66. Maria Ward Lambin, "This Business of Dancing," *Survey*, 15 July 1924, 459. See also Ella Gardner, "Dance Hall Dangers," *Woman's Journal*, April 1930, 10–11,

41–42, and Gregory Mason, "Satan in the Dance-Hall," *American Mercury*, June 1924, 177–82.

67. Appier, *Policing Women*, 98–100.

68. Headlines quoted in Roger Daniels and Harry H. L. Kitano, *American Racism: Exploration of the Nature of Prejudice* (Englewood Cliffs, N.J.: Prentice Hall, 1970), 67.

69. Quoted in Ronald Takaki, *Strangers from a Different Shore: A History of Asian Americans* (Boston: Little, Brown, 1989), 329.

70. Gregory, *American Exodus*, esp., 104–8.

71. Interview by James Earl Wood, n.d. (but definitely in the 1930s, when Wood conducted his fieldwork), Wood Papers, folder 9.

72. The literature on the New Deal is extensive. Classic texts include William E. Leuchtenburg, *Franklin D. Roosevelt and the New Deal, 1932–1940* (New York: Harper & Row, 1963), and Paul K. Conkin, *The New Deal* (New York: Crowell, 1967). For New Left perspectives, see, for example, Barton J. Bernstein, "The New Deal: The Conservative Achievements of Liberal Reform," in *Past Imperfect: Alternative Essays in American History*, ed. Blanche Wiesen Cook, Alice Kessler Harris, and Ronald Radosh (New York: Knopf, 1973), 2:159–75, and Frank Freidel, "The New Deal in Historical Perspective," in *Twentieth-Century America: Recent Interpretations*, ed. Barton J. Bernstein and Allen J. Matusow (New York: Harcourt, Brace & World, 1969), 246–82. On women and the New Deal, see Susan Ware, *Beyond Suffrage: Women in the New Deal* (Cambridge, Mass.: Harvard University Press, 1981), and Lois Scharf, *To Work and to Wed: Female Employment, Feminism, and the Great Depression* (Westport, Conn.: Greenwood Press, 1980). On New Deal programs and the working class, see Lizabeth Cohen, *Making a New Deal: Industrial Workers in Chicago, 1919–1939* (Cambridge: Cambridge University Press, 1990). For regional aspects and effects of the New Deal, see Lowitt, *New Deal and the West*. For discussions of New Deal policies and their disintegration in the Ronald Reagan years, see Steve Fraser and Gary Gerstle, eds., *The Rise and Fall of the New Deal Order, 1930–1980* (Princeton, N.J.: Princeton University Press, 1989).

73. Edward A. Williams, *Work, Relief, and Security*, Publication of Works Progress Administration, Social Problems Series (Washington, D.C.: Government Printing Office, 1941): 13.

74. Eric H. Thomson, "Why Plan Security for the Migratory Laborer?" (paper for "Conference of Social Work," San José, Calif., 12 May 1937), Federal Writers' Project, Bancroft Library, University of California, Berkeley.

75. Casiano Coloma, "A Study of the Filipino Repatriation Movement" (master's thesis, University of Southern California, 1939).

76. Benecio T. Catapusan, "Filipino Immigrants and Public Relief in the United States," *Sociology and Social Research* 23, no. 4 (1939): 546–54.

77. Scharf, *To Work and to Wed*. On gender and welfare policies in general, see Dorothy C. Miller, *Women and Social Welfare: A Feminist Analysis* (New York: Praeger, 1990).

78. Scharf, *To Work and to Wed*, 115, esp. chap. 6. See also Dolores Janiewski, "Flawed Victories: The Experiences of Black and White Women Workers in Durham During the 1930s," in *Decades of Discontent: The Women's Movement, 1920–1940*, ed. Lois Scharf and Joan M. Jensen (Westport, Conn.: Greenwood Press, 1983), 85–109.

79. Mrs. F. Marcuello, interview by James Earl Wood, 6 February 1930, transcript, Wood Papers.

80. Cressy, *Taxi-Dance Hall*, 12.

81. Odem, "Single Mothers," 30. See also Winifred D. Wandersee, "The Economics of Middle-Income Family Life: Working Women During the Great Depression," in *Decades of Discontent*, ed. Scharf and Jensen, 45–58. On women and retail jobs, see Susan Porter Benson, *Counter Cultures: Saleswomen, Managers, and Customers in American Department Stores, 1890–1940* (Urbana: University of Illinois Press, 1988).

82. Louis B. Perry and Richard S. Perry, *A History of the Los Angeles Labor Movement, 1911–1941* (Berkeley: University of California Press, 1963), 237–317; Rose Pesotta, *Bread upon the Waters* (New York: Dodd, Mead, 1944); Rosalinda M. Gonzalez, "Chicanas and Mexican Immigrant Families, 1920–1940: Women's Subordination and Family Exploitation," in *Decades of Discontent*, ed. Scharf and Jensen, 59–84; Odem, "Single Mothers." See also Sánchez, *Becoming Mexican American*, chap. 11.

83. See, for example, Vicki Ruiz, *Cannery Women/Cannery Lives: Mexican Women, Unionization, and the California Food Processing Industry, 1930–1950* (Albuquerque: University of New Mexico Press, 1987).

84. Interview, in Vedder, "Analysis of the Taxi Dance Hall," 133.

85. Juana Martinez, interview by Luis Felipe Recinos, 6 April 1927, transcript, Gamio Papers.

86. Vedder, "Analysis of the Taxi Dance Hall," 70.

87. Herminia Meñez and Helen Brown, "Pioneer Filipino Musicians" (manuscript, photocopy, in author's possession).

88. Robert Park Antolin, "Sweet Music," in *Turning Shadows into Light: Art and Culture of the Northwest's Early Asian/Pacific Community*, ed. Mayumi Tsutakawa and Alan Chong Lau (Seattle: Young Pine Press/Asian Multi-Media Center, 1982), 60. On Filipino musicians, see also Fred Cordova, *Filipinos: Forgotten Asian Americans*, ed. Dorothy Cordova (Seattle: Demonstration Project for Asian Americans, 1983), 89–92.

89. Recinos, "Observaciones," Gamio Papers.

90. *Filipino Observer-Spokesman* (Los Angeles), 30 October 1935.

91. Carlos Malla, n.d., interview PNW 81-Fil-005ba, transcript, Filipino American National Historical Society, Seattle, Wash.

92. Antonio Cabanag, interview by author, 26 June 1993, San Francisco, Calif.

93. Cressy, *Taxi-Dance Hall*, 73.

94. Martinez interview, Gamio Papers.

95. Interview, in Cressy, *Taxi-Dance Hall*, 88. "Wanda" eventually married a Filipino she met at the taxi dance hall.

96. Gloria Navas, interview by Luis Felipe Recinos, 16 April 1927, transcript, Gamio Papers.

97. Quoted in Jane Logan, *Chicago Daily Times*, 1 February 1930.

98. Bowler, "Social Hygiene in Racial Problems," 455.

99. Mason, "Satan in the Dance-Hall," 178.

100. Recinos, "Observaciones," Gamio Papers.

101. See the list of slang words in Corpus, "Analysis of the Racial Adjustment Activities and Problems of the Filipino-American Christian Fellowship in Los Angeles," 26–27.

102. Ibid.

103. See, for example, the collection of essays in Elliott West and Paula Petrik, eds., *Small Worlds: Children and Adolescents in America, 1850–1950* (Lawrence: University Press of Kansas, 1992).

104. Stan Singer, "Vaudeville in Los Angeles, 1910–1926: Theaters, Management, and the Orpheum," *Pacific Historical Review* 61, no. 1 (1992): 103–13.

105. Kelley, "'We Are Not What We Seem,'" 84–85.

106. Severino Corpus, interview by Berkley Walker, 24 May 1937, transcript, "Racial Minority Survey: Filipinos," FWP.

107. Ibid.

108. See, for example, Marcelino A. Foronda Jr., "Vigan: A Study of Mexican Cultural Influences in the Philippines" *Journal of Social History* (Manila, Philippines) 21, nos. 1–2 (1976): 1–12.

109. Ibid., 4. The minor influence of Spanish in the Ilocos and northern regions is mainly because very few Spaniards and Mexicans lived in these provinces. Tagalog, the dialect of Manila and its surrounding environs, contains significantly more Spanish because large populations of Spanish-speaking people settled in these areas.

110. Renato Constantino, *The Miseducation of the Filipino*, 2d ed. (Quezon City, Philippines: Foundation for Nationalist Studies, 1983), 3.

111. Interview by James Earl Wood, n.d. (but definitely in the 1930s, when Wood conducted his fieldwork), Wood Papers, folder 3.

112. On the FFA, see Steffi San Buenaventura, "Nativism and Ethnicity in a Filipino-American Experience" (Ph.D. diss., University of Hawaii, 1990).

113. *Associated Filipino Press* (Los Angeles), 15 February 1939 (emphasis in original).

114. Sigme Windam, interview by author, 17 September 1994, San Francisco, Calif.

115. Alfronso Perales Dangaran, quoted in Cordova, *Filipinos*, 215.

116. Interview by James Earl Wood, n.d. (but definitely in the 1930s, when Wood conducted his fieldwork), Wood Papers, folder 3.

117. Ibid.

118. Buaken, *I Have Lived with the American People*, 103. Amazingly, only one Filipino, Fermin Tovera, died.

119. Duncan Aikman, quoted in "Causes of California's Race Riots," *Literary Digest*, 15 February 1930, 12.

120. On subverting and inverting icons of the dominant culture, see, for example, George Lipsitz, *Time Passages: Collective Memory and American Popular Culture* (Minneapolis: University of Minnesota Press, 1990), 233–53.

121. Howard A. De Witt, *Violence in the Fields: California Farm Labor Unionization During the Great Depression* (San Francisco: R and E Research Associates, 1980).

122. David R. Roediger, *The Wages of Whiteness: Race and the Making of the American Working Class* (London: Verso, 1991), 12.

123. Ibid., 106, 107.

124. Roxanne Dunbar-Ortiz, "One or Two Things I Know About Us: 'Okies' in American Culture," *Radical History Review* 59, no. 1 (1994): 6.

125. Quoted in Vedder, "Analysis of the Taxi Dance Hall," 48.

126. Los Angeles Police Department, "Rules Governing Taxi Dance Halls, 1943," Los Angeles Public Library, Central Branch, Los Angeles, Calif.

127. Alice Wells, "Policewomen of Los Angeles, California," in *Proceedings of the National Conference of Charities and Corrections* (Chicago: Hildmann Printing, 1915), 412.

128. Ibid.

129. August Vollmer, *Police Conditions in the United States: A Report to the National Commission on Law Observance and Enforcement* (Washington, D.C.: Government Printing Office, 1931), 116. The nature of policewomen's duties and responsibilities within the LAPD, however, changed as the 1930s progressed. See Appier, *Policing Women*, esp. chap. 5.

130. Los Angeles Police Department, "Rules Governing Taxi Dance Halls, 1943."

5. The War Years

1. Carey McWilliams, *North from Mexico: The Spanish-Speaking People of the United States*, rev. ed. (New York: Greenwood press, 1990), 224. For an analysis of the disturbances that focuses on the Mexican American zoot suiters and U.S. servicemen, see Mauricio Mazón, *The Zoot-Suit Riots: The Psychology of Symbolic Annihilation* (Austin: University of Texas Press, 1984). On racism and the zoot suit riots, see Chester Himes, "Zoot Riots Are Race Riots," in *Black on Black: Baby Sister and Selected Writings* (New York: Doubleday, 1973), 220–25.

2. *Los Angeles Times*, 10 June 1943.

3. This description of the evolution of the zoot suit style is geared more toward the urban Southwest, especially Los Angeles. East Coast youths, including white middle-class teenagers in New York and, especially, working-class African Americans in Harlem, also wore the drape shape as an emblem of fashion and opposition at about this time, but variations on the complete zoot togs existed among its wearers. Among African Americans, for example, the coiffure most associated with the ensemble is the "conk," straightened (and sometimes colored) hair. See Robin D. G. Kelley, "The Riddle of the Zoot: Malcolm Little and Black Cultural Politics During World War II,"

in *Generations of Youth: Youth Cultures and History in Twentieth-Century America*, ed. Joe Austin and Michael Willard (New York: New York University Press, 1998), 136–56.

4. Stuart Cosgrove, "The Zoot-Suit and Style Warfare," *History Workshop Journal* 18 (1984): 78.

5. James Earl Wood Papers, box 1, folder 10, Bancroft Library, University of California, Berkeley.

6. Kelley, "Riddle of the Zoot," 140.

7. Lalo Guerréro, interview by author, 26 May 1995, Cathedral City, Calif.

8. Steve Chibnall, "Whistle and Zoot: The Changing Meaning of a Suit of Clothes," *History Workshop Journal* 20 (1985): 57.

9. Guerréro interview.

10. On Mexican American artists and the development of Los Angeles–based Latino music and musical styles, see George Lipsitz, *Time Passages: Collective Memory and American Popular Culture* (Minneapolis: University of Minnesota Press, 1990), 133–60, and Steven Loza, *Barrio Rhythm: Mexican American Music in Los Angeles* (Urbana: University of Illinois Press, 1993). On the African American music scene in Los Angeles, see, for example, Johnny Otis, *Upside Your Head! Rhythm and Blues on Central Avenue* (Hanover, N.H.: University Press of New England, 1993).

11. Lipsitz, *Time Passages*, 136.

12. Lizbeth Cohen, *Making a New Deal: Industrial Workers in Chicago, 1919–1939* (Cambridge: Cambridge University Press, 1990), 105. For a comparative analysis of how race, class, and age affected the laborers' experiences with mass culture, see chap. 20.

13. The Tydings-McDuffie Act of 1934, which included a provision for Philippine independence within ten years, also established an annual quota of fifty Filipino immigrants to the U.S. mainland.

14. U.S. Department of Commerce, Bureau of the Census, *Sixteenth Census of the United States, 1940* (Washington, D.C.: Government Printing Office, 1943), table 39.

15. Ibid.

16. Johnny Rallonza, telephone interview by author, 17 May 1995.

17. *Los Angeles Times*, 5 June 1943.

18. Gerald D. Nash, *The American West Transformed: The Impact of the Second World War* (Bloomington: Indiana University Press, 1985). While recognizing Nash's contributions to narratives of economic growth in the urban West, scholars argue about the extent of World War II as a force in revolutionizing the West. These scholars point out that the war only accelerated, particularly in California, economic trends that had existed since the beginning of the twentieth century. Further, some argue that Nash's hypothesis neglected the social developments, particularly ethnic popular culture, that played key roles in the transformation of the West. See, for example, the articles on the American West and World War II in *Pacific Historical Review* 63, no. 3 (1994).

19. Arthur C. Verge, "The Impact of the Second World War on Los Angeles," *Pacific Historical Review* 63, no. 3 (1994): 290, 293.

20. On the female workforce during World War II, see, for example, Sherna Berger Gluck, *Rosie the Riveter Revisited: Women, The War, and Social Change* (Boston: Twayne, 1987).

21. Lin-chi Wang, "The Politics of Assimilation and Repression," in Sucheng Chan, *Asian Americans: An Interpretive History* (Boston: Twayne, 1991), 121.

22. Lawrence Brooks de Graaf, "Negro Migration to Los Angeles, 1930–1950" (Ph. D. diss., University of California, Los Angeles, 1962). See also Lawrence B. de Graaf and Quintard Taylor, "Introduction: African Americans in California History, California in African American History," in *Seeking El Dorado: African Americans in California*, ed. Lawrence B. de Graaf, Kevin Mulroy, and Quintard Taylor (Los Angeles: Autry Museum of Western Heritage, 2001), 3–69, and Lonnie G. Bunch, "A Past Not Necessarily Prologue: The Afro-Americans in Los Angeles," in *Twentieth-Century Los Angeles: Power, Promotion, and Social Conflict*, ed. Norman M. Klein and Martin J. Schiesl (Claremont, Calif.: Regina Books, 1991), 117.

23. Marilyn Domer, "The Zoot-Suit Riot: A Culmination of Social Tensions in Los Angeles" (master's thesis, Claremont Graduate School, 1955), 27.

24. On race relations in Los Angeles during the war years, see, for example, Kevin Allen Leonard, "Years of Hope, Days of Fear: The Impact of World War II in Los Angeles" (Ph.D. diss., University of California Davis, 1992).

25. Chan, *Asian Americans*, esp. chap. 7.

26. There are a significant number of publications on Japanese and Japanese American evacuation and internment. See, for example, Greg Robinson, *By Order of the President: FDR and the Internment of Japanese Americans* (Cambridge, Mass.: Harvard University Press, 2003), and Roger Daniels, *Prisoners Without Trial: Japanese Americans in World War II* (New York: Hill and Wang, 1993), and *Concentration Camps USA: Japanese Americans and World War II* (New York: Holt, Rinehart and Winston, 1972). Several books also focus on specific internment camps. On the evacuation of Japanese Americans from Cortez, California, and their experiences in Amache, Colorado, see Valerie J. Matsumoto, *Farming the Home Place: A Japanese American Community in California, 1919–1982* (Ithaca, N.Y.: Cornell University Press, 1993). On Manzanar, located in California's Owens Valley and one of the best-known camps, see Jeanne Wakatsuki Houston and James D. Houston, *Farewell to Manzanar* (Boston: Houghton Mifflin, 1973). On oral testimonies of internees, see Arthur A. Hansen, ed., *Japanese American World War II Evacuation Oral History Project*, 4 vols. (Westport, Conn.: Meckler, 1991). Japanese and their descendents were also interned in other countries in North and South America. On Canada, see Henry Moritsugu's oral history "To Be More Japanese," in Joann Faung Jean Lee, *Asian Americans: Oral Histories of First to Fourth Generation Americans from China, the Philippines, Japan, India, the Pacific Islands, Vietnam, and Cambodia* (New York: New Press, 1992), 99–103. On Latin America, see C. Harvey Gardiner, *Pawns in a Triangle of Hate: The Peruvian Japanese and the United States* (Seattle: University of Washington Press, 1981).

27. George J. Sánchez, "'The Other Los Angeles': Chicanos, Jews, and Japanese on the Eastside, 1925–1945" (photocopy, in author's possession).

28. Quoted in Leonard, "Years of Hope, Days of Fear," 72.

29. Donald Teruo Hata Jr. and Nadine Ishitani Hata, "Asian-Pacific Angelinos: Model Minorities and Indispensable Scapegoats," in *Twentieth-Century Los Angeles*, ed. Klein and Schiesl, 61–99.

30. Lon Kurashige, *Japanese American Celebration and Conflict: A History of Ethnic Identity and Festival in Los Angeles, 1934–1990* (Berkeley: University of California Press, 2002).

31. Yuri Kochiyama, "Then Came the War," interview in Lee, *Asian Americans*, 13. See also Yuri Kochiyama, *Passing It On* (Los Angeles: UCLA Asian American Studies Center Press, 2004).

32. On the effects of World War II on ethnic relations and domestic policies in the United States, see, for example, George Lipsitz, "'Frantic to Join . . . the Japanese Army': Beyond the Black-White Binary," in *The Possessive Investment in Whiteness: How White People Profit from Identity Politics* (Philadelphia: Temple University Press, 1998), 184–210.

33. Leonard, "Years of Hope, Days of Fear," 61. See also Kevin Allen Leonard, "'In the Interest of All Races': African Americans and Interracial Cooperation in Los Angeles During and After World War II," in *Seeking El Dorado*, ed. de Graaf, Mulroy, and Taylor, 309–40.

34. Guerréro interview. On the Mexican repatriation campaigns during the Depression, see, for example, Douglas Monroy, *Rebirth: Mexican Los Angeles from the Great Migration to the Great Depression* (Berkeley: University of California Press, 1999).

35. Kochiyama, "Then Came the War," 12.

36. Mary Paik Lee, *Quiet Odyssey: The Life of a Pioneer Korean American Woman* (Seattle: University of Washington Press, 1990), 94.

37. Ibid., 95–96.

38. On other Asian groups' attempts to distance themselves from Japanese and Japanese Americans, see Yen Le Espiritu, *Asian American Panethnicity: Bridging Institutions and Identities* (Philadelphia: Temple University Press, 1992).

39. Hyung-chan Kim and Wayne Patterson, *The Koreans in America, 1882–1974*, quoted in Ronald Takaki, *Strangers from a Different Shore: A History of Asian Americans* (Boston: Little, Brown, 1989), 364.

40. Quoted in Hata and Hata, "Asian-Pacific Angelinos," 78.

41. Felix Pascua, interview by author, 30 September 1993, Los Angeles, Calif. Pascua was drafted into the U.S. Army in the midst of this campaign. The substitute pastor proceeded with the protest in accordance with Pascua's last request before leaving for boot camp. Unfortunately, nobody remembers the results.

42. Paul Valdez, interview in Roberto V. Vallangca, *Pinoy: The First Wave* (San Francisco: Strawberry Hill Press, 1977).

43. On "Oriental" as a racial category and stereotypes of certain Asian American

groups in specific historical moments, see Robert G. Lee, *Orientals: Asian Americans in Popular Culture* (Philadelphia: Temple University Press, 1999).

. 44. *Time*, 22 December 1941, 33.

45. Harold R. Isaacs, *Images of Asia: American Views of China and India*, quoted in Chan, *Asian Americans*, 121.

46. De Graaf, "Negro Migration to Los Angeles," 282–84. See also de Graaf and Taylor, "Introduction: African Americans in California History, California in African American History," 3–69, and Bunch, "Past Not Necessarily Prologue," 110–19.

47. "Remedial Measures for Minority Problems," Carey McWilliams Papers, Charles E. Young Research Library, University of California, Los Angeles. See also de Graaf, "Negro Migration to Los Angeles."

48. National Housing Authority to Izak Subcommittee, quoted in de Graaf, "Negro Migration to Los Angeles," 284.

49. On Little Tokyo, see William H. Warren, "Maps: A Spatial Approach to Japanese American Communities in Los Angeles," *Amerasia Journal* 13, no. 2 (1986–1987): 137–51.

50. R. T. Feria, "War and the Status of Filipino Immigrants," *Sociology and Social Research* 31, no. 2 (1946): 49.

51. *Associated Filipino Press* (Los Angeles), 25 July 1945.

52. McWilliams, *North from Mexico*, 206–11. See also Sleepy Lagoon Defense Committee, *The Sleepy Lagoon Case* (Hollywood, Calif.: Mercury Printing, 1943).

53. Bill Henry, in *Los Angeles Times*, n.d., McWilliams Papers.

54. Lorenzo U. Pimentel, interview by Cynthia Mejia, 14 November 1975, interview FIL-KNG 75-34cm, transcript, Washington State Oral/Aural History Program, Washington State Archives, Olympia (hereafter cited as WSOAHP).

55. Manuel Buaken, "Our Fighting Love of Freedom," *Asia and the Americas*, June 1943, 357. Filipino civilians in the United States were not granted citizenship until after the war, in 1946, when the Philippines gained its independence.

56. Attorney General Robert W. Kenney to District Attorney John P. Fitzgerald, n.d., reprinted in *Filipino Echo* (Calexico, Calif.), May 1943.

57. Feria, "War and the Status of Filipino Immigrants."

58. Toribio Castillo, interview by author, 1 March 1992, Los Angeles, Calif. Castillo eventually bought his own land and continued farming until he retired in 1975.

59. Bienvenido N. Santos, "Filipinos in War," *Far Eastern Survey* 11, no. 24 (1942): 249–50.

60. Takaki, *Strangers from a Different Shore*, 359.

61. Fred Cordova, *Filipinos: Forgotten Asian Americans*, ed. Dorothy Cordova (Seattle, Wash.: Demonstration Project for Asian Americans, 1983), 217–18. See also James G. Wingo, "The First Filipino Regiment," *Asia*, October 1942, 562–63.

62. Vincent Mendoza, interview by Cynthia Mendoza, 13 January 1976, interview FIL-KNG 76-40cm, transcript, WSOAHP.

63. Mariano Angeles, interview by Cynthia Mejia, 6 November 1975, interview

FIL-KNG 75-32cm, transcript, WSOAHP. Angeles eventually applied for citizenship before he was discharged from the army so he could bring his family to the United States.

64. A. B. Santos, "We Have to Show the Americans that We Can Be as Good as Anybody," interview in Yen Le Espiritu, *Filipino American Lives* (Philadelphia: Temple University Press, 1995), 42.

65. Manuel Buaken, "Life in the Armed Forces," *New Republic*, 30 August 1943, 280.

66. Miguel Lawagan, interview by author, 26 June 1993, San Francisco, Calif.

67. Quoted in Buaken, "Our Fighting Love of Freedom," 357.

68. Buaken, "Life in the Armed Forces," 280.

69. The description of the uniform comes from Buaken, "Our Fighting Love of Freedom," 357.

70. Cordova, *Filipinos*, 218.

71. Quentin A. Ramil, "The Eagle—A Symbol of Democracy," *Associated Filipino Press* (Los Angeles), 4 August 1944.

72. *Associated Filipino Press* (Los Angeles), 11 August 1944.

73. Buaken, "Life in the Armed Forces," 280.

74. Casiano P. Coloma, "A Study of the Filipino Repatriation Movement" (master's thesis, University of Southern California, 1939).

75. Pimentel interview, FIL-KNG 75-34cm, transcript, WSOAHP.

76. Quoted in Wingo, "First Filipino Regiment," 562. On Filipino laborers, inter-ethnic conflicts, and unionization efforts in the Pullman Company, see Barbara M. Posadas, "Ethnic Life and Labor in Chicago's Pre–World War II Filipino Community," in *Labor Divided: Race and Ethnicity in United States Labor Struggles, 1835–1960*, ed. Robert Asher and Charles Stephenson (Albany: State University of New York Press, 1990), 63–80.

77. Martin H. Neumeyer, "Wartime Trends in Recreation," *Sociology and Social Research* 27, no. 5 (1944): 362.

78. Joe Morella, Edward Z. Epstein, and John Griggs, *The Films of World War II* (Secaucus, N.J.: Citadel Press, 1973), 13.

79. Constance Chandler, "Recreation Among Women War Workers: A Study in San Bernardino," *Sociology and Social Research* 27, no. 1 (1943): 30–36.

80. Morella, Epstein, and Griggs, *Films of World War II*, 16.

81. The last motion picture that focuses on the war in the Philippines is Twentieth Century Fox's *American Guerrilla in the Philippines*, released in 1950. It was shot on location in postwar Luzon. The film, featuring more than a thousand Filipino extras, with fifty-five Filipinos in speaking roles, stars Tyrone Power as a PT boat officer who joins a band of Filipino guerrillas led by Juan Torena after the Japanese destroy his vessel. Torena, a Filipino American actor, returned to the Philippines after a twenty-six-year absence in order to play the part.

82. *Bataan*, prod. Irving Starr, dir. Tay Garnett, original screenplay by Robert D. Andres, 114 min., Metro-Goldwyn-Mayer, 1943.

83. Quoted in Clayton R. Koppes and Gregory D. Black, *Hollywood Goes to War:*

How Politics, Profits, and Propaganda Shaped World War II (Berkeley: University of California Press, 1990), 258.

84. Kathryn Kane, *Visions of War: Hollywood Combat Films of World War II* (Ann Arbor, Mich.: UMI Research Press, 1982), 72.

85. Dana Polan, *Power and Paranoia: History, Narrative, and the American Cinema, 1940–1950* (New York: Columbia University Press, 1986), 47.

86. *Back to Bataan*, prod. Robert Fellows, dir. Edward Dmytryk, screenplay by Ben Barzman and Richard H. Landau, based on an original story by Aeneas MacKenzie and William Gordon, 98 minutes, RKO Radio Pictures, 1945.

87. Ibid.

88. Ibid.

89. Edward Dmytryk, *It's a Hell of a Life but Not a Bad Living* (New York: Times Books, 1978), 66.

90. The Katipunan was a secret society organized and led by Andres Bonifacio around 1892 to fight against the Spanish. See Reynaldo C. Ileto, *Pasyon and Revolution: Popular Movements in the Philippines, 1840–1910*, 3d ed. (Quezon City, Philippines: Ateneo de Manila University Press, 1989), and Renato Constantino, *The Philippines: A Past Revisited*, 14th ed. (Quezon City, Philippines: Foundation for Nationalist Studies, 1993).

91. Ben Barzman, "The Duke and Me," *Los Angeles Magazine*, January 1989, 6.

92. *Associated Filipino Press* (Los Angeles) 19 January 1945.

93. Quoted in *Nation*, 28 July 1945, 71. On hostilities directed against Filipino workers in the post–World War II years, see Arleen Garcia de Vera, "An Unfinished Agenda: Filipino Immigrant Workers in the Era of McCarthyism: A Case Study of the Cannery Workers and Farm Laborers Union, 1948–1955" (master's thesis, University of California, Los Angeles, 1990).

94. Fabian Bergano, interview by Fredrick A. Cordova Jr., 15 April 1975, interview FIL-KNG 75-7jr, transcript, WSOAHP.

95. Celestino Gloria, interview by author, 30 March 1993, Stockton, Calif. After earning his M.A., Gloria reenlisted in the U.S. Army and served in the Korean and Vietnam Wars.

96. Sammy Escalona, interview by author, 3 January 1992, Stockton, Calif.

97. Lawagan interview.

98. Feria, "War and the Status of Filipino Immigrants," 49.

99. Data calculated from Immigration and Naturalization Service, Military Service Records, "Military Petitions for Naturalization, 1918–1946," boxes 13 and 14, National Archives/Pacific Southwest Regional Branch, Laguna Niguel, Calif.

100. Ibid.

101. Ibid.

102. U.S. Department of Commerce, Bureau of the Census, *Seventeenth Census of the United States, 1950* (Washington, D.C.: Government Printing Office, 1953), table 6.

103. Ibid, table 25.

104. On the *bracero* program, see, for example, Erasmo Gamboa, "Braceros in the Pacific Northwest: Laborers on the Domestic Front, 1942–1947," *Pacific Historical Review* 56, no. 3 (1987): 378–98.

105. Sam Figueras, interview by Cynthia Mejia, 5 January 1976, interview FIL-KNG 76-39cm, transcript, WSOAHP.

106. Juan V. Mina, interview by Carolina Apostol, 30 May 1976, interview FIL-KNG 76-47cma, transcript, WSOAHP.

6. Reformulating Communities

1. Quoted in Kristine C. Mosqueda, "Dream Now a Reality: L.A. Declares Establishment," *Balita* (Los Angeles), 3–9 August 2002.

2. The majority of post-1965 and contemporary immigrants, however, tend to settle in the suburbs. In Los Angeles County, cities like Carson, Long Beach, Cerritos, Diamond Bar, and West Covina contain significant Filipino communities. On reforms in U.S. immigration legislation and patterns of Filipino and Asian immigration and settlements since 1965, see Eric Lai and Dennis Arguelles, eds., *The New Face of Asian Pacific America: Numbers, Diversity, and Change in the Twenty-first Century* (Berkeley, Calif.: Consolidated Printers, 2003).

3. David Brodsly, *L.A. Freeway* (Berkeley: University of California Press, 1981), 39. See also Eric H. Monkkonen, *America Becomes Urban: The Development of U.S. Cities and Towns, 1780–1980* (Berkeley: University of California Press, 1988).

4. Brodsly, *L.A. Freeway*, 39.

5. *Manila Post Herald* (Los Angeles), 30 April 1945, 15 March 1945.

6. R. T. Feria, "War and the Status of Filipino Immigrants," *Sociology and Social Research* 31, no. 2 (1946): 50.

7. Raymond Chandler, *The High Window* (New York: Knopf, 1942), 65.

8. Rodolfo F. Acuña, *A Community Under Siege: A Chronicle of Chicanos East of the Los Angeles River, 1945–1975* (Los Angeles: UCLA Chicano Studies Research Center, 1984), 68–70.

9. Nellie Foster, "Legal Status of Filipino Intermarriages in California," *Sociology and Social Research* 16, no. 5 (1932): 441–54. For a fuller discussion of antimiscegenation laws as they applied to Asian immigrants, see Megumi Dick Osumi, "Asians and California's Anti-Miscegenation Laws," in *Asian and Pacific American Experiences: Women's Perspectives*, ed. Nobuya Tsuchida (Minneapolis: Asian/Pacific American Learning Resource Center, University of Minnesota, 1982), 1–37. On race, gender, and the development of antimiscegenation laws in the West, see, for example, Peggy Pascoe, "Race, Gender, and the Privileges of Property: On the Significance of Miscegenation Laws in the U.S. West," in *Over the Edge: Remapping the American West*, ed. Valerie J. Matsumoto and Blake Allmendinger (Berkeley: University of California Press, 1999), 215–30. The California Supreme Court repealed the state's antimiscegenation laws in 1948; the U.S. Supreme Court declared antimiscegenation legislation unconstitutional in 1967.

10. See, for example, Caroline Chung Simpson, "'Out of an Obscure Place': Japanese War Brides and Cultural Pluralism in the 1950s," *Differences: A Journal of Feminist Cultural Studies* 10, no. 3 (1998): 47–81. For interviews with some Filipina war brides, see Caridad Concepcion Vallangca, *The Second Wave: Pinay and Pinoy (1945–1960)* (San Francisco: Strawberry Hill Press, 1987).

11. Valentin R. Aquino, "The Filipino Community in Los Angeles" (master's thesis, University of Southern California, 1952), 49.

12. *Philippine Pictorial* (Los Angeles), 17 May 1940.

13. *Sentinel* (Brawley, Calif.), 15 March 1946.

14. Benecio T. Catapusan, "The Filipino Occupational and Recreational Activities in Los Angeles" (master's thesis, University of Southern California, 1934), 13.

15. Benecio T. Catapusan, "The Social Adjustment of Filipinos in the United States" (Ph.D. diss., University of Southern California, 1940).

16. Aquino, "Filipino Community in Los Angeles," 42.

17. The space spared from the construction of the Harbor Freeway in the original community on Weller Street has been absorbed into the Weller Court shopping center and its parking lot in Little Tokyo. Weller Street does not even exist anymore: in 1986, it was renamed Onizuka Street as a tribute to astronaut Ellison Onizuka, the first Japanese American in space, who perished when the space shuttle *Challenger* burst into flames. On the redevelopment of Little Tokyo, see Lon Kurashige, *Japanese American Celebration and Conflict: A History of Ethnic Identity and Festival in Los Angeles, 1934–1990* (Berkeley: University of California Press, 2002).

18. Norman M. Klein, *The History of Forgetting: Los Angeles and the Erasure of Memory* (London: Verso, 1997).

BIBLIOGRAPHY

Government Records and Publications

California Commission on Immigration and Housing. *Second Annual Report.* Sacramento, 1916.

California Department of Industrial Relations. *Facts About Filipino Immigration into California.* 1930. Reprint, San Francisco: R and E Research Associates, 1972.

California State Athletic Commission on Boxing and Wrestling. California State Archives, Sacramento.

Immigration and Naturalization Service, Military Service Records. "Military Petitions for Naturalization, 1918–1946." National Archives/Pacific Southwest Regional Branch, Laguna Niguel, Calif.

Los Angeles Police Department. *Annual Report of the Police Department, 1936–37.* Los Angeles Public Library, Central Branch, Los Angeles, Calif.

———. *Annual Report of the Police Department, 1937–38.* Los Angeles Public Library, Central Branch, Los Angeles, Calif.

———. "Rules Governing Taxi Dance Halls, 1943." Los Angeles Public Library, Central Branch, Los Angeles, Calif.

State Relief Administration of California. Division of Special Surveys and Studies. *Transients in California.* Sacramento: State of California, 1936.

U.S. Department of Agriculture, Farm Security Administration. *A Study of 6655 Migrant Households in California.* Washington, D.C.: Government Printing Office, 1938.

U.S. Department of Commerce, Bureau of the Census. *Sixteenth Census of the United States, 1940.* Washington, D.C.: Government Printing Office, 1943.

———. *Seventeenth Census of the United States, 1950.* Washington, D.C.: Government Printing Office, 1953.

———. *Twenty-second Census of the United States, 2000.* Available at: http://www.census.gov.

U.S. National Commission on Law Observance. *Report on Crime and the Foreign Born.* Washington, D.C.: Government Printing Office, 1931.

Vollmer, August. *Police Conditions in the United States: A Report to the National Commission on Law Observance and Enforcement.* Washington, D.C.: Government Printing Office, 1931.

Webb, John N. *The Transient Unemployed.* Publication of Works Progress Administration, Division of Social Research. Washington, D.C.: Government Printing Office, 1935.

Williams, Edward A. *Work, Relief, and Security.* Publication of Works Progress Administration, Social Problems Series. Washington, D.C.: Government Printing Office, 1941.

Works Progress Administration, Federal Writers' Project Collection. Bancroft Library, University of California, Berkeley.

Works Progress Administration, Federal Writers' Project Collection. "Racial Minority Survey: Filipinos." Department of Special Collections, Charles E. Young Research Library, University of California, Los Angeles.

Manuscripts and Collections

Bagley, Charles Leland. Collection. Department of Special Collections, University of Southern California, Los Angeles.

Bulosan, Carlos. Papers. Manuscripts and University Archives Division, Suzzallo Library, University of Washington, Seattle.

California State Athletic Commission. California State Archives, Sacramento.

Gamio, Manuel. Papers. Bancroft Library, University of California, Berkeley.

McWilliams, Carey. Papers. Department of Special Collections, Charles E. Young Research Library, University of California, Los Angeles.

Sports Library. Amateur Athletic Foundation, Los Angeles, Calif.

Wood, James Earl. Papers. Bancroft Library, University of California, Berkeley.

Oral History Collections

Department of Special Collections, Charles E. Young Research Library, University of California, Los Angeles

McWilliams, Carey. "Honorable in All Things." Interview by Joel Gardner, 13 July 1978, transcript.

Federal Writers Project, "Racial Minority Survey: Filipinos." Charles E. Young Research Library, University of California, Los Angeles

Anonymous Filipino. Interview by Lundy, 2 February 1937, transcript.

Cardoz, Maria Garcia. Interview by Lundy, 9 February 1937, transcript.

Corpus, Severino. Interview by Berkley Walker, 24 May 1937, transcript.

Diaz, Santa Maria. Interview by Lundy, 20 January 1937, transcript.

Fiores, Manuel. Interview by Lundy, 2 March 1937, transcript.

Garcia, Johnny. Interview by Lundy, 18 January 1937, transcript.

Gonzales, Arturo. Interview by Lundy, 25 February 1937, transcript.

Manzoa, Eddie. Interview by Lundy, 10 February 1937, transcript.

Miguel, Carl (Carlos). Interview by Lundy, 10 March 1937, transcript.

Tardez, Immanuel. Interview by Lundy, 18 February 1937, transcript.

Weiss, George. Interview by Lundy, 16 February 1937, transcript.

Oral History Project, the National Pinoy Archives. Filipino American National Historical Society, Seattle, Wash.

Corpus, Ray Edralin. Interview by Bob Antolin, 22 September 1981. Interview PNW81-Fil-028ba, transcript.

Malla, Carlos. Interview PNW81-Fil-005ba, n.d., transcript.

Tapang, Bruno. Interview PNW81-Fil-007, n.d., transcript.

Washington State Oral/Aural History Program. Washington State Archives, Olympia

Aliwanag, Leo. Interview by Cynthia Mejia, 19 August 1976. Interview FIL-KNG 76-50cm, transcript.

Angeles, Mariano. Interview by Cynthia Mejia, 6 November 1975. Interview FIL-KNG 75-32cm, transcript.

Bergano, Fabian. Interview by Fredrick A. Cordova Jr., 15 April 1975. Interview FIL-KNG 75-7jr, transcript.

Dumlao, Felipe G. Interview by Cynthia Mejia, 21 November 1975. Interview FIL-KNG 75-35cm, transcript.

Figueras, Sam. Interview by Cynthia Mejia, 5 January 1976. Interview FIL-KNG 76-39cm, transcript.

Guiang, Marino F. Interview by Dorothy Cordova, 24 September 1976. Interview FIL-KNG 76-52dc, transcript.

Lopez, Sammy R. Interview by Cynthia Mejia, 24 November 1975. Interview FIL-KNG 75-36cm, transcript.

Martin, Toribio. Interview by Dorothy Cordova, 27 April 1976. Interview FIL-KNG 76-44dc, transcript.

Mendoza, John. Interview by Dorothy Cordova, 6 April 1976. Interview FIL-KNG 76-42dc, transcript.

Mendoza, Vincent. Interview by Cynthia Mejia, 13 January 1976. Interview FIL-KNG 76-40cm, transcript.

Mensalvas, Chris. Interview by Carolina N. Koslosky, 10 and 11 February 1975. Interview FIL-KNG 75-1ck, transcript.

Mina, Juan V. Interview by Carolina Apostol, 30 May 1976. Interview FIL-KNG 76-47cma, transcript.

Pimentel, Lorenzo U. Interview by Cynthia Mejia, 14 November 1975. Interview FIL-KNG 75-34cm, transcript.
Quintero, Peter. Interview by Dorothy Cordova, 8 June 1976. Interview FIL-KNG 76-48dc, transcript.

Taped, by Linda España-Maram

Brown, Helen. 25 May 1995. Los Angeles, Calif.
Cabanag, Antonio. 26 June 1993. San Francisco, Calif.
Castillo, Toribio. 1 March 1992. Los Angeles, Calif.
Castro, Ann. 2 April 1993. French Camp, Calif.
Castro, John. 1 April 1993. French Camp, Calif.
Escalona, Leo. 26 June 1993. San Francisco, Calif.
Escalona, Samuel (Sammy). 2 and 3 January 1993. Stockton, Calif.
Gloria, Celestino. 30 March 1993. Stockton, Calif.
Guerréro, Eduardo (Lalo). 26 May 1995. Cathedral City, Calif.
Lawagan, Miguel. 26 June 1993. San Francisco, Calif.
Morales, Royal. 24 April 1992. Los Angeles, Calif.
Ordinario, Adoration. 23 April 1994. Altadena, Calif.
Ordinario, Pedro. 23 April 1994. Altadena, Calif.
Pascua, Felix. 12 April 1992 and 30 September 1993. Los Angeles, Calif.
Samaoang, Fanny. 30 September 1993. Seattle, Wash.
Windam, Sigme. 17 September 1994. San Francisco, Calif.
Zapata, Socorro (Coring). 30 September 1993. Seattle, Wash.

Untaped, by Linda España-Maram

Bayhon, Larry. 3 January 1993. Stockton, Calif.
Butado, Remigio. 30 March 1993. Stockton, Calif.
Fabay, Manuel. 5 February 1993. Long Beach, Calif.
Pascua, Felix, Toribio Castillo, and Johnny Rallonza. 12 April 1992. Los Angeles, Calif.
Rallonza, Jean Heff. 23 April 1992. Downey, Calif.
Rallonza, Johnny. 23 April 1992 and 17 May 1995. Downey, Calif.

Newspapers, Filipino American (Calif.)

Ang Bantay (*The Guardian*) (Los Angeles), 1929.
Associated Filipino Press (Los Angeles), 1938–1945.
Cosmopolitan Bulletin (Los Angeles), 1939.
Filipino Eagle (Los Angeles), 1940.
Filipino Echo (Calexico), 1943.
Filipino Observer-Spokesman (Los Angeles), 1935, 1937.

Filipino Pioneer (Stockton), 1938.
Little Manila Times (Los Angeles), 1939.
Los Angeles Filipino Bulletin (Los Angeles), 1992.
Manila Post Herald (Los Angeles), 1944–1945.
Philippine Commonwealth Times (Santa Maria), 1936–1942.
Philippine Enterprise (Sacramento), 1935–1936.
Philippine Examiner (Stockton), 1935–1937.
Philippine News-Herald (Los Angeles), 1944.
Philippine News Reporter (Los Angeles), 1938.
Philippine Pictorial (Los Angeles), 1940.
Philippine Tribune (San Francisco), 1936–1938.
Philippines Herald Tribune (Los Angeles), 1936.
Philippines Review (Los Angeles), 1935–1937.
Sentinel (Brawley), 1946.
Three Stars (Stockton), 1929.

Books and Articles

Acuña, Rodolfo F. *A Community Under Siege: A Chronicle of Chicanos East of the Los Angeles River, 1945–1975*. Los Angeles: UCLA Chicano Studies Research Center, 1984.

Agoncillo, Teodoro A. *A Short History of the Philippines*. New York: New American Library, 1969.

Alarilla, Joey G. "L.A. Designates Official 'Historic Filipinotown.'" *Global Nation* (Manila, Philippines). Available at: http://www.inq7.net/gbl/2002/aug/28/gbl_3-1.htm.

Alidio, Kimberly. "'When I Get Home I Want to Forget': Memory and Amnesia in the Occupied Philippines, 1901–1904." *Social Text* 17, no. 2 (1999): 145–60.

Almirol, Edwin B. "Exclusion and Acceptance of Filipinos in America." *Asian Profile* 13, no. 5 (1985): 395–407.

——. "Filipino Voluntary Associations: Balancing Social Pressures and Ethnic Images." *Ethnic Groups* 2 (1978): 65–92.

——. "Rights and Obligations in Filipino American Families." *Journal of Comparative Family Studies* 13, no. 3 (1982): 291–305.

"Amerasia Forum: Strangers from a Different Shore." *Amerasia Journal* 16, no. 2 (1990): 63–154.

Anderson, Robert N., Richard Coller, and Rebecca F. Pestano. *Filipinos in Rural Hawaii*. Honolulu: University of Hawaii Press, 1984.

Angelou, Maya. *I Know Why the Caged Bird Sings*. New York: Bantam Books, 1971.

Antolin, Robert Park. "Sweet Music." In *Turning Shadows into Light: Art and Culture of the Northwest's Early Asian/Pacific Community*, edited by Mayumi Tsutakawa and Alan Chong Lau. Seattle: Young Pine Press/Asian Multi-Media Center, 1982.

Appier, Janis. *Policing Women: The Sexual Politics of Law Enforcement and the LAPD*. Philadelphia: Temple University Press, 1998.

Arabe, Arlene. "Pilipinos' Past in Los Angeles: Searching for the Old Manila Town." *Pacific Ties* 14, no. 2 (1990): 36.

Arcellana, Francisco. "American Influence in Philippine Literature." *Solidarity* 2, no. 6 (1967): 89–94.

Armstrong, Henry. *Gloves, Glory, and God: An Autobiography.* Westwood, N.J.: Revell, 1956.

Astor, Gerald. ". . . *And a Credit to His Race": The Hard Life and Times of Joseph Louis Barrow, a.k.a. Joe Louis.* New York: Saturday Review Press/Dutton, 1974.

Austin, Joe, and Michael Nevin Willard, eds. *Generations of Youth: Youth Cultures and History in Twentieth-Century America.* New York: New York University Press, 1999.

Bacho, Peter. "A Manong's Heart." In *Dark Blue Suit and Other Stories.* Seattle: University of Washington Press, 1997.

Bakhtin, Mikhail M. *The Dialogic Imagination.* Edited by Michael Holquist. Translated by Caryl Emerson and Michael Holquist. Austin: University of Texas Press, 1981.

———. *Rabelais and His World.* Translated by Helene Iswolsky. Bloomington: Indiana University Press, 1984.

Barthes, Roland. *Mythologies.* Translated by Annette Lavers. 7th ed. New York: Hill and Wang, 1976.

Barzman, Ben. "The Duke and Me." *Los Angeles Magazine,* January 1989.

Bederman, Gail. *Manliness and Civilization: A Cultural History of Gender and Race in the United States, 1880–1917.* Urbana: University of Illinois Press, 1996.

Benson, Susan Porter. *Counter Cultures: Saleswomen, Managers, and Customers in American Department Stores, 1890–1940.* Urbana: University of Illinois Press, 1988.

Bernstein, Barton J. "The New Deal: The Conservative Achievements of Liberal Reform." In *Past Imperfect: Alternative Essays in American History,* edited by Blanche Wiesen Cook, Alice Kessler Harris, and Ronald Radosh, 2:159–75. New York: Knopf, 1973.

Blair, Karen J. *The History of American Women's Voluntary Organizations, 1810–1969.* Boston: Hall, 1989.

Bogardus, Emory S. "American Attitudes Towards Filipinos." *Sociology and Social Research* 14, no. 1 (1929): 59–69.

———. *Anti-Filipino Race Riots: A Report Made to the Ingram Institute of Social Science of San Diego.* San Diego, Calif., 15 May 1930.

Bonus, Rick. *Locating Filipino Americans: Ethnicity and the Cultural Politics of Space.* Philadelphia: Temple University Press, 2000.

Bowler, Alida C. "Social Hygiene in Racial Problems—The Filipino." *Journal of Social Hygiene* 18, no. 8 (1932): 452–56.

Brodsly, David. *L.A. Freeway.* Berkeley: University of California Press, 1981.

Bromberg, Lester. *Boxing's Unforgettable Fights.* New York: Ronald Press, 1962.

Buaken, Iris Brown. "My Brave New World." *Asia and the Americas,* May 1943, 268–70.

Buaken, Manuel. *I Have Lived with the American People.* Caldwell, Idaho: Caxton Printers, 1948.

——. "Life in the Armed Forces." *New Republic*, 30 August 1943, 279–80.

——. "Our Fighting Love of Freedom." *Asia and the Americas*, June 1943, 357–59.

Bulosan, Carlos. *America Is in the Heart: A Personal History.* New York: Harcourt, Brace, 1946. Reprint, Seattle: University of Washington Press, 1979.

Bunch, Lonnie G. "A Past Not Necessarily Prologue: The Afro-Americans in Los Angeles." In *Twentieth-Century Los Angeles: Power, Promotion, and Social Conflict*, edited by Norman M. Klein and Martin J. Schiesl, 100–130. Claremont, Calif.: Regina Books, 1991.

Burrill, Bob. *Who's Who in Boxing.* New Rochelle, N.Y.: Arlington House, 1974.

Butterworth, J. S., and Charles A. Poindexter, "An Electrocardiographic Study of the Effects of Boxing." *American Heart Journal* 23 (1942).

Campomanes, Oscar. "Filipinos in the United States and Their Literature of Exile." In *Reading the Literatures of Asian America*, edited by Shirley Geok-lin Lim and Amy Ling, 49–78. Philadelphia: Temple University Press, 1992.

Carr, Harry. *Los Angeles: City of Dreams.* New York: Appleton-Century, 1935.

Carroll, Edward J., Jr. "Punch-Drunk." *American Journal of the Medical Sciences*, May 1936, 706–12.

Castillo, Adelaida. "Filipino Migrants in San Diego, 1900–1946." *Journal of San Diego History* 22, no. 3 (1976): 26–35.

Catapusan, Benecio T. "Filipino Immigrants and Public Relief in the United States." *Sociology and Social Research* 23, no. 4 (1939): 546–54.

——. "Filipino Intermarriage Problems in the United States." *Sociology and Social Research* 22, no. 3 (1938): 265–72.

——. "Leisure Time Problems of Filipino Immigrants." *Sociology and Social Research* 24, no. 1 (1940): 541–49.

——. "Problems of Filipino Students in America." *Sociology and Social Research* 26, no. 2 (1941): 146–53.

"Causes of California's Race Riots." *Literary Digest*, 15 February 1930.

Chan, Anthony B. *Perpetually Cool: The Many Lives of Anna May Wong (1905–1961).* Lanham, Md.: Scarecrow Press, 2003.

Chan, Sucheng. *Asian Americans: An Interpretive History.* Boston: Twayne, 1991.

Chandler, Constance. "Recreation Among Women War Workers: A Study in San Bernardino." *Sociology and Social Research* 27, no. 1 (1943): 30–36.

Chandler, Raymond. *The High Window.* New York: Knopf, 1942.

Chang, Gordon H. "Asian Americans and the Writing of Their History." *Radical History Review* 53, no. 1 (1992): 105–14.

Chauncey, George. *Gay New York: Gender, Urban Culture, and the Making of the Gay Male World, 1890–1940.* New York: Basic Books, 1994.

Cheng, Lucie. "Free, Indentured, Enslaved: Chinese Prostitutes in Nineteenth-Century America." In *Labor Immigration Under Capitalism: Asian Workers in the United States Before World War II*, edited by Lucie Cheng and Edna Bonacich, 402–30. Berkeley: University of California Press, 1984.

Cheng, Lucie, and Edna Bonacich, eds. *Labor Immigration Under Capitalism: Asian*

Workers in the United States Before World War II. Berkeley: University of California Press, 1984.

Chibnall, Steve. "Whistle and Zoot: The Changing Meaning of a Suit of Clothes." *History Workshop Journal* 20 (1985): 56–81.

Choy, Catherine Ceniza. *Empire of Care: Nursing and Migration in Filipino American History*. Durham, N.C.: Duke University Press, 2003.

———. "Relocating the Struggle: Filipino Nurses Organize in the United States." In *Asian/Pacific Islander American Women: A Historical Anthology*, edited by Shirley Hune and Gail M. Nomura, 335–49. New York: New York University Press, 2003.

Chuh, Kandice, and Karen Shimakawa, eds. *Orientations: Mapping Studies in the Asian Diaspora*. Durham, N.C.: Duke University Press, 2001.

Chung Simpson, Caroline. "'Out of an Obscure Place': Japanese War Brides and Cultural Pluralism in the 1950s." *Differences: A Journal of Feminist Cultural Studies* 10, no. 3 (1998): 47–81.

Cohen, Lizabeth. *Making a New Deal: Industrial Workers in Chicago, 1919–1939*. Cambridge: Cambridge University Press, 1990.

Conkin, Paul K. *The New Deal*. New York: Crowell, 1967.

Constantino, Renato. "Identity and Consciousness: The Philippine Experience." Paper presented at the eighth World Sociology Congress, Toronto, August 1974.

———. "The Miseducation of the Filipino." *Weekly Graphic*, 8 June 1966.

———. *The Miseducation of the Filipino*. 2d ed. Quezon City, Philippines: Foundation for Nationalist Studies, 1983.

———. *The Philippines: A Past Revisited*. 14th ed. Quezon City, Philippines: Foundation for Nationalist Studies, 1993.

Cordova. Dorothy. "Voices from the Past: Why They Came." In *Making Waves: An Anthology of Writings by and About Asian American Women*, edited by Asian Women United of California, 42–49. Boston: Beacon Press, 1989.

Cordova, Fred. *Filipinos: Forgotten Asian Americans*. Edited by Dorothy Cordova. Seattle: Demonstration Project for Asian Americans, 1983.

Cordova, Joan May T. and Alexis S. Canillo, eds. *Voices: A Filipino-American Oral History*. Santa Rosa, Calif.: Northwestern Graphics, 1984.

Corpus, Severino F. "Second Generation Filipinos." *Sociology and Social Research* 22, no. 5 (1938): 446–51.

Cortez, Ruben. "A History of the Mexican-American in Los Angeles: The Zoot Suit Riots." *Probe,* May–June 1969, 6–7.

Cosgrove, Stuart. "The Zoot-Suit and Style Warfare." *History Workshop Journal* 18 (1984): 77–91.

Counter, Cross. "Garcia Thrills Again!" *Ring*, December 1939.

Cressy, Paul. *The Taxi-Dance Hall: A Sociological Study in Commercialized Recreation and City Life*. New York: Greenwood Press, 1932.

Cruz, Hermenegildo. "Problems of Filipino Emigration." In *Problems of the Pacific: Proceedings of the Fourth Conference of the Institute of Pacific Relations, 1931*, edited by Bruno Lasker. Chicago: University of Chicago Press, 1932.

Czitrom, Daniel. "Underworlds and Underdogs: Big Tim Sullivan and Metropolitan Politics in New York, 1889–1913." *Journal of American History* 78, no. 2 (1991): 536–58.

Daniels, Roger. *Concentration Camps USA: Japanese Americans and World War II.* New York: Holt, Rinehart and Winston, 1972.

———. *Prisoners Without Trial: Japanese Americans in World War II.* New York: Hill and Wang, 1993.

De Certeau, Michel. "On the Oppositional Practices of Everyday Life." *Social Text* 3 (1980): 3–43.

De Forest, Jimmy. "How to Control Weight." *Ring,* February 1925.

De Graaf, Lawrence B., Kevin Mulroy, and Quintard Taylor, eds. *Seeking El Dorado: African Americans in California.* Los Angeles: Autry Museum of Western Heritage, 2001.

De Graaf, Lawrence B., and Quintard Taylor. "Introduction: African Americans in California History, California in African American History." In *Seeking El Dorado: African Americans in California,* edited by Lawrence B. de Graaf, Kevin Mulroy, and Quintard Taylor, 3–69. Los Angeles: Autry Museum of Western Heritage, 2001.

Dela Cruz, Melany, and Pauline Agbayani-Siewert. "Swimming With and Against the Tide." In *The New Face of Asian Pacific American: Numbers, Diversity, and Change in the Twenty-first Century,* edited by Eric Lai and Dennis Arguelles, 45–50. Berkeley, Calif.: Consolidated Printers, 2003.

Demetrio, Francisco R. "Themes in Philippine Folk Tales." *Asian Studies* 10, no. 1 (1972): 6–17.

Denning, Michael. *Mechanic Accents: Dime Novels and Working-Class Culture in America.* London: Verso, 1987.

De Vera, Arleen. "The Tapia-Saiki Incident: Interethnic Conflict and Filipino Responses to the Anti-Filipino Exclusion Movement." In *Over the Edge: Remapping the American West,* edited by Valerie J. Matsumoto and Blake Allmendinger, 201–14. Berkeley: University of California Press, 1999.

De Witt, Howard A. *Anti-Filipino Movements in California.* San Francisco: R and E Research Associates, 1976.

———. *Violence in the Fields: California Farm Labor Unionization During the Great Depression.* San Francisco: R and E Research Associates, 1980.

Dmytryk, Edward, *It's a Hell of a Life but Not a Bad Living.* New York: Times Books, 1978.

Dorgan, John L. (Ike). "Grim Reaper Removes Two Fistic Stars." *Ring,* September 1925.

Dunbar-Ortiz, Roxanne. "One or Two Things I Know About Us: 'Okies' in American Culture." *Radical History Review* 59, no. 1 (1994): 4–34.

Elumba, H. A. "Sports Slants." *Filipino Pioneer* (Stockton, Calif.), 16 December 1938.

Espiritu, Yen Le. *Asian American Panethnicity: Bridging Institutions and Identities.* Philadelphia: Temple University Press, 1992.

————. *Filipino American Lives*. Philadelphia: Temple University Press, 1995.

————. *Home Bound: Filipino American Lives Across Cultures, Communities, and Countries*. Berkeley: University of California Press, 2003.

"Essays into American Empire in the Philippines: Culture, Community, and Capital." *Amerasia Journal* 24, no. 3 (1998).

"Essays into American Empire in the Philippines: Legacies, Heroes, and Identity." *Amerasia Journal* 24, no. 2 (1998).

Ewen, Elizabeth. *Immigrant Women in the Land of Dollars: Life and Culture on the Lower East Side, 1880–1925*. New York: Monthly Review Press, 1985.

Fabian, Ann. *Card Sharps, Dream Books, and Bucket Shops: Gambling in Nineteenth-Century America*. Ithaca, N.Y.: Cornell University Press, 1990.

Feng, Peter X., ed. *Screening Asian Americans*. New Brunswick, N.J.: Rutgers University Press, 2002.

Feria, R. T. "War and the Status of Filipino Immigrants." *Sociology and Social Research* 31, no. 2 (1946): 48–53.

Fernandez, Doreen G. "Philippine-American Cultural Interaction." University of the Philippines, Third World Studies Discussion Papers, no. 21, December 1980.

"Filipinos in American Life." *Amerasia Journal* 13, no. 1 (1986–1987).

Flamming, Douglas. "Becoming Democrats: Liberal Politics and the African American Community in Los Angeles, 1930–1965." In *Seeking El Dorado: African Americans in California*, edited by Lawrence B. de Graaf, Kevin Mulroy, and Quintard Taylor, 279–308. Los Angeles: Autry Museum of Western Heritage, 2001.

————. *Bound for Freedom: Black Los Angeles in Jim Crow America*. Berkeley: University of California Press, 2005.

Fleischer, Nat. "Louis Tops for 1939." *Ring*, February 1940.

Fong, Timothy. *The Contemporary Asian American Experience: Beyond the Model Minority*. Upper Saddle River, N.J.: Prentice Hall, 1998.

Fong, Timothy, and Larry H. Shinagawa, eds. *Asian Americans: Experiences and Perspectives*. Upper Saddle River, N.J.: Prentice Hall, 2000.

Foronda, Marcelino A., Jr. "America Is in the Heart: Ilocano Immigration to the United States, 1906–1930." *Journal of Social History* (Manila, Philippines) 21, nos. 1–2 (1976): 24–37.

————. "Vigan: A Study of Mexican Cultural Influences in the Philippines." *Journal of Social History* (Manila, Philippines) 21, nos. 1–2 (1976): 1–12.

Foster, Nellie. "Legal Status of Filipino Intermarriage in California." *Sociology and Social Research* 16, no. 5 (1932): 441–54.

Fraser, Steve, and Gary Gerstle, eds. *The Rise and Fall of the New Deal Order, 1930–1980*. Princeton, N.J.: Princeton University Press, 1989.

Freidel, Frank. "The New Deal in Historical Perspective." In *Twentieth-Century America: Recent Interpretations*, edited by Barton J. Bernstein and Allen J. Matusow, 246–82. New York: Harcourt, Brace & World, 1969.

Friday, Chris. *Organizing Asian American Labor: The Pacific Coast Canned Salmon Industry, 1870–1942*. Philadelphia: Temple University Press, 1995.

Fujita Rony, Dorothy. *American Workers, Colonial Power: Philippine Seattle and the Transpacific West, 1919–1941.* Berkeley: University of California Press, 2003.

Gaerlan, Barbara S. "The Pursuit of Modernity: Trinidad H. Pardo de Tavera and the Educational Legacy of the Philippines Revolution." *Amerasia Journal* 24, no. 2 (1998): 87–108.

Gamboa, Erasmo. "Braceros in the Pacific Northwest: Laborers on the Domestic Front, 1942–1947." *Pacific Historical Review* 56, no. 3 (1987): 378–98.

Gardiner, C. Harvey. *Pawns in a Triangle of Hate: The Peruvian Japanese and the United States.* Seattle: University of Washington Press, 1981.

Gardner, Ella. "Dance Hall Dangers." *Woman's Journal,* April 1930, 10–11, 41–42.

Gillis, James. *Catholic World,* July 1924, 533.

———. "Prize Fighting." *Catholic World,* September 1927, 834–37.

Gleeck, Lewis E., Jr. *American Institutions in the Philippines (1898–1941).* Quezon City, Philippines: Garcia, 1976.

Glenn, Evelyn Nakano. "The Dialectics of Wage Work: Japanese American Women and Domestic Service, 1905–1940." In *Unequal Sisters: A Multi-Cultural Reader in U.S. Women's History,* edited by Ellen Carol DuBois and Vicki L. Ruiz, 345–72. New York and London: Routledge, 1990.

Gluck, Sherna Berger. *Rosie the Riveter Revisited: Women, the War, and Social Change.* Boston: Twayne, 1987.

Gonzalez, Rosalinda M. "Chicanas and Mexican Immigrant Families, 1920–1940: Women's Subordination and Family Exploitation." In *Decades of Discontent: The Women's Movement, 1920–1940,* edited by Lois Scharf and Joan M. Jensen, 59–84. Westport, Conn.: Greenwood Press, 1983.

Gonzalo, D. F. "Social Adjustment of Filipinos." *Sociology and Social Research* 14, no. 2 (1929): 166–73.

Gorn, Elliott J. *The Manly Art: Bare-Knuckle Prize Fighting in America.* Ithaca, N.Y.: Cornell University Press, 1986.

Gramsci, Antonio. *An Antonio Gramsci Reader: Selected Writings, 1916–1935.* Edited by David Forgacs. New York: Schocken Books, 1988.

———. *Selections from the Prison Notebooks.* Edited by Quintin Hoare and Geoffrey Nowell Smith. New York: International , 1971.

Gregory, James N. *American Exodus: The Dust Bowl Migration and Okie Culture in California.* New York: Oxford University Press, 1989.

Gutman, Allen. *Women's Sports: A History.* New York: Columbia University Press, 1991.

Hagedorn, Jessica. "Asian Women in Film: No Joy, No Luck." In *Signs of Life in the USA: Readings on Popular Culture for Writers,* 2d ed., edited by Sonia Maasik and Jack Solomon, 306–14. Boston: Bedford Books, 1997.

Hall, Stuart. "Notes on Deconstructing 'the Popular.'" In *People's History and Socialist Theories,* edited by Raphael Samuel, 227–39. London: Routledge and Kegan Paul, 1981.

———. "The Rediscovery of 'Ideology': Return of the Repressed in Media Studies."

In *Culture, Society, and the Media*, edited by Michael Gurevitch, 56–90. London: Methuen, 1982.

Hallburton, Richard. "Half a Mile of History." *Readers Digest*, October 1937, 70–75.

Haller, Mark H. "Policy Gambling, Entertainment, and the Emergence of Black Politics: Chicago from 1900 to 1940." *Journal of Social History* 24, no. 3 (1991): 719–39.

Hamamoto, Darrell Y., and Sandra Liu, eds. *Countervisions: Asian American Film Criticism* Philadelphia: Temple University Press, 2000.

Hansen, Arthur A., ed. *Japanese American World War II Evacuation Oral History Project*. 4 vols. Westport, Conn.: Meckler, 1991.

Hareven, Tamara K., and Randolph Langenbach. *Amoskeag: Life and Work in an American Factory-City*. New York: Pantheon Books, 1978.

Harring, Sidney L. *Policing a Class Society: The Experience of American Cities, 1865–1915*. New Brunswick, N.J.: Rutgers University Press, 1983.

Hata, Donald Teruo, Jr., and Nadine Ishitani Hata. "Asian-Pacific Angelinos: Model Minorities and Indispensable Scapegoats." In *Twentieth-Century Los Angeles: Power, Promotion, and Social Conflict*, edited by Norman M. Klein and Martin J. Schiesl, 61–99. Claremont, Calif.: Regina Books, 1991.

Hazzard-Gordon, Katrina. *Jookin': The Rise of Social Dance Formation in African-American Culture*. Philadelphia: Temple University Press, 1990.

Henry, Bill. "Ceferino Garcia Loses Game Fight to Ross." *Los Angeles Times*, 24 October 1937.

Herrera-Sobek, Maria. "The Corrido as Hypertext: Undocumented Mexican Immigrant Films and the Mexican/Chicano Ballad." In *Culture Across Borders: Mexican Immigration and Popular Culture*, edited by David R. Maciel and Maria Herrera-Sobek, 227–58. Tucson: University of Arizona Press, 1998.

———. *The Mexican Corrido: A Feminist Analysis*. Bloomington: Indiana University Press, 1990.

Himes, Chester B. "Zoot Riots Are Race Riots." In *Black on Black: Baby Sister and Selected Writings*, 220–25. New York: Doubleday, 1973.

Hoganson, Kristin L. *Fighting for American Manhood: How Gender Politics Provoked the Spanish-American and Philippine-American Wars*. New Haven, Conn.: Yale University Press, 1998.

Houston, Jeanne Wakatsuki, and James D. Houston. *Farewell to Manzanar*. Boston: Houghton Mifflin, 1973.

"How to Tell Your Friends from the Japs." *Time*, 22 December 1941, 33.

Hughes, Ed. "We Mourn His Loss." *Ring*, September 1925.

Hune, Shirley, and Gail M. Nomura, eds. *Asian/Pacific Islander American Women: A Historical Anthology*. New York: New York University Press, 2003.

Ileto, Reynaldo C. "Outlines of a Non-Linear Emplotment of Philippine History." In *Reflections on Development in Southeast Asia*, edited by Lim Teek Ghee, 130–59. Singapore: Institute of Southeast Asian Studies, 1988.

———. *Pasyon and Revolution: Popular Movements in the Philippines, 1840–1910*. 3d ed. Quezon City, Philippines: Ateneo de Manila University Press, 1989.

James, C. L. R. *Beyond a Boundary*. London: Paul, 1963. Reprint, Durham, N.C.: Duke University Press, 1993.

Jameson, Fredric. "Reification and Utopia in Mass Culture." *Social Text* 1, no. 1 (1979): 130–48.

Janiewski, Dolores. "Flawed Victories: The Experiences of Black and White Women Workers in Durham During the 1930s." In *Decades of Discontent: The Women's Movement, 1920–1940*, edited by Lois Scharf and Joan M. Jensen, 85–109. Westport, Conn.: Greenwood Press, 1983.

Johnson, Alexander. *Ten—And Out! The Complete Story of the Prize Ring in America*. 3d ed. New York: Ives Washburn, 1947.

Jones, Jacqueline. *Labor of Love, Labor of Sorrow: Black Women, Work, and the Family from Slavery to the Present*. New York: Basic Books, 1985.

Jones, Wally, and Jim Washington. *Black Champions Challenge American Sports*. New York: McKay, 1972.

Kane, Kathryn. *Visions of War: Hollywood Combat Films of World War II*. Ann Arbor, Mich.: UMI Research Press, 1982.

Karnow, Stanley. *In Our Image: America's Empire in the Philippines*. New York: Ballantine Books, 1989.

Kelley, Robin D. G. *Hammer and Hoe: Alabama Communists During the Great Depression*. Chapel Hill: University of North Carolina Press, 1990.

———. "Notes on Deconstructing 'the Folk.'" *American Historical Review* 97, no. 5 (1992): 1400–1408.

———. *Race Rebels: Culture, Politics, and the Black Working Class*. New York: Free Press, 1994.

———. "The Riddle of the Zoot: Malcolm Little and Black Cultural Politics During World War II." In *Generations of Youth: Youth Cultures and History in Twentieth-Century America*, edited by Joe Austin and Michael Willard, 136–56. New York: New York University Press, 1998.

———. "'We Are Not What We Seem': Rethinking Black Working-Class Opposition in the Jim Crow South." *Journal of American History* 80, no. 1 (1993): 75–112.

Kim, Elaine H. "Defining Asian American Realities Through Literature." *Cultural Critique* 6 (1987): 87–111.

Kitano, Harry H. L., and Roger Daniels. *Asian Americans: Emerging Minorities*. Englewood Cliffs, N.J.: Prentice Hall, 1988.

Klein, Norman M. *The History of Forgetting: Los Angeles and the Erasure of Memory*. London: Verso, 1997.

Klein, Norman M., and Martin J. Schiesl, eds. *Twentieth-Century Los Angeles: Power, Promotion, and Social Conflict*. Claremont, Calif.: Regina Books, 1991.

Kochiyama, Yuri. *Passing It On*. Los Angeles: UCLA Asian American Studies Center Press, 2004.

———. "Then Came the War." Interview in Joann Faung Jean Lee, *Asian Americans: Oral Histories of First to Fourth Generation Americans from China, the Philippines, Japan, India, the Pacific Islands, Vietnam, and Cambodia*. New York: New Press, 1992.

Kofoed, Jack. "A Dirge for Baseball." *North American Review*, July 1929.

Koppes, Clayton R., and Gregory D. Black. *Hollywood Goes to War: How Politics, Profits and Propaganda Shaped World War II*. Berkeley: University of California Press, 1990.

Koppman, Lionel, and Bernard Postal. *Guess Who's Jewish in American History*. 2d ed. New York: Steimatzky, 1986.

Kurashige, Lon. *Japanese American Celebration and Conflict: A History of Ethnic Identity and Festival in Los Angeles, 1934–1990*. Berkeley: University of California Press, 2002.

Lai, Eric, and Dennis Arguelles, eds. *The New Face of Asian Pacific America: Numbers, Diversity, and Change in the Twenty-first Century*. Berkeley, Calif.: Consolidated Printers, 2003.

Lambin, Maria Ward. "This Business of Dancing." *Survey*, 15 July 1924, 457–61.

Lardizabal, Amparo S., and Felicitas Tensuan-Leogardo, eds. *Readings on Philippine Culture and Social Life*. Manila, Philippines: Rex Printing, 1976.

Larkin, John A. "Philippine History Reconsidered: A Socioeconomic Perspective." *American Historical Review* 87, no. 3 (1982): 595–628.

Lasker, Bruno. *Filipino Immigration to the Continental United States and Hawaii*. Chicago: University of Chicago Press, 1931.

Lazarus, Neil. "Cricket and National Culture in the Writings of C. L. R. James." In *C. L. R. James's Caribbean*, edited by Paget Henry and Paul Buhle, 92–110. Durham, N.C.: Duke University Press, 1992.

Lee, Joann Faung Jean. *Asian Americans: Oral Histories of First to Fourth Generation Americans from China, the Philippines, Japan, India, the Pacific Islands, Vietnam, and Cambodia*. New York: New Press, 1992.

Lee, Mary Paik. *Quiet Odyssey: The Life of a Pioneer Korean American Woman*. Seattle: University of Washington Press, 1990.

Lee, Robert G. *Orientals: Asian Americans in Popular Culture*. Philadelphia: Temple University Press, 1999.

Leonard, Kevin Allen. "'In the Interest of All Races': African Americans and Interracial Cooperation in Los Angeles During and After World War II." In *Seeking El Dorado: African Americans in California*, edited by Lawrence B. de Graaf, Kevin Mulroy, and Quintard Taylor, 309–40. Los Angeles: Autry Museum of Western Heritage, 2001.

Leong, Russell, ed. *Moving the Image: Independent Asian Pacific American Media Arts*. Los Angeles: UCLA Asian American Studies Center and Visual Communications, 1991.

Leuchtenburg, William E. *Franklin D. Roosevelt and the New Deal, 1932–1940*. New York: Harper & Row, 1963.

Levine, Lawrence W. *Black Culture and Black Consciousness: Afro-American Thought from Slavery to Freedom*. Oxford: Oxford University Press, 1977.

Levine, Peter. *Ellis Island to Ebbets Field: Sport and the American Jewish Experience*. New York: Oxford University Press, 1992.

Levine, Rhonda F. *Class Struggle and the New Deal: Industrial Labor, Industrial Capital, and the State.* Lawrence: University Press of Kansas, 1988.

Light, Ivan. "The Ethnic Vice Industry, 1880–1944." *American Sociological Review* 42, no. 3 (1977): 464–79.

———."From Vice District to Tourist Attraction: The Moral Career of American Chinatowns, 1880–1940." *Pacific Historical Review* 43, no. 3 (1974): 367–94.

———. "Numbers Gambling Among Blacks: A Financial Institution." *American Sociological Review* 42, no. 6 (1977): 892–904.

Limón, José E. *Mexican Ballads, Chicano Poems: History and Influence in Mexican-American Social Poetry.* Berkeley: University of California Press, 1992.

Lipsitz, George. "'Frantic to Join . . . the Japanese Army': Beyond the Black–White Binary." In *The Possessive Investment in Whiteness: How White People Profit From Identity Politics*, 184–210. Philadelphia: Temple University Press, 1998.

———. *A Life in the Struggle: Ivory Perry and the Culture of Opposition.* Philadelphia: Temple University Press, 1988.

———. "Listening to Learn and Learning to Listen: Popular Culture, Cultural Theory, and American Studies." *American Quarterly* 42, no. 4 (1990): 615–36.

———. *The Possessive Investment in Whiteness: How White People Profit from Identity Politics.* Philadelphia: Temple University Press, 1998.

———. *Rainbow at Midnight: Labor and Culture in the 1940s.* Urbana: University of Illinois Press, 1994.

———. "The Struggle for Hegemony." *Journal of American History* 75, no. 1 (1988): 146–50.

———. *Time Passages: Collective Memory and American Popular Culture.* Minneapolis: University of Minnesota Press, 1990.

Lipsyte, Robert. *SportsWorld: An American Dreamland.* New York: Quadrangle Books, 1975.

Long, Garnette Malbeuf. "A Dust Bowl Perspective." *American Papers* 12 (1992): 5–11.

Louis, Joe. *My Life Story.* 2d ed. New York: Duell, Sloan and Pearce, 1947.

Lowitt, Richard. *The New Deal and the West.* Bloomington: Indiana University Press, 1984.

Loza, Stephen J. *Barrio Rhythm: Mexican American Music in Los Angeles.* Urbana: University of Illinois Press, 1993.

Madrid-Barela, Arturo. "In Search of the Authentic Pachuco: An Interpretive Essay." *Aztlán* 4, no. 1 (1973): 31–57.

Manalansan, Martin F., IV. "*Biyuti* in Everyday Life: Performance, Citizenship, and Survival Among Filipinos in the United States." In *Orientations: Mapping Studies in the Asian Diaspora*, edited by Kandice Chuh and Karen Shimakawa, 153–71. Durham, N.C.: Duke University Press, 2001.

———. *Global Divas: Filipino Gay Men in the Diaspora.* Durham, N.C.: Duke University Press, 2003.

——, ed. *Cultural Compass: Ethnographic Explorations of Asian America*. Philadelphia: Temple University Press, 2000.

Mann, Arthur. "The Prize-Fighting Racket." *American Mercury*, August 1934, 408–14.

Manzon, Maximo C. *The Strange Case of the Filipinos in the United States*. New York: American Committee for the Protection of the Foreign Born, 1938.

Mark, Gregory Y. "Gambling in Oakland Chinatown: A Case of Constructive Crime?" In *Frontiers of Asian American Studies*, edited by Gail Nomura, Russell Endo, Stephen H. Sumida, and Russell C. Leong, 14–24. Pullman: Washington State University Press, 1989.

Martland, Harrison. "Punch-Drunk." *Journal of the American Medical Association* 91 (1928): 1103–7.

Mason, Gregory. "Satan in the Dance-Hall." *American Mercury*, June 1924, 177–82.

Matsumoto, Valerie J. *Farming the Home Place: A Japanese American Community in California, 1919–1982*. Ithaca, N.Y.: Cornell University Press, 1993.

Matsumoto, Valerie J., and Blake Allmendinger, eds. *Over the Edge: Remapping the American West*. Berkeley: University of California Press, 1999.

Maynard, Richard A. *Propaganda on Film: A Nation at War*. Rochelle Park, N.J.: Hayden Book, 1975.

Mazón, Mauricio. *The Zoot-Suit Riots: The Psychology of Symbolic Annihilation*. Austin: University of Texas Press, 1984.

McCoy, Alfred W., and Ed C. de Jesus, eds. *Philippine Social History: Global Trade and Local Transformations*. Quezon City, Philippines: Ateneo de Manila University Press, 1982.

McWilliams, Carey. *Brothers Under the Skin*. 1942. Reprint, Boston: Little, Brown, 1964.

——. *Factories in the Field: The Story of Migratory Farm Labor in California*. Boston: Little, Brown, 1939. Reprint, Hamden, Conn.: Archon Books, 1969.

——. *North from Mexico: The Spanish-Speaking People of the United States*. Rev. ed. New York: Greenwood Press, 1990.

——. *Southern California: An Island on the Land*. 7th ed. Salt Lake City: Peregrine Smith Books, 1988.

Mears, Eliot Grinnell. *Resident Orientals on the American Pacific Coast: Their Legal and Economic Status*. Chicago: University of Chicago Press, 1928.

Mei, June. "Socioeconomic Developments Among the Chinese in San Francisco, 1848–1906." In *Labor Immigration under Capitalism: Asian Workers in the United States before World War II*, edited by Lucie Cheng and Edna Bonacich, 370–401. Berkeley: University of California Press, 1984.

Melendy, H. Brett. *Asians in America: Filipinos, Koreans, and East Indians*. Boston: Hall, 1977.

Meñez, Herminia Quimpo. "Agyu and the Skyworld: The Philippine Folk Epic and Multicultural Education." *Amerasia Journal* 13, no. 1 (1987–1987): 135–49.

——. *Folklore Communication Among Filipinos in California*. New York: Arno Press, 1980.

Messick, Hank, and Burt Goldblatt. *The Only Game in Town: An Illustrated History of Gambling*. New York: Crowell, 1976.

Miller, Dorothy C. *Women and Social Welfare: A Feminist Analysis*. New York: Praeger, 1990.

Miller, Sally, ed. *The Ethnic Press in America*. Westport, Conn.: Greenwood Press, 1987.

Mills, Norris C. "Filipino Boxing Invasion Coming." *Ring*, September 1925.

Modell, John. *The Economics and Politics of Racial Accommodation: The Japanese of Los Angeles, 1900–1942*. Urbana: University of Illinois Press, 1977.

Monkkonen, Eric H. *America Becomes Urban: The Development of U.S. Cities and Towns, 1780–1980*. Berkeley: University of California Press, 1988.

Monroy, Douglas. "Like Swallows at the Old Mission: Mexicans and Racial Politics of Growth in Los Angeles in the Interwar Period." *Western Historical Quarterly* 14, no. 4 (1983): 435–58.

———. "'Our Children Get So Different Here': Film, Fashion, Popular Culture and the Process of Cultural Syncretization in Mexican Los Angeles, 1900–1935." *Aztlán* 19, no. 1 (1988–1990): 79–108.

———. *Rebirth: Mexican Los Angeles from the Great Migration to the Great Depression*. Berkeley: University of California Press, 1999.

Morales, Royal F. *Makibaka: The Pilipino American Struggle*. Los Angeles: Mountainview, 1974.

Morawska, Ewa. "The Sociology and Historiography of Immigration." In *Immigration Reconsidered: History, Sociology, and Politics*, edited by Virginia Yans-McLaughlin, 187–238. New York: Oxford University Press, 1990.

Morella, Joe, Edward Z. Epstein, and John Griggs. *The Films of World War II*. Secaucus, N.J.: Citadel Press, 1973.

Moritsugu, Henry. "To Be More Japanese." Interview in Joann Faung Jean Lee, *Asian Americans: Oral Histories of First to Fourth Generation Americans from China, the Philippines, Japan, India, the Pacific Islands, Vietnam, and Cambodia*, 99–103. New York: New Press, 1992.

Morley, David, and Kuean-Hsing Chen, eds. *Stuart Hall: Critical Dialogues in Cultural Studies*. New York: Routledge, 1996.

Mosqueda, Kristine C. "Dream Now a Reality: L.A. Declares Establishment." *Balita* (Los Angeles, California), 3–9 August 2002.

Muñoz, Alfredo N. *Filipinos in America*. Los Angeles: Mountainview, 1971.

Nakano Glenn, Evelyn. *Issei, Nisei, War Bride*. Philadelphia: Temple University Press, 1986.

Nash, Gerald. *The American West Transformed: The Impact of the Second World War*. Bloomington: Indiana University Press, 1985.

———. *World War II and the West: Reshaping the Economy*. Lincoln: University of Nebraska Press, 1990.

Neumeyer, Martin H. "Wartime Trends in Recreation." *Sociology and Social Research* 27, no. 5 (1944).

Niiya, Brian, ed. *More than a Game: Sport in the Japanese American Community*. Los Angeles: Japanese American National Museum, 2000.

Nomura, Gail M. "Filipina American Journal Writing: Recovering Women's History." In *Asian/Pacific Islander American Women: A Historical Anthology*, edited by Shirley Hune and Gail M. Nomura, 138–52. New York: New York University Press, 2003.

Ochoa, Dante. "Little Manila Revisited." *Philippine Beat Magazine*, January–February 1989, 14–16.

Odem, Mary. "Single Mothers, Delinquent Daughters, and the Juvenile Court in Early 20th Century Los Angeles." *Journal of Social History* 25, no. 1 (1991): 27–43.

Ong, Paul, and Tania Azores. "The Migration and Incorporation of Filipino Nurses." In *The New Asian Immigration in Los Angeles and Global Restructuring*, edited by Paul Ong, Edna Bonacich, and Lucie Cheng, 164–95. Philadelphia: Temple University Press, 1994.

Ong, Paul, Edna Bonacich, and Lucie Cheng, eds. *The New Asian Immigration in Los Angeles and Global Restructuring*. Philadelphia: Temple University Press, 1994.

Osumi, Megumi Dick. "Asians and California's Anti-Miscegenation Laws." In *Asian and Pacific American Experiences: Women's Perspectives*, edited by Nobuya Tsuchida, 1–37. Minneapolis: Asian/Pacific American Learning Resource Center, University of Minnesota, 1982).

Otis, Johnny. *Upside Your Head! Rhythm and Blues on Central Avenue*. Hanover, N.H.: University Press of New England, 1993.

Palmer, Albert W. *Orientals in American Life*. New York: Friendship Press, 1934.

Palmer, Phyllis. *Domesticity and Dirt: Housewives and Domestic Servants in the United States, 1920–1945*. Philadelphia: Temple University Press, 1989.

Panunzio, Constantine. "Intermarriage in Los Angeles, 1924–1933." *American Journal of Sociology* 45, no. 5 (1942): 690–701.

Paredes, Américo. *"With His Pistol in His Hand": A Border Ballad and Its Hero*. Austin: University of Texas Press, 1958.

Pascoe, Peggy. "Race, Gender, and the Privileges of Property: On the Significance of Miscegenation Laws in the U.S. West." In *Over the Edge: Remapping the American West*, edited by Valerie J. Matsumoto and Blake Allmendinger, 215–30. Berkeley: University of California Press, 1999.

Pasquil, Cornelio. "Filipino Boxers Make History in America." *Los Angeles Filipino Bulletin*, 21 April–20 May 1992.

Peiss, Kathy. *Cheap Amusements: Working Women and Leisure in Turn-of-the-Century New York*. Philadelphia: Temple University Press, 1986.

Peiss, Kathy, and Christina Simmons, eds. *Passion and Power: Sexuality in History*. Philadelphia: Temple University Press, 1989.

Perry, Louis B., and Richard S. Perry. *A History of the Los Angeles Labor Movement, 1911–1941*. Berkeley: University of California Press, 1963.

Pesotta, Rose. *Bread upon the Waters*. New York: Dodd, Mead, 1944.

Phillips, A. D. "Boxing Commissions at Fault, Failure to Set Aside Jealousies and Respect Each Other's Ruling a Tremendous Detriment to the Game." *Ring*, January 1925.

Polan, Dana. *Power and Paranoia: History, Narrative, and the American Cinema, 1940–1950*. New York: Columbia University Press, 1986.

Popenoe, Paul. "How Can Young People Get Acquainted?" *Journal of Social Hygiene* 18, no. 4 (1932): 218–24.

Posadas, Barbara M. "Ethnic Life and Labor in Chicago's Pre–World War II Filipino Community." In *Labor Divided: Race and Ethnicity in United States Labor Struggles, 1835–1960*, edited by Robert Asher and Charles Stephenson, 63–80. Albany: State University of New York Press, 1990.

Posadas, Barbara M., and Roland L. Guyotte, "Aspiration and Reality: Occupational and Educational Choice Among Filipino Migrants to Chicago, 1900–1935." *Illinois Historical Journal* 85, no. 2 (1992): 89–104.

"Punchy: Prize-Fighters Walk on Their Heels After Getting Numerous Hooks to Chin." *Literary Digest*, 10 April 1937, 39–40.

Radway, Janice. *Reading the Romance: Women, Patriarchy, and Popular Literature*. Chapel Hill: University of North Carolina Press, 1984.

Rafael, Vicente L. "White Love: Surveillance and Nationalist Resistance in the U.S. Colonization of the Philippines." In *Cultures of United States Imperialism*, edited by Amy Kaplan and Donald E. Pease, 185–218. Durham, N.C.: Duke University Press, 1993.

——. *White Love and Other Events in Filipino History*. Durham, N.C.: Duke University Press, 2000.

——, ed. *Discrepant Histories: Translocal Essays on Filipino Cultures*. Philadelphia: Temple University Press, 1995.

Ramil, Quentin A. "The Eagle—A Symbol of Democracy." *Associated Filipino Press* (Los Angeles), 4 August 1944.

Rauch, Basil. *The History of the New Deal, 1933–38*. 2d ed. New York: Octagon Books, 1975.

Rickard, "Tex." "Boxers of World Ranked in 1924." *Ring*, February 1925.

Riess, Steven A. "Only the Ring Was Square: Frankie Carbo and the Underworld Control of American Boxing." *International Journal of the History of Sport* 5, no. 1 (1988): 29–52.

——. "Sport and the American Dream: A Review Essay." *Journal of Social History* 14, no. 2 (1980): 295–303.

——. "Sport and the Redefinition of American Masculinity." *International Journal of the History of Sport* 8, no. 1 (1991): 5–27.

Robinson, Greg. *By Order of the President: FDR and the Internment of Japanese Americans*. Cambridge, Mass.: Harvard University Press, 2003.

robles, al. "taxi dance." In *rappin' with ten thousand carabaos in the dark*. Los Angeles: UCLA Asian American Studies Center, 1996.

Roediger, David R. *The Wages of Whiteness: Race and the Making of the American Working Class*. London: Verso, 1991.

Rojo, Trinidad A. "Social Maladjustment Among Filipinos in the United States." *Sociology and Social Research* 21, no. 5 (1937): 447–57.

Rollins, Judith. *Between Women: Domestics and Their Employers*. Philadelphia: Temple University Press, 1985.

Rony, Fatimah Tobing. *The Third Eye: Race, Cinema, and Ethnographic Spectacle*. Durham, N.C.: Duke University Press, 1996.

Rosenzweig, Roy. *Eight Hours for What We Will: Workers and Leisure in an Industrial City*. Cambridge: Cambridge University Press, 1983.

Ruck, Rob. *Sandlot Seasons: Sport in Black Pittsburgh*. Urbana: University of Illinois Press, 1987.

Ruiz, Vicki. *Cannery Women/Cannery Lives: Mexican Women, Unionization, and the California Food Processing Industry, 1930–1950*. Albuquerque: University of New Mexico Press, 1987.

———. "'Star Struck': Acculturation, Adolescence, and Mexican American Women, 1920–1950." In *Small Worlds: Children and Adolescents in America, 1850–1950*, edited by Elliott West and Paula Petrik, 61–80. Lawrence: University Press of Kansas, 1992.

Rydell, Robert W. *All the World's a Fair: Visions of Empire at American International Expositions, 1876–1916*. Chicago: University of Chicago Press, 1984.

Saldívar, José David. "Américo Paredes and Decolonization." In *Border Matters: Remapping American Cultural Studies*, 36–56. Berkeley: University of California Press, 1997.

Sammons, Jeffrey T. *Beyond the Ring: The Role of Boxing in American Society*. Urbana: University of Illinois Press, 1988.

Samson, Johnny. "History of Boxing in the Philippines." In *The Making of Champions in California*, by DeWitt Van Court. Los Angeles: Premier Printing, 1926.

San Buenaventura, Steffi. "The Master and the Federation: A Filipino-American Social Movement in California and Hawaii." *Social Process in Hawaii* 33 (1991): 169–93.

Sánchez, George J. *Becoming Mexican American: Ethnicity, Culture, and Identity in Chicano Los Angeles, 1900–1945*. New York: Oxford University Press, 1993.

Sandmeyer, Elmer Clarence. *The Anti-Chinese Movement in California*. Urbana: University of Illinois Press, 1939.

Santos, Bienvenido N. "Filipinos in War." *Far Eastern Survey* 11, no. 24 (1942): 249–50.

Saxton, Alexander. *The Indispensable Enemy: Labor and the Anti-Chinese Movement in California*. Berkeley: University of California Press, 1971.

Scharf, Lois. *To Work and to Wed: Female Employment, Feminism, and the Great Depression*. Westport, Conn.: Greenwood Press, 1980.

Scharlin, Craig, and Lilia V. Villanueva, eds. *Philip Vera Cruz: A Personal History of Filipino Immigrants and the Farmworkers Movement*. 3d ed. Seattle: University of Washington Press, 2000.

Schulberg, Budd. "Champions for Sale: The Mike Jacobs Story." *Collier's*, 22 April 1950, 19, 48–52.

Scott, James C. *Domination and the Arts of Resistance: Hidden Transcripts*. New Haven, Conn.: Yale University Press, 1990.

Seitz, Don C. "The Millionaire Art of Self-Defense: Some Reflections Concerning Plutocracy in the Prize Ring." *Outlook*, 6 October 1926, 179–80.

"Shades of L.A.: A Search for Visual Ethnic History." Department of History, Los Angeles Public Library, Central Branch, Los Angeles.

Shah, Nayan. *Contagious Divides: Epidemics and Race in San Francisco's Chinatown*. Berkeley: University of California Press, 2001.

Shumsky, Neil Larry. "Tacit Acceptance: Respectable Americans and Segregated Prostitution, 1870–1910." *Journal of Social History* 19, no. 4 (1986): 664–79.

Singer, Stan. "Vaudeville in Los Angeles, 1910–1926: Theaters, Management, and the Orpheum." *Pacific Historical Review* 61, no. 1 (1992): 103–13.

Sleepy Lagoon Defense Committee. *The Sleepy Lagoon Case*. Hollywood, Calif.: Mercury Printing, 1943.

Smith, Harry B. "California's Classy Fighters." *Ring*, April 1939.

Stein, Walter J. *California and the Dust Bowl Migration*. Westport, Conn.: Greenwood Press, 1973.

Stott, Richard B. *Workers in the Metropolis: Class, Ethnicity, and Youth in Antebellum New York City*. Ithaca, N.Y.: Cornell University Press, 1990.

Taggaoa, Fernando A. "No Cause For Regret." *Asia*, October 1942, 567.

Tajima, Renee E. "Lotus Blossoms Don't Bleed: Images of Asian Women." In *Making Waves: An Anthology of Writings by and about Asian American Women*, edited by Asian Women United of California, 308–17. Boston: Beacon Press, 1989.

Takaki, Ronald. *Strangers from a Different Shore: A History of Asian Americans*. Boston: Little, Brown, 1989.

Tambolero, W. L. "Fight for Title a Drawing Card Far Beyond Expectations of Matchmakers." *Philippines Review* (Los Angeles), 23 February 1937.

Tilly, Charles. "Transplanted Networks." In *Immigration Reconsidered: History, Sociology, and Politics*, edited by Virginia Yans-McLaughlin, 79–95. New York: Oxford University Press, 1990.

Tsutakawa, Mayumi, and Alan Chong Lau, eds. *Turning Shadows into Light: Art and Culture of the Northwest's Early Asian/Pacific Community*. Seattle: Young Pine Press/Asian Multi-Media Center, 1982.

Tung, Charlene. "Caring Across Borders: Motherhood, Marriage, and Filipina Domestic Workers in California." In *Asian/Pacific Islander American Women: A Historical Anthology*, edited by Shirley Hune and Gail M. Nomura, 301–15. New York: New York University Press, 2003.

Vallangca, Caridad Concepcion. *The Second Wave: Pinay and Pinoy (1945–1960)*. San Francisco: Strawberry Hill Press, 1987.

Vallangca, Roberto V. *Pinoy: The First Wave*. San Francisco: Strawberry Hill Press, 1977.

Van, Bill. "'Speedy' Dado Is a Pancho Villa." *Knockout*, 21 February 1931.

Vergara, Benito M., Jr. "Betrayal, Class Fantasies, and the Filipino Nation in Daly City." In *Cultural Compass: Ethnographic Explorations of Asian America*, edited by Martin F. Manalansan IV, 139–58. Philadelphia: Temple University Press, 2000.

Verge, Arthur C. "The Impact of the Second World War on Los Angeles." *Pacific Historical Review* 43, no. 3 (1994): 289–314.

Villa, Pancho. "My Hardest Fight." *Ring*, April 1925.

Vinassa, Gene. "Brown Bomber in Miniature." *Ring*, September 1939.

Vite, Doroteo V. "A Filipino Rookie in Uncle Sam's Army." *Asia*, October 1942, 564–66.

Walters, Ronald G. *American Reformers, 1815–1860*. New York: Hill and Wang, 1978.

Wandersee, Winifred D. "The Economics of Middle-Income Family Life: Working Women During the Great Depression." In *Decades of Discontent: The Women's Movement, 1920–1940*, edited by Lois Scharf and Joan M. Jensen, 45–58. Westport, Conn.: Greenwood Press, 1983.

Ware, Susan. *Beyond Suffrage: Women in the New Deal*. Cambridge, Mass.: Harvard University Press, 1981.

Warren, William H. "Maps: A Spatial Approach to Japanese American Communities in Los Angeles." *Amerasia Journal* 13, no. 2 (1986–1987): 137–51.

Weinberg, S. Kirson, and Henry Avond. "The Occupational Culture of the Boxer." *American Journal of Sociology* 57, no. 5 (1952): 460–69.

Wells, Alice Stebbins. "Policewomen of Los Angeles, Calif." In *Proceedings of the National Conference of Charities and Correction*. Chicago: Hildmann Printing, 1915.

White, Kevin. *The First Sexual Revolution: The Emergence of Male Heterosexuality in Modern America*. New York: New York University Press, 1993.

Wickberg, Edgar. *The Chinese in Philippine Life*. New Haven, Conn.: Yale University Press, 1965.

———. "The Chinese Mestizo in Philippine History." *Journal of Southeast Asian History* 5 (1964): 62–100.

Williams, Raymond. *Marxism and Literature*. Oxford: Oxford University Press, 1977.

Wingo, James G. "The First Filipino Regiment." *Asia*, October 1942, 562–63.

Worster, Donald. *Dust Bowl*. New York: Oxford University Press, 1979.

Zia, Helen. *Asian American Dreams: The Emergence of an American People*. New York: Farrar, Straus and Giroux, 2000.

Theses, Dissertations, and Other Unpublished Papers

Alidio, Kimberly. "Between Civilizing Mission and Ethnic Assimilation: Racial Discourse, U.S. Colonial Education, and Filipino Ethnicity, 1901–1946." Ph.D. diss., University of Michigan, 2001.

Aquino, Valentin R. "The Filipino Community in Los Angeles." Master's thesis, University of Southern California, 1952.

Ave, Mario Paguia. "Characteristics of Filipino Social Organizations in Los Angeles." Master's thesis, University of Southern California, 1956.

Azores, Tania. "Filipinos in the Los Angeles Labor Force: Placemaking in Little Manila." 1983. Photocopy, in author's possession.

Berbano, Marcos P. "The Social Status of the Filipino in Los Angeles County." Master's thesis, University of Southern California, 1931.

Castillo-Tsuchida, Adelaida. "Filipino Migrants in San Diego, 1900–1946." Master's thesis, University of San Diego, 1979.

Catapusan, Benecio T. "The Filipino Occupational and Recreational Activities in Los Angeles." Master's thesis, University of Southern California, 1934.

——. "The Social Adjustment of Filipinos in the United States." Ph.D. diss., University of Southern California, 1940.

Coloma, Casiano P. "A Study of the Filipino Repatriation Movement." Master's thesis, University of Southern California, 1939.

Corpus, Severino F. "An Analysis of the Racial Adjustment Activities and Problems of the Filipino-American Christian Fellowship in Los Angeles." Master's thesis, University of Southern California, 1938.

De Graaf, Lawrence Brooks. "Negro Migration to Los Angeles, 1930–1950." Ph.D. diss., University of California, Los Angeles, 1962.

De Vera, Arleen Garcia. "An Unfinished Agenda: Filipino Immigrant Workers in the Era of McCarthyism: A Case Study of the Cannery Workers and Farm Laborers Union, 1948–1955." Master's thesis, University of California, Los Angeles, 1990.

Domer, Marilyn. "The Zoot-Suit Riot: A Culmination of Social Tensions in Los Angeles." Master's thesis, Claremont Graduate School, 1955.

Espiritu, Augusto Fauni. "The Rise and Fall of the Filipino Town Campaign in Los Angeles: A Study in Filipino American Leadership." Master's thesis, University of California, Los Angeles, 1992.

Ferguson, Charles K. "Political Problems and Activities of Oriental Residents in Los Angeles and Vicinity." Master's thesis, University of California, Los Angeles, 1942.

Gonzalves, Theodore. "When the Lights Go Down: Performing in the Filipina/o Diaspora." Ph.D. diss., University of California, Irvine, 2001.

Ibañez, Rosemarie D. "'Birds of Passage': Filipino Immigrants in the 1920s and 1930s." 1990. Photocopy, in author's possession.

Jones, Solomon James. "The Government Riots of Los Angeles, June 1943." Master's thesis, University of California, Los Angeles, 1969.

Leader, Leonard J. "Los Angeles and the Great Depression." Ph.D. diss., University of California, Los Angeles, 1972.

Leonard, Kevin Allen. "Years of Hope, Days of Fear: The Impact of World War II in Los Angeles." Ph.D. diss., University of California, Davis, 1992.

Lim, Shirley. "Gender, Race, and Film in the West: Anna May Wong." Paper presented at the "American Dreams, Western Images" Conference, Part One: "Representation and Identity: The West and the Westerner," Los Angeles, 19–20 November 1993.

Lipsitz, George. "Con Safos: Can Cultural Studies Read the Writing on the Wall?" 1991. Photocopy, in author's possession.

Mariano, Honorante. "The Filipino Immigrants in the United States." Master's thesis, University of Oregon, 1933.

McDannold, Thomas Allen. "Development of the Los Angeles Chinatown: 1850–1970." Master's thesis, California State University, Northridge, 1973.

Meñez, Herminia, and Helen Brown. "Pioneer Filipino Musicians." Manuscript, photocopy, in author's possession.

Pet, Catherine Ceniza. "Pioneers/Puppets: The Legacy of the *Pensionado* Program." B.A. senior thesis, Pomona College, 1991.

Provido, Generoso Pacificar. "Oriental Immigration from an American Dependency." Master's thesis, University of California, Los Angeles, 1931.

Ragan, Rex. "The Economic Effects on the Pacific Coast of Filipino Immigration to the United States." M.B.A. thesis, University of Southern California, 1928.

Rodríguez, Gregory S. "'Palaces of Pain'—Arenas of Mexican-American Dreams: Boxing and the Formation of Ethnic Mexican Identities in Twentieth-Century Los Angeles." Ph.D. diss., University of California, San Diego, 1999.

San Buenaventura, Steffi. "Nativism and Ethnicity in a Filipino-American Experience." Ph.D. diss., University of Hawaii, 1990.

Sánchez, George. "'The Other Los Angeles': Chicanos, Jews, and Japanese on the Eastside, 1925–1945." Photocopy, in author's possession.

Santos, Amparo Eugenio. "Marital Adjustment of Filipino Couples in Los Angeles." Master's thesis, University of Southern California, 1962.

Thomson, Eric H. "Why Plan Security for the Migratory Laborer?" Paper for "Conference of Social Work," San José, Calif., 12 May 1937. Federal Writers' Project, Bancroft Library, University of California, Berkeley.

Vedder, Clyde Bennett. "An Analysis of the Taxi-Dance Hall as a Social Institution, with Special Reference to Los Angeles and Detroit." Ph.D. diss., University of Southern California, 1947.

Wallovits, Sonia Emily. "The Filipinos in California." Master's thesis, University of Southern California, 1966.

Woods, Joseph Gerald. "The Progressives and the Police: Urban Reform and the Professionalization of the Los Angeles Police." Ph.D. diss., University of California, Los Angeles, 1973.

Films and Performances

Back to Bataan. Produced by Robert Fellows. Directed by Edward Dmytryk. Screenplay by Ben Barzman and Richard Landau, based on an original story by Aeneas MacKenzie and William Gordon. 98 min. RKO Radio Pictures, 1945.

Bataan. Produced by Irving Starr, directed by Tay Garnett. Original screenplay by Robert D. Andres. 114 min. Metro-Goldwyn-Mayer, 1943.

Bontoc Eulogy. Written and directed by Marlon Fuentes. 57 min. Videocassette.

The Day the Dancers Came. Directed by Daniel Tirtawinata. UCLA School of Theater, Film, and Television, 1993.

A Dollar a Day, Ten Cents a Dance: A Historic Portrait of Filipino Farm Workers in America. Produced by George Ow Jr., Geoffrey Dunn, and Mark Schwartz. Directed by Mark Schwartz. 40 min. Impact Productions, 1984. Videocassette.

Dreaming Filipinos. Produced by Manny Reyes and Herky del Mundo. Directed by Manny Reyes. National Asian American Telecommunications Association, 1990. Videocassette.

The Fall of the I Hotel. Produced by Crosscurrent Media. Directed by Curtis Choy. National Asian American Telecommunications Association, 1983. Videocassette.

Filipino Americans: Discovering Their Past for the Future. Produced by J. F. Wehman and Associates for the Filipino American National Historical Association (FANHS). Directed by John Wehman. National Asian American Telecommunications Association, 1994. Videocassette.

The Great Pinoy Boxing Era: Three Decades of Filipino-American Boxers. Produced by Corky Pasquil. Edited by Bernard Espinosa. Videocassette.

In No One's Shadow: Filipinos in America. Produced by Naomi de Castro and Antonio de Castro. Directed by Naomi de Castro. National Asian American Telecommunications Association, 1988. Videocassette.

Manong. Produced and directed by Linda Mabalot. Visual Communications, 1978.

peregriNasyon (Is America in the Heart?). Written by Chris B. Millado. Performance at the Center for the Arts Forum, San Francisco, 27 August 1994.

Unforgivable Blackness: The Rise and Fall of Jack Johnson. Directed by Ken Burns. 4 hours. Florentine Films/PBS, 2004. DVD.

A World on Display. Written and directed by Eric Breitbart. Produced by Eric Breitbart and Mary Lance. 53 min. New Deal Films, 1996. Videocassette.

INDEX